From John Cabot
to Henry Hudson

ALSO BY JAMES F. HANCOCK

*From Ponce de León to Sir Walter Raleigh:
Early European Arrivals in Southeastern
North America* (McFarland, 2025)

# From John Cabot to Henry Hudson

*Early European Arrivals
in Northeastern and Mid-Atlantic
North America*

JAMES F. HANCOCK

McFarland & Company, Inc., Publishers
*Jefferson, North Carolina*

ISBN (print) 978-1-4766-9577-8
ISBN (ebook) 978-1-4766-5492-8

LIBRARY OF CONGRESS CATALOGING DATA ARE AVAILABLE

Library of Congress Control Number 2025010288

© 2025 James F. Hancock. All rights reserved

*No part of this book may be reproduced or transmitted in any form or by any means, electronic or mechanical, including photocopying or recording, or by any information storage and retrieval system, without permission in writing from the publisher.*

Front cover image: colorized detail from a 1562 map titled "Americae sive qvartae orbis partis nova et exactissima descriptio," Lessing J. Rosenwald Collection (Library of Congress).

Printed in the United States of America

McFarland & Company, Inc., Publishers
Box 611, Jefferson, North Carolina 28640
www.mcfarlandpub.com

# Table of Contents

| | |
|---|---:|
| *Preface* | 1 |
| *Introduction: North Atlantic America Before the Europeans Arrived* | 3 |
| **One**. Newfoundland: The First European Touchpoint, 1497–1527 | 11 |
| **Two**. Jacques Cartier's Voyages of Discovery: 1534–1542 | 19 |
| **Three**. Fool's Gold: The Arctic Expeditions of Martin Frobisher, 1576–1578 | 34 |
| **Four**. The Arctic Voyages of John Davis: 1585–1587 | 46 |
| **Five**. English and French Expeditions to the North Atlantic: 1578–1621 | 57 |
| **Six**. L'Acadie: The French Begin a Fur Trading Empire, 1588–1603 | 71 |
| **Seven**. Pierre Dugua de Monts's Colonies at Saint Croix and Port Royal: 1603–1606 | 85 |
| **Eight**. English Expeditions to New England: 1602–1605 | 105 |
| **Nine**. Samuel de Champlain and the Founding of Québec: 1608–1635 | 118 |
| **Ten**. The Virginia Companies and the First Two Attempts to Settle Maine: 1607–1608 | 130 |
| **Eleven**. The Founding of Jamestown by the London Company: 1606–1608 | 140 |

**TWELVE.** Jamestown Teeters but Survives: 1608–1622   153

**THIRTEEN.** John Smith's Chesapeake Voyages: 1608   165

**FOURTEEN.** The Enduring Dream of Ferdinando Gorges: 1611–1619   175

**FIFTEEN.** Henry Hudson and the Early Dutch Expeditions: 1609–1621   186

*Epilogue: Northern Atlantic America in the Early Seventeenth Century*   201

*Bibliography*   207

*Index*   213

# Preface

This book describes the English, French, and Dutch expeditions to northern Atlantic America before the Pilgrims arrived at Plymouth in 1620. It features the firsthand accounts of the explorers themselves and is meant as a companion to another volume, *Ponce de León to Sir Walter Raleigh: Early European Arrivals in Southeastern North America*, which covers the Spanish expeditions into southeastern America and early Spanish entanglements with the French and English.

During this precolonial period when the eastern coastline of Atlantic America and its people were first revealed to Europe, much happened that has been largely forgotten. Students are taught about the Pilgrims and the great English diaspora that followed, but very little is presented on the rich period of discovery that preceded the establishment of Plymouth.

This book covers the period from Cabot's discovery of Newfoundland in 1497 through the founding of Jamestown in the early 1600s and the events that followed soon after, including Henry Hudson's explorations. It describes the precolonial activities of the French, English, and Dutch at essentially six geographic hotspots: the Grand Banks of Newfoundland and the Gulf of Maine, Baffin Island and Labrador, Cape Cod Bay and Nantucket Sound, New York Harbor and the Hudson River, the St. Lawrence River and Valley, and the Chesapeake Bay Region. Absent from this book are the two northern excursions that Pedro Menéndez sent from Florida to the Chesapeake Region and Giovanni da Verrazzano's northern touchdowns in Massachusetts and Maine. These expeditions are described in the companion book, *Ponce de León to Sir Walter Raleigh: Early European Arrivals in Southeastern North America*.

This book describes many events that are not widely known. For example:

- North America was regularly visited by European cod fishermen long before Columbus's voyage in 1492.
- Martin Frobisher led a massive mining expedition to Greenland in 1577, only to return with "fool's gold."

- The Indigenous people of North America suffered a huge population crash due to European diseases, making vast areas of farmland available for European settlement.
- The prime mover in the Jamestown colony of Virginia was a man named Bartholomew Gosnold, who established an even earlier colony in Cape Cod.
- John Smith, once the governor of Jamestown, is credited with the first good map of the coast of Maine and New England.
- Many of the expeditions sent to New England in the early 1600s were in search of sassafras, then considered a wonder drug.
- Dozens of Indigenous people were abducted by the English in the sixteenth and seventeenth centuries for use as pilots and interpreters.
- The first Dutch expedition to North America was led by an Englishman, Henry Hudson.

This book describes the neglected story of how North Atlantic America was revealed to the Europeans and the many events that preceded their conquest of Atlantic America. It reports on the lives of the Indigenous peoples, how they interacted with the European explorers and early settlers, and how the European onslaught impacted their tribal cultures.

As in my book on the southern explorations, I rely heavily on the eyewitness reports of the explorers themselves whenever possible, taking the liberty to modernize the original English accounts or translations except in a few instances to add flavor. I also have provided descriptions of each Indigenous group's lifeways at the ends of the chapters.

This book benefited greatly from several earlier vibrant histories of the precolonial period written 50 to 125 years ago. These include Henry P. Biggar's *The Early Trading Companies of New France* (1901), Henry S. Burrage's *Early English and French Voyages Chiefly from Hakluyt* (1906), Henry F. Howe's *Prologue to New England* (1969), Samuel L. Morison's *The European Discovery of America: The Northern Voyages* (1971), Carl O. Sauer's *Sixteenth Century North America* (1971), and David B. Quinn's *England and the Discovery of America, 1481–1620* (1974).

# Introduction

## North Atlantic America Before the Europeans Arrived

European explorers' examination of eastern North America started at its geological and environmental extremes—Newfoundland and Florida. The first to reach Newfoundland was Venetian John Cabot in 1497, following the trails of the French and Spanish fishermen who had begun plying the rich fisheries of the Great Banks. The first to Florida was the Spaniard Ponce de León in 1512, who came after the slave traders in search of new captives to replace the vanishing Caribbean Taíno.

Then came a slow but steady period of exploration of Atlantic America that revealed a great continent and its people. In 1524, Giovanni Verrazzano, sailing for France, was the first to travel up the entire Eastern Seaboard, touching down in the Outer Banks of North Carolina, Cape Cod, New York Harbor, and the Gulf of Maine. In the south, Ponce de León would be followed by Hernando de Soto, Pánfilo de Narváez, and Pedro Menéndez de Avilés in a Spanish attempt to take ownership of Florida and southeastern America. The French would make a brief foray into Florida before being routed by the Spanish and chased north. There Cartier, Champlain, Smith, Hudson, and many others would chart the coast of Maritime Canada, the Gulf of Maine, and the New England coast.

For more than a century, Europeans would explore the nooks and crannies of Atlantic America before successfully establishing a colony at Jamestown. As will unfold in this book, there were six primary touchpoints where early European explorers would probe northern Atlantic America, including Newfoundland and the Gulf of Maine, Baffin Island and Labrador, the St. Lawrence Seaway and Valley, New York Harbor and the Hudson River, Cape Cod and the Nantucket Sound, and the Chesapeake Bay Region. As the Europeans probed these locations, they found a rich, diverse ecology that was already overflowing with people.

## The Climate and Vegetation of North America

The climate of North America ranged from an icy, barren Arctic north to a humid, subtropical south. The native vegetation shifted from a treeless North Atlantic to forests of hemlock and white pine along the Gulf of Maine; oak and chestnut in upper New England; mixed forests of beech, tulip tree, basswood, sugar maple, buckeye, chestnut, red oak, white oak, and hemlock in southern New England and the upper South; and mixed evergreens in the lower South. Rich estuaries teemed with life at regular intervals along the coast, and fertile bottomlands flanked the rivers and streams leading to the interior (Sauer 1941).

Those explorers who first visited Arctic Canada found what they considered a generally uninviting, barren, and cold landscape. In 1534 Jacques Cartier found the coast of Labrador to be

> a most rocky and inhospitable shore. He complained that ... he did not see enough soil to fill a cartload and ... found only moss and small stunted trees. It was a landscape ... so barren and rocky that it must be that which God gave to Cain, in retribution for his sins. The coastal areas of southern Labrador and northern Newfoundland are unlike any landscape with which Cartier might have been familiar.... The mossy ground, that from a distance resembles meadowland, could only have been a grave disappointment [Dickenson 2008, 30].

Cartier and the other early explorers' perception of North America changed dramatically when they entered the Gulf of St. Lawrence, where they were on land more familiar to them. Cartier waxed eloquently on the bounty of plants along the shores as he traveled down the St. Lawrence River. Dickenson (2008, 31) suggests that Cartier found on the other side of the ocean a landscape very analogous to what he knew in Europe but more temperate than Spain. He saw what he thought looked like wild wheat and oats, white and red currants, roses, plums, figs (perhaps serviceberry), nuts, apples, and beans growing wild. In northern New Brunswick, he found "land made for the plow, with lovely meadows and fields, and in the highlands in from the coast, were mountains covered in great trees—mast trees, suitable for vessels of 300 tons or more" (Dickenson 2008, 31).

These accounts give the impression that Cartier had entered a world of "vegetable abundance, a natural garden yielding produce sweeter and larger than that of Europe, and without effort" (Dickenson, 2008, 32). Sauer (1941, 159) also noted that for western European explorers and settlers, the New World was a "lustier land," with more sun; warmer, wetter summers; taller trees; and thicker forests than Europe.

In fact, the early explorers and settlers would find the vegetation of the Eastern Seaboard of North America to be quite familiar to them. As Sauer (1941, 159) relates:

In most cases, the colonists were at no loss to identify the native plants and animals that they found on the western side of the Atlantic. It would be impossible, indeed, to cross an ocean anywhere else and find as little that is unfamiliar in nature on the opposite side.

However, the explorers found several hardwoods unique to northern Europe, including chestnut, walnut, hickory, pecan, and tulip trees. They knew chestnuts and walnuts from Mediterranean climes, but the hickories and pecans were unknown to them, and they would have to call them by their Amerindian names. They misnamed the tulip tree as "yellow poplar" (Sauer 1941, 159).

Despite the similarity in vegetation, the colonists would find that the Atlantic Seaboard had hotter summers and colder winters than their home countries. Also, there was a more abrupt change between seasons and more intense rains of shorter duration than in coastal Europe. Captain John Smith suggested that the summers of Virginia were like those of Spain and its winters like those of England. "The thunder and lightning purify the air," he said, "I have seldom either seen or heard in Europe" (Sauer 1941, 158). The air from the ocean generally flows over the European shores of the Atlantic, but the air that flows over the Atlantic Seaboard of the United States generally comes from the west, and it is heated in summer and cooled in winter as it flows over the continent.

## First Encounters

When Europeans first arrived on the Atlantic Coast, they would land on a densely settled and richly fecund homeland to hundreds of nations. About four million people were in North America when the Europeans first arrived (Denevan 1992). Hundreds of tribal groups dotted the Atlantic Coast from Florida to Newfoundland, and the Europeans would encounter powerful nations at all their touchpoints. Among the nations first encountered by Europeans in the Northeast were the Beothuk of Newfoundland, the Inuit of Arctic Canada, and the Wabanaki of Acadia and the Gulf of Maine. In southern Ontario and New England were the St. Lawrence Iroquoians, the Lenni Lenape surrounding New York Harbor, and the Narragansett along the coast of Rhode Island. In Cape Cod and Nantucket Sound were the Wampanoag and Nauset.

The societies scattered along the Atlantic shore had unique cultural aspects, but they also shared many similarities. Their leaders were usually chosen from a small group of men belonging to families of great esteem. Each village had its own leader, who might serve under a greater leader of multiple villages who received a tribute for protection from warring nations. The chieftain held the position until death, unless people lost confidence in them and left the village. The chieftain settled disputes, granted land to individuals for farming and foraging, and dealt with outsiders, but all decisions were subject to the consensus of family heads and elders of the community. Most major decisions were made during springtime gatherings of the whole nation.

The Indigenous people of Atlantic America also, in general, shared a similar way of life (Sauer 1941). Houses were made of poles set upright and covered with strips of heavy bark. Most Indigenous groups made dugout canoes by hollowing the trunk of a tree or used bark canoes. Household vessels were also largely made of wood and bark. Before the Europeans arrived, stone was used to tip their arrows, spears, harpoons, knives, and hide scrapers. Most villages were located along streams and bodies of water. For defense, islands and land partly enclosed by stream confluences were sometimes chosen.

The hard maples were tapped for the spring sap, which was boiled down to sugar. From the woods, berries and edible roots were gathered in quantity. Walnuts, hickory nuts, chestnuts, and the sweeter acorns provided winter foods of importance. They hunted with stone-tipped bows and arrows and with spears. Woodland browse and glade and marsh grasses supported game in an amount and variety that greatly impressed the newly arrived Europeans, who rarely had been given the chance to hunt at home. Deer was particularly important to them and provided food, clothing, blankets, and tools made of antler and bone. To fish, they used a wide array of methods including hooks, nets, poisoned spears, weirs, and dugout canoes.

Women planted, harvested, prepared food, tanned hides, gathered firewood, carried water, made clothing, weaved baskets, took care of the children, and carried supplies on journeys. Men felled trees, cleared the land, built wigwams, constructed dugouts and animal traps, fished and hunted, and protected their families. The much revered old people knitted nets; made clay bowls, wampum beads, and stone implements; and scraped and dressed the pelts for clothing.

Remarkably, most of the eastern societies grew a common assemblage of crops that was unknown in the Eastern Hemisphere—maize, beans, chili peppers, and gourds. The level of agricultural development varied widely across the different cultures depending on geography. The importance of farming was greatest in the southeast and gradually diminished in importance northward to a little above the border of today's Maine. Further north the soil was too weak and the summers too short to support agriculture.

The Indigenous people of what is now the eastern United States did not subsist on crops alone; they also gathered acorns, fruit, and nuts from the forest and fish, clams, and lobster from the waterways. Their food was prepared mostly by boiling or baking on hot coals. Maize was pounded into a coarse flour, soaked in weak lye water obtained from wood ash, and boiled in a soup. They made many kinds of bread, mush, and dumplings from fresh or dried maize, pulses, acorns, and nuts. Corn and beans were combined to make succotash. Cornmeal mush and pounded nuts were used as a base for vegetable, meat, and fish stews. They also boiled meat, fish, pulses, and squash separately.

Fields were cleared by the girdling of trees that let enough full sunlight onto the forest floor in a few months' time for planting. The understory was burned before planting to free it of dead branches and the other herbaceous vegetation that was present. The forest topsoil that remained was dark and rich in potash, making it perfect for maize and their other crops. In a few years' time, wind and decay completed the task of bringing down the dead timber. The planting was usually done in hills by setting several kinds of seed, such as corn, beans, and squash, in heaped mounds of earth. The nations used digging sticks and hoes for cultivation in irregular fields, disregarding stumps. They did not have draft animals or equipment other than hoe or mattock.

The people of the central coast were mostly sedentary with permanent settlements, but during the winter they followed the migration of various hunted animals. They lived in villages, which could number as many as one hundred homes. Some villages were protected by wooden palisades; each house boasted an extensive garden, in which were grown corn, beans, peas, squash, pumpkin, and sunflower. Tobacco, primarily used for ceremonial purposes, was grown apart from the rest of the crops.

Societies in the Northeast typically congregated in villages that were moved seasonally or at intervals of several years. Even the most nomadic people of Labrador gathered in villages in the summer. In northeastern New England, the Wabanaki lived in villages for part of the year and went through an annual cycle of migration—southward to seashore camps for the summer, northward to deep woods hunting camps in the fall and winter, returning to villages along the rivers for late fall feasting and spring fishing and planting—while in southern New England, New York, and New Jersey a more agricultural population lived in villages of some permanence (Day 1953). They generally stayed in place for 10 years or more.

## Myth of the "Pristine Forest"

By the time the Europeans arrived on America's soils, the eastern forests were by no means pristine—all had been disturbed to varying degrees by Amerindian activity. Several biogeographers have made this very clear.

Willian Denevan (1992, 371) describes the state of the woodlands prior to European occupation:

> Agricultural clearing and burning had converted much of the forest into successional (fallow) growth and into semi-permanent grassy openings (meadows, barrens, plains, glades, savannas, prairies), often of considerable size. Much of the mature forest was characterized by an open, herbaceous understory, reflecting frequent ground fires.

Michael Williams (1989, 33) agrees:

> Much of the "natural" forest remained, but the forest was not the vast, silent, unbroken, impenetrable and dense tangle of trees beloved by many writers in their romantic accounts of the forest wilderness.

William Cronon (1983, 49–51) likewise explains what confronted the Europeans in the so-called New World:

> The result [of this human activity] was a forest of large, widely spaced trees, few shrubs, and much grass and herbage.... Selective Indian burning thus promoted the mosaic quality of New England ecosystems, creating forests in many different states of ecological succession.

The first European settlers would find a great, wide-open space—previously cleared by the Indigenous people—that they could exploit for farming.

## *The Clash of Cultures*

When the Europeans began to explore Atlantic America, they were disappointed to find that there were no great, organized, hierarchical societies like the Incas and Aztecs to conquer and plunder as the Spanish had in Mesoamerica and South America. They were confronted instead by groups of farmers and hunter-gatherers, who operated with little hierarchy in a society without metal tools or beasts of burden.

The societies of the two hemispheres had domesticated very different crops and utilized different forms of agriculture. In Europe, the most important crop was wheat, grown in rows plowed by oxen, while in America maize was the primary staple, grown in mounds with beans and squash, all planted by hand with a stick.

The Europeans would find it difficult to understand the complex cultural and intellectual wealth of these Indigenous people they called Indians. Their religious and cultural biases and their concept of land ownership kept them from appreciating and understanding the people who were in it. The people of North America did not have all the advanced technologies of the Europeans, but they had a society just as complex as their ultimate conquerors. Just like the Europeans, the Amerindians knew how to use natural resources to their advantage, adapt to regional environments, forge alliances, build trade networks, and develop strong social bonds.

A major stumbling block in negotiations between the Indigenous people and the colonists would revolve around their concept of land ownership. To the Amerindians, the land could not be owned and was like the life-giving forces of air and sunlight. Humans had the right to use the land, to plant and hunt on it, but they did not possess it. The Amerindians felt that while one might allow another person to hunt, fish, and trap on a piece of property, the original "owner" was not permanently dispossessed from the use of the land. The lessee could use the land but could not exclude all others from entry. To the Europeans, land could be owned by a person or persons, and its use could be restricted. This difference in attitude would cause great misunderstandings and bloodshed as the Europeans began to expand their American footprint.

The introduction of European trade goods into the Amerindian world also instituted a great change in Indigenous culture. They would become very interested and even dependent on things that the explorers and early colonists could provide. Soon, the Indigenous people began using these new materials in their everyday lives. Native hunters were happy to trade hides and pelts for colored cloth and metal tools such as axes, hoes, and knives. It did not take long for the Amerindians to put aside their bows and arrows for European firearms, powder, and lead shot. The desire to get European goods had a dramatic effect on the Indigenous peoples' ancient trading patterns, as hunting animals for food and clothing almost became less important than getting animal hides to trade. The European trade across the Atlantic Ocean would change the Indigenous culture forever.

## *The Great Dying*

The Indigenous populations would be hit with multiple waves of epidemics that overwhelmed their immune systems, which had evolved in isolation from the Eurasians for 13,000 years. The infectious diseases that were carried from the Old World to the New included bubonic plague, chicken pox, malaria, measles, smallpox, typhus, and whooping cough. Because the Indigenous people had no previous contact with Old World diseases, they had not built up any immunological defenses (Koch et al. 2019). Dobyns (1983, 34) suggests that "before the invasion of peoples of the New World by pathogens that evolved among inhabitants of the Old World, Native Americans lived in a relatively disease-free environment."

The illnesses spread through both direct contact with explorers and colonists and secondary contacts through Amerindian trade. Perhaps only one in 10 natives survived this onslaught. Just before the Pilgrims arrived in 1620, the Wampanoag had suffered three disease epidemics in the previous 10 years, which had killed as many as three-quarters of their entire population.

European diseases were accidentally introduced to the Indigenous people of North America, and neither the colonists nor the nations had any idea why this was happening. However, disease wound up playing a major, if not pivotal, role in the European conquest of America, freeing land for colonist cultivation and reducing the number of warriors to combat the European advance.

## One

# Newfoundland
### The First European Touchpoint, 1497–1527

## Setting the Stage: The Real European Discovery of America

The discovery of America by a European is generally credited to Columbus in 1492, but in fact, the Scandinavian Vikings were in North America long before he was. Sailing westward from settlements in Iceland and Greenland, the Norse crossed the Davis Strait in the tenth century, traveled down the coasts of Baffin Island and Labrador, and built a settlement at the northern tip of Newfoundland, known as L'Anse aux Meadows (Wallace 2003). It was a small settlement of no more than 75 people and did not last for more than 20 years, but it was the first known European footprint in North America.

In the interlude between the Vikings at L'Anse aux Meadows and Columbus's landing at Hispaniola, countless other Europeans visited North American waters. Basques from northern Spain were fishing cod during the summer along Newfoundland's Grand Banks as early as the thirteenth or fourteenth century. No one knows for sure when the first English fisherman landed on the eastern coast of North America, but word of an important fishing ground must have reached Bristol by the late 1470s. In 1480, a merchant named John Day is known to have outfitted a ship to search for the mythical island of "Brazil," thought to be far west of Ireland (Pringle 1997). Buffeted by storms, Day's ship did not make it very far out to sea before returning home without success.

## Cabot's Early Voyage of Discovery

The first European explorer to travel to North America was Venetian John Cabot (a.k.a. Giovanni Caboto), commissioned by Henry VII of

England. He made two trips in 1497 and 1498, just a few years after the first Caribbean trip of Columbus.

Little is known about Cabot's life before this voyage. He enters the historical record first in 1461, when he moved from Genoa to Venice and became a naturalized Venetian citizen. He likely was involved in trade at the great markets of Mecca, where spices, perfumes, silks, and precious stones from the Far East were offered for barter. In his 1911 book *The Precursors of Jacques Cartier*, Henry Percival Biggar suggests that

> it occurred to him [Cabot] that this merchandise might be transported to Europe by sailing straight across the western ocean. Compared with the long camel route from northeastern Asia to Mecca and thence to Alexandria and Venice. The voyage by water from Asia to Europe would affect a veritable revolution in trade. The first step in such a change was to find the course across the western ocean from Europe to Asia [Biggar 1911, vii].

Consumed with this idea, Cabot traveled to London in about 1484 on a Venetian galley and made his thoughts known to the merchants of Bristol, who were already conducting extensive trade with Iceland. It was decided that they should first seek the mythical island of "Brazil" shown on many medieval maps and use this island as a stepping stone to Asia across the western sea. Missions were sent out in 1491 and 1492, presumably under Cabot's direction, to find this island, but they came up empty-handed.

About this time, word reached the English court that Christopher Columbus had sailed west across the ocean from Spain and had reached the Indies, provoking great excitement. Henry VII got wind of Cabot's plan and, on March 5, 1496, publicly indicated his support:

> Be it known and made manifest that we have given and granted ... to our well-beloved John Cabot, citizen of Venice, and to Lewis, Sebastian and Sancio, sons of the said John, and to the heirs and deputies of them, and of any one of them, full and free authority, faculty and power to sail to all parts, regions and coasts of the eastern, western and northern sea, under our banners, flags and ensigns, with five ships or vessels of whatsoever burden and quality they may be, and with so many and such mariners and men as they may wish to take with them in the said ships, at their own proper costs and charges, to find, discover and investigate whatsoever islands, countries, regions or provinces of heathens and infidels, in whatsoever part of the world placed, which before this time were unknown to all Christians [Biggar 1911, ix].

On May 2, 1497, in the *Matthew*, manned by 18 men, Cabot set sail from Bristol to find a Northwest Passage to the Orient. No published account of the voyage is known. There are only references to it in a couple of letters, and some marginal notes written by John Cabot's son Sebastian on a 1551 map of the world by Sancho Gutiérrez. On the margin of the Gutiérrez map is printed (Merás 1993, 119):

> This land was discovered by Johannes Caboto, venetian and Sebastian Caboto, his son, in the year of the birth of our Lord Jesus Christ MCCCCXCIV, 24th of June in the morning. They put to it the name "prima terra vista" [...] This big island was named Saint John, as it was discovered on Saint John holiday. People there wander wearing animal furs. They use bows and arrows to fight, javelins and darts, and wooden batons and slings. This is a very sterile land, there are a lot of white bears and very big deer, big as horses, and many other animals. As well there are infinite fish: plaices, salmons, very long soles, 1-yard long, and many other varieties of fish. Most of them are called cod. And there are also black hawks, black as ravens, eagles, partridges, and many other birds.

On his voyage, Cabot is thought to have rounded Ireland, steered north, and then westward. After 52 days at sea, he and his crew sighted their first land and set foot on southern Labrador, the island of Newfoundland, or Cape Breton Island. Wherever he landed, Cabot was convinced that he had reached the northeastern coast of Asia.

When Cabot set ashore in the Americas, he and his crew found evidence of human settlement and fire, but the locals stayed out of their sight. The people who inhabited the area were probably the Beothuk, who had lived in Newfoundland for thousands of years. Beothuk means "the people" or "true people" in their now-extinct language. It is likely that they had already come up against European fishermen and perhaps Vikings centuries before, which made them cautious.

## Cabot's Return

On Sunday, August 6, 1497, the *Matthew* dropped anchor back in Bristol Harbor after catching the westerlies home. Cabot hurried to court and reported that he had been to what he thought must be China and there were vast quantities of fish. A delighted Henry gave Cabot a present of £10 for his discovery and promised him a large fleet to sail to China the next spring. Cabot was also given an annual pension of £20, a lavish reward at that time as a house then rented for £2 a year (Morison 1971).

New letters of patent were issued by Henry, and Cabot set off in May 1498 with five vessels. He likely stopped off at Greenland and Newfoundland and might have explored as far south as Chesapeake Bay or even the Caribbean. However, no one knows for sure, as there are no published records of his return (Jones 2008).

There is a long-held legend at Grates Cove in Newfoundland that Cabot did get ashore with some of the crew, but they died there either by starvation or at the hands of local Beothuk. The first published report of Cabot's landing appeared in William Cormack's narrative *A Journey*

*Across the Island of Newfoundland in 1822*. In it, he asserts that Cabot's landing was documented "by [his] cutting an inscription, still perfectly legible, on a large block of rock that stands on the shore" (1928, 116). This story was repeated numerous times by a series of historians over the next 125 years. However, the rock is now missing (if it ever existed), so we will never know if the long-held story is true.

## Like Father, Like Son—Sebastian Cabot

From the sixteenth to the nineteenth century there was an erroneous belief that John Cabot's son, Sebastian, led the two expeditions of his father in 1497 and 1498. This was based in part on Sebastian's marginal notes on the Gutiérrez map. However, he would have been only 13 or 14 at the time and was unlikely to have been on the voyage (Skelton 2003).

Sebastian did, however, conduct some of his own missions to the North Atlantic after his father's death. In 1504, he led a fishing expedition from Bristol to the New World in two ships: *Jesus* and *Gabriel*. Few details survive of this mission, except that, on April 3, 1505, Cabot was given an annuity of £10 by Henry VII for his discovery of the newfound lands (Ruddock 1974). In 1508–9, Cabot led a more extensive mission to find the Northwest Passage to the Far East. There are also few details of this voyage, except two accounts that report he passed through Hudson Strait to the mouth of Hudson Bay. This journey was depicted in maps drawn by him in later life and by several other cartographers in the sixteenth century.

## Other Early Expeditions to Newfoundland

Cabot's initial return to Bristol elicited a tremendous interest in further exploring the North Atlantic and its great cod fisheries.

Henry VII granted patents to at least five groups from 1501 to 1504 to explore the West (Biggar 1911). Little is known about most of these missions, except that Francis Fernandez and João Gonzales participated in many of them, working with Bristol merchants. These two adventurers may have been the first to abduct Beothuk and bring them back to Europe as trophies. They returned from one of their expeditions with "three men brought out of an Land forre beyonde Irelond, the which were clothed in Beestes skynnes and ate raw flessh and were rude in their demeanure as Beestes" (Biggar 1911, xx). This sad practice of abducting Amerindians would become common among European explorers.

In 1500 and 1501, Gaspar Corte-Real and his brother Miguel, members of the Portuguese royal household, sailed to Greenland, Labrador, and possibly Newfoundland (Hiller 2004). In 1501 Gaspar made another voyage to the Canadian Atlantic with three caravels and explored the east coast of Labrador. Two of Gaspar's three ships returned to Lisbon in October 1501, but the third, with the leader of the expedition, did not return.

Gaspar's brother Michael set out on May 10, 1502, to search for him with three vessels (Biggar 1911). When the group reached Newfoundland in June, it was decided that each vessel would explore a different part of the coast and meet up on August 20 at St. John's. As the boats searched, all had multiple friendly trade opportunities with the Beothuk. One of the vessels explored the area beyond Placentia Bay where Gaspar was lost and found a boat of his but no survivors. As planned on August 20, they returned to the agreed rendezvous point at St. John's and found one of the other boats, but Michael's ship was now missing. After waiting in vain for some time, these two returned home alone.

In 1508, Thomas Aubert, a navigator from Dieppe, was given command of *La Pensée* for a fishing and reconnoitering voyage in the New World in the service of the prominent shipowner Jean Ango (Lanctot, 2003a). Little detail exists of this voyage, but it is known that he brought back the first Beothuk seen in France. Their costumes, arms, and canoes caused great excitement in Rouen, where they were baptized with great pomp.

As the sixteenth century progressed, ever-increasing numbers of Breton and Norman vessels were annually crossing the Atlantic for cod (Biggar 1903). A ship called the *La Pensée*, of Dieppe, led a group of fishing boats in 1508 to the harbors north of Cape Bonavista in Newfoundland. Few details of this voyage remain except that one of the vessels brought back seven captive Beothuk and one of their canoes.

In 1520, a Portuguese nobleman, João Álvares Fagundes, explored the southern coast of Newfoundland and may have reached as far as the mouth of the St. Lawrence River and the Nova Scotia coast. He received a captaincy to the lands he had found from King Manuel of Portugal and established the first European colony in North America on Cape Breton at today's Ingonish in 1521.

Few details are known of this settlement, except that it was established by Fagundes and several families, mostly from the Azores (Morison 1971). They set up a fishing community, but after a year to 18 months, the local Beothuk began cutting their fishing lines, destroying their homes, and ultimately killing them all, or forcing them to move to unknown parts. The Beothuk already had a history of abuse from the Europeans, and probably when they realized that the colonists had come to stay, rather than visit to fish and trade, they decided they had to go.

In 1523, Estêvão Gomes (a.k.a. Esteban Gómez) of Portugal convinced Emperor Charles V to fund another expedition to find the Northwest Passage (Hiller 2004). Gomes had sailed with Magellan as a pilot of the *San Antonio* in the first circumnavigation of the earth, but at the Strait of Magellan in May 1521, he deserted and returned to Spain. He and several other deserters were put in prison but were released in September 1522 when the remainder of Magellan's crew reached Spain and told of their harrowing experiences.

A 50-ton caravel, *La Anunciada*, was built for Gomes's expedition, and it sailed on September 24, 1524, from A Coruña, with a crew of 29 men. He likely first landed in Cuba and then headed north. There is no written account of his journey, so his itinerary is largely unknown. He may have gone north as far as the Cabot Strait and Cape Breton, and likely entered the upper reaches of New York Bay and the Hudson River. Along the way he passed along the coast of Maine, where he thought for sure that the estuary of the Penobscot River was the Northwest Passage. He returned to Spain on August 21, 1525, after abducting more than 50 Beothuk to sell as slaves (Vigneras 2003). This would have been five to 10 percent of the whole Beothuk population in Newfoundland.

In 1527, John Rut from Essex was chosen by Henry VIII to make an expedition to North America in search of the Northwest Passage (De Costa 1884). Rut set sail from Plymouth with two ships, *Samson* and *Mary Guildford*. As they crossed the Atlantic Ocean, the *Samson* was lost in a storm and the *Mary Guildford* met heavy ice, but it managed to reach the Labrador coast near St. Lewis Inlet and then set sail for St. John's Harbor. Remarkably, at St. John's, they came upon 11 Norman, one Breton, and two Portuguese fishing boats. Rut then proceeded southward to Puerto Rico, then Santo Domingo, and after being fired upon by a Spanish fort, headed home.

## *The Lifeways of the Beothuk*

The inhabitants of Newfoundland were the Beothuk, who were scattered across the northeastern, western, and southern coasts of Newfoundland and had a precontact population of only about 500 to one thousand (Tuck et al. 2022; Holly 2000). They were to suffer mightily from the effects of the European invasion, and by the early 1800s, the last of their race went extinct.

They were organized in bands ranging from 35 to 50 individuals belonging to seven to 10 families (Pastore 1998). They hunted harp seals on the coast in late winter and early spring, caught smelt in the rivers in

May, and took advantage of the salmon runs in late summer. They hunted caribou during their fall migrations (Marshall 1996). The Beothuk constructed fences consisting of long lines of poles with flapping straps of skin attached to them and then herded the caribou into the water where they were easier to catch and slaughter. They also hunted beavers, martens, and otter for their furs.

The Beothuk were bow hunters on land and fished with harpoons and spears. They built beautiful, lightweight, easily reparable birch bark canoes, some of which were capable of making long sea trips (Marshall 1996). They also used birch bark to make light, strong containers for food and water. Their clothing was made of warm and light caribou skin. They were sewn together with sinew from the back leg of the caribou.

Before the Europeans arrived, the Beothuk used stone points to tip their arrows, spears, harpoons, knives, and scrapers. After the Europeans began establishing fishing camps, the Beothuk began to salvage metal objects that the fishermen left behind and reworked nails, fishhooks, and scrapes of iron into arrowheads, blades, and other tools. By the end of the seventeenth century, the Beothuk had largely replaced their stone technology.

> The most distinctive of Beothuk artifacts are carved bone, antler and ivory pendants intricately decorated with carved patterns. Many of these items were recovered from grave sites in caves or rock shelters in the late 19th and early 20th centuries [Gallant and Filice 2022].

The Beothuk played bowl-and-dice games, where dice were thrown into the air and scored by whether a marked side fell up or down. Games were played for both entertainment and spiritual reasons, e.g., to cure an illness or lead souls to the other world. Their preparation for these rituals included dreaming, fasting, and sacrifices (Marshall 1998).

The Beothuk traditionally lived in temporary, cone-shaped structures made by placing sheets of bark or hides over a framework of light poles. Spruce boughs were sometimes piled around the perimeter of the tipi for added insulation. After the European contact, they began building more permanent structures as they moved away from the coast to avoid the fishermen. These houses were multisided and often about six to seven meters in diameter. They were built by first excavating a shallow depression in the ground and then sticking short poles, perhaps a meter or so in length, into the ground. Other poles were then tied to the tops of these posts to form a roof. Birch bark was used for the roof and siding, and soil was piled around the perimeter of the structure.

They also built special houses that were oval in shape for feasts. These could be nine to 10 meters in length and four to five meters wide and had a hearth running down the middle. The feasts included cakes made of caribou bone marrow, produced by grinding up the bones, boiling them, and then skimming off the marrow and collagen that rose to the surface and pressing it into cakes. The Beothuk made widespread use of powdered hematite, or red ochre, which they painted on their canoes, artifacts, and bodies. In their grave sites were found intricately carved bone, antler, and ivory.

The Beothuk "adorned themselves dramatically" (Marshall 1998). They painted their whole body with a mixture of red ochre and grease. Both men and women wore a cloak made from several caribou skins sewn together that was wrapped around the body and held tight with a belt. Their coats were sleeveless, and their arms were protected with separate covers. They wore mittens, and their feet were protected by leg-skin boots and moccasins secured by a drawstring thong.

## *Beothuk's Response to Europeans*

While there is evidence of some early friendly interactions between the Beothuk and the Europeans (Holly et al. 2010), the Beothuk were greatly outnumbered during the fishing season and mostly avoided the Europeans. As time went on, most of their contact with Europeans became the scavenging of the seasonally abandoned fishing rooms.

Before the arrival of the Europeans, the Beothuk inhabited most of the island. By the mid-1700s, the majority had moved to secluded Notre Dame Bay and the watershed of the Exploits River and Red Indian Lake to escape the encroachments of the Europeans. Eventually, the Europeans also moved into these regions to hunt and fish, leading to acts of violence on both sides.

The Beothuk did not have guns, so they were largely unable to defend themselves against the European onslaught. Their population numbers began to steadily decline through starvation, European diseases, and harassment from Europeans. Other native groups began to move onto the island and compete with the Beothuk (Pope 2015). The Beothuk went extinct in the late 1820s.

## Two

# Jacques Cartier's Voyages of Discovery
## 1534–1542

### Setting the Stage: The French Get into the Action

About the time that Spaniard Cabeza de Vaca was emerging from the wilderness of Texas, the French explorer Jacques Cartier was beginning his first exploration of Canada. He would follow the trail blazed by Cabot and a host of French, English, and Portuguese sailors fishing for cod along the Grand Banks of Newfoundland. Cartier would travel with the support of Francis I of France, who wanted to build on Verrazzano's discoveries and counterbalance the Holy Roman Emperor Charles V's control of large sections of southeastern Atlantic America.

Cartier would make three voyages between 1534 and 1542. He traveled along the west coast of Newfoundland, which already boasted active Basque whaling stations and a fishery. He then would discover Prince Edward Island, sail up the St. Lawrence River as far as the island of Montréal, and claim already well-populated northern North America for France.

We are fortunate that Cartier kept and published journals of all these voyages. Herein, I quote from a compilation of these voyages published by Henry Burrage in 1906: *Early English and French Voyages Chiefly from Hakluyt 1534–1608*.

### Who Was Jacques Cartier?

Jacques Cartier was a native of Saint-Malo, the principal port of Brittany. Few details exist on his early life, except that he was likely employed as a mariner at a young age and probably sailed along the coast of France,

Newfoundland, and Brazil as a sailor and then as an officer (Allaire 2013). He may also have accompanied Giovanni da Verrazzano on his epic voyage up the Atlantic coast of America and his last trip to Brazil.

Henry Burrage writes in his introduction to *Early English and French Voyages* (1906, 3):

> On fishing voyages in his [Cartier's] earlier years he became interested in western discovery, and in 1533, in a letter addressed to Philippe de Chabot, Sieur de Brion, High Admiral of France, he proposed a voyage to the American coast, continuing the discoveries commenced by Verrazzano in 1524. Through him the interest of the king was enlisted in the enterprise; and with two vessels of sixty tons each, Cartier sailed from the port of St. Malo, April 20, 1534.

## Cartier's First Voyage

On April 20, 1534, Cartier set sail, hoping to discover a western passage to Asia. Enjoying perfect weather, Cartier reached Newfoundland in only 20 days and then sailed throughout the Maritime area, visiting Prince Edward Island, Labrador, and New Brunswick. Along the way, he had brief encounters with small groups of Beothuk and Eastern Wabanaki (Mi'kmaq or Micmac).

Alfred Bailey (1969, 6) relates:

> At Paspebiac Point, in Chaleur Bay, a group of Micmacs attracted Cartier's attention by exhibiting furs which they held up on sticks, and by making signs to the Bretons to come ashore. But in spite of their seeming friendliness, Cartier was wary of their great numbers, and he repelled their advances by shooting two small cannons over their heads and by scattering fire-lances among them. Clearly the strangers who controlled the thunder were heavily endowed with Manito [spirit], but even the displeasure of the gods could not keep the Micmacs from the source of iron, for iron saved them from days of drudgery and enabled them to vanquish their enemies who were yet armed only with stone, bone and wood implements. They returned the next day and signified their willingness to barter. This time Cartier was more venturesome. There was a red cap for the chief and knives, beads, and hatchets for others, all of whom gave furs in exchange.... "And so much at ease did the savages feel in our presence that at length we bartered with them, hand to hand, for everything they possessed, so that nothing was left them but their naked bodie."

During one stop at Île aux Oiseaux in the Magdalen Islands, Cartier would discover an island densely covered with great auks. The ravenous crew harvested birds in the thousands. Cartier writes:

> In less than half an hour we filled two boats full of them as if they had been stones so that besides them which we did not eat fresh, every ship did powder and salt five or six barrels full of them [Burrage 1906, 5].

Thus would begin a sad practice repeated by all explorers of the Maritimes until the last auk was slaughtered in 1840. When Cartier first arrived, great auks were widely distributed across the north Atlantic seas and roosted mostly in water except during their breeding season when they settled on only a few islands between Newfoundland and Norway. Galasso (2014) reports:

> Prior to the 16th century, the species was so abundant that colonies consisting of hundreds of thousands packed the shores during the month-long breeding season. The Little Ice Age of the 16th to the 19th centuries slightly reduced their numbers and territory when their breeding islands became accessible to polar bears, but even with their natural predators encroaching upon their territory, they were a robust species.

## Cartier Meets the Innu and St. Lawrence Iroquoians

After visiting New Brunswick, Cartier headed west and crossed Chaleur Bay to the Gaspé Peninsula. Here Cartier came upon a group of Innu on their annual seal hunt. As Cartier describes:

> We with our boats went on shore in many places, and among the rest we entered into a goodly river, but very shallow, which we named The river of boats, because that there we saw boats full of wild men that were crossing the river. We had no other notice of the said wild men: for the wind came from the sea, and so beat against the shore, that we were constrained to retire ourselves with our boats toward our ships. Till the next day morning at Sunne rising ... we saw a man running after our boats that were going along the coast, who made signs unto that we should return toward the said Cape again. We seeing such signs, began to turn toward him, but he seeing us come, began to flee: so soon as we came on shore, we set a knife before him and a woolen girdle on a little staff, and then came to our ships again [Burrage 1906, 16].

A little later, Cartier's ships were greeted by two fleets of 40 to 50 canoes and a great number of men on shore beckoning them to come and trade. The large numbers of Indigenous people scared the Frenchman, and Cartier frightened them away by firing light artillery.

The following day, another nine canoes approached the ship and the visitors held up furs to show they wanted to trade. This time, Cartier responded favorably and sent two men ashore with iron goods and knives to barter. As Cartier remembers:

> Two of our men ventured to go on land to them, and carry them knives with other iron wares, and a red hat to give unto their Captain. When they saw, they also came on land and brought some of their skins, and so began to deal with us, seeming to be very glad to have our ironware and other things, still

dancing with many other ceremonies, as with their hands to cast sea water on their heads. They gave us whatsoever they had, not keeping anything, so that they were constrained to go back again naked, and made signs that the next day they would come again, and bring more skins with them [Burrage 1906, 20].

This began a period of congenial trade, and the explorers concluded, "These people might very easily be converted to our religion."

This experience made it clear that the Innu had encountered Europeans before and knew exactly what they wanted. The Amerindians would literally trade the clothes off their backs.

Cartier also had some contact in the area with the shyer Beothuk, although it was by no means as extensive as with the Innu. He described their practice of rubbing red ochre over their bodies, hair, clothing, and other items.

At Gaspé Bay, Cartier encountered a group of 300 St. Lawrence Iroquoians, who had come down the St. Lawrence River from Québec. Cartier noted that they slept underneath their overturned canoes and wore little—only breechcloths and a few skins over their shoulders. They welcomed the French with songs and dances and proved to be inventive thieves of knives, combs, and other small articles.

## A Foul Deed by Cartier

On July 24, Cartier took symbolic possession of the Gaspé Peninsula by planting a tall, wooden cross overlooking Gaspé Bay, in front of a huge group of people, about 200 men, women, and children. The imposing cross was about 10 meters high, and at its center it bore a metal plaque with the words "Long Live the King of France." At first, the interaction was pleasant, but the mood turned sour when the locals realized that Cartier was claiming possession of their homeland. Cartier relates:

> After we returned to our ships, their Captain clad with an old bears skin, with three of his sons, and a brother of his, came unto us in one of their boats, but not as near as they wanted and made a long oration unto us, showing us the cross we had set up, and making a cross with two fingers, then did he showed us all the country about us [Burrage 1906, 25].

The leader of this group was Donnacona, the chief of the St. Lawrence Iroquoians village of Stadacona (located at the present site of Québec City), and he had made it very clear that he was not happy about the cross that had been put into the ground on his land.

Once Donnacona's oration had ended, Cartier offered the Iroquoians an axe as a gift. Cartier relates what happened as their boats got near:

> One of our fellows that was in our boat, took hold of theirs, and suddenly leaped into it, with two or three more, who enforced them to enter into our ships, whereat they were greatly astonished. But our Captain did [straightaway] assure them, that they should have no harm, nor any injuries offered them at all, and entertained them very friendly, making them eat and drink. Then did we shew them with signs, that the crosse was but one set up to be as light and leader which ways to enter into the port, and that we would shortly come again, and bring good store of iron wares and other things, but that we would take two of his children with us, and afterward bring them to the said port again [Burrage 1906, 25].

What Cartier had done was abduct two sons of Donnacona—Taignoagny and Domagaya. The action was certainly part of a plan that had been hatched long before the deed was done. One can only imagine the horror and fear that these two abductees must have felt. In his journal, Cartier made light of the event and suggested that the Iroquoians were easily placated about their fate. He writes:

> And so we clothed two of them in shirts, and colored coats, with red caps, and put about everyone's neck a copper chain, whereat they were greatly contented: then gave they their old clothes to their fellows that went back again, and we gave to each one of those three that went back, a hatchet, and some knives, which made them very glad. After these were gone, and had told the news unto their fellows, in the afternoon there came to our ships six boats of them, with five or six men in everyone, to take their farewells of those two we had detained to take with us and brought them some fish, uttering many words which we did not understand, making signs that they would not remove the crosse we had set up [Burrage 1906, 25–26].

After the abduction, Cartier continued to explore the area surrounding the entrance to the St. Lawrence River between the Gaspé Peninsula and Anticosti Island but was unable to travel further inland due to strong winds and opposing tides. At this point, it seemed prudent to head home. Cartier describes:

> We assembled together all our captains, masters, and mariners, to have their advice and opinion what was best to be done: and after that everyone had said, considering that the easterly winds began to beare away, and blow, ... and that the tempests began to reign in Newfoundland, and that we were so far from home, not knowing the perils and dangers that were behind, for either we must agree to return home again, or else to stay there all the year. Moreover, we did consider, that if the northern winds did take us, it was not possible for us to depart thence. All which opinions being heard and considered, we altogether determined to address ourselves homeward [Burrage 1906, 28].

Cartier would return home with the two captive Iroquoians and many great tales of potential riches. Taignoagny and Domagaya likely supported him with their own embroidered stories of the Kingdom of Saguenay, no doubt hoping to be returned to Canada as soon as possible.

Barbara Huck (2002, 25) suggests: "What they told Cartier and his sponsors, including the king, was apparently enough to convince them to launch a larger expedition the following spring."

## Cartier's Second Voyage

In 1535, Cartier was rewarded for his efforts with another mission to America. The goal would be to establish a colony that would remain through the winter. On May 19, he set off on a second voyage with three ships and 110 men including Taignoagny and Domagaya. His ships were named the *Great Stoat*, the *Lesser Stoat*, and the *Merlin*. They landed first in Newfoundland and then headed to "the Island of Birds," where they filled two boats with auks (Burrage 1906).

As before, Cartier continued to move down the Maritime coast and reached the St. Lawrence Seaway, but this time he was able to sail upriver and came upon the Iroquoian village of Stadacona where Chief Donnacona ruled. Here Cartier relates:

> We took our two wild men with us, meeting with many of these country people who would not at all approach unto us, but rather fled from us until our two men began to speak unto them, telling them that they were Taignoagny and Domagaya, who as soon as they had taken acquaintance of them, began greatly to rejoice, dancing and showing many sorts of ceremonies and many of them came to our boats and brought many eels and other sorts of fishes, with two or three burdens of great millet wherewith they make their bread, and many great musk melons [pumpkins]. The same day came also many other boats full of those countrymen and women to see and take acquaintance of our two men, all of which were as courteously received and friendly entertained by our captain as possibly could be. And to have them better acquainted with him and make them his friends, he gave them many small gifts, but of small value; nevertheless, they were greatly contented with them [Burrage 1906, 46].

At Stadacona, Cartier makes the first reference in his journal to the name "Canada," which he used to identify the region. The name came from the Iroquoian word *kanata*, which means "village" but was misinterpreted by Cartier to represent the newly discovered land. Cartier would also name the inhabitants of the area "Canadians" and call the St. Lawrence River "Canada River."

After these encounters, Cartier left his two largest ships behind and continued in the smallest one upriver towards what was the chief Iroquoian village of Hochelaga, located where Montréal now stands.

Donnacona tried to discourage his further travel upriver, not wanting him to learn about the greatest city of the St. Lawrence Iroquoians. Donnacona was worried he would lose his hoped-for role as a middleman if Carter were to establish relations there. To dissuade him from going to Hochelaga, Donnacona told Cartier "that his Lord did greatly sorrow that he would go to Hochelaga, and that he would not by any means permit that any of them should go with him, because the river was of no importance." The Iroquoians even tried to scare them away by dressing "up three men as devils, arraying them in black and white dog-skins, with horns as long as one's arm and their faces colored black as coal, and unknown to us put them into a canoe" (Burrage 1906, 50). Taignoagny also warned Cartier that their god Cudouagny had announced that there would be much ice and snow at Hochelaga, and they would all perish in it. Cartier ignored this warning, and while such conditions did not come to pass at this time, it proved to be prophetic later when he decided to overwinter in Stadacona.

Cartier arrived at the village on October 2, 1535, and even though he had been discouraged from visiting, once there, he was warmly received. In his journal, he records:

> We came across on the way many of the country's people, who brought us fish and other provisions while dancing and showing great joy at our coming. And in order to win and keep their friendship, the Captain made them a present of some knives, beads, and other small trifles, whereat they were greatly pleased. And on reaching Hochelaga, there came to meet us more than a thousand persons, men, women, and children, who gave us as good a welcome as any father ever gave to his son, making great signs of joy [Burrage 1906, 57].

At Hochelaga, the river was blocked by rapids, and Cartier could progress no further. In spite of this, he was convinced that he had found the Northwest Passage and that the rapids were all that was between him and China. He named the rapids "Lachine" after the French *la Chine*, which means "China."

Cartier found Hochelaga to be a vast fortified city surrounded by agricultural fields. In the first European description of an Amerindian village, he relates:

> We went along, and about a mile and a half farther, we began to find goodly and large fields.... In the midst of those fields is the city of Hochelaga, placed near, and as it was joined to the great mountain that is tilled roundabout, very fertile, on the top of which you may see very far, we named it Mount Royal. The city of Hochelaga is round, compassed about with timber, with three courses of rampires, one within another framed like a sharp spire, but laid across above.... The rampires are framed and fashioned with pieces of timber, laid along on the ground, very well and cunningly joined together after their fashion. This enclosure is in height about two rods. It hath but one gate or entry,

which is shut with piles, stakes, and barres. Over it, and also in many places of the wall, there be places to run along, and ladders to get up, all full of stones, for the defense of it. There are in the town about fifty houses, about fifty paces long, and twelve, or fifteen broad, built all of wood, covered over with the bark of the wood.... Within the said houses, there are many rooms, lodgings, and chambers. In the middle of everyone, there is a great court, whereof they make their fire. They live in common together.... They have also on the top of their house's certain garrets, wherein they keep their corn to make their bread [Burrage 1906, 59].

Cartier spent two days at Hochelaga before returning to Stadacona on October 11 to spend the winter. His men built a small fort, stacked firewood, and salted down game and fish as provisions. Then came a monster winter. From mid–November 1535 to mid–April 1536, the French fleet was frozen solid in ice over a fathom (1.8 meters) thick with snow four feet (1.2 meters) deep ashore. Within a few months, scurvy broke out among the crew. Cartier describes:

Unknown sickness began to spread itself amongst us after the strangest sort that ever was either heard of or seen, insomuch as some did lose all their strength, and could not stand on their feet, then did their legs swell, their sinews shrine as black as any coal. Others also had all their skins spotted with spots of blood of a purple color: then did it ascend up to their ankles, knees, thighs, shoulders, arms, and neck: their mouth became stinking, their gums so rotten, that all the flesh did fall off, even to the roots of the teeth, which did also almost all fall out. With such infection did this sickness spread itself in our three ships, that about the middle of February, of a hundred and ten persons that we were, there were not ten whole, so that one could not help the other, a most horrible and pitiful case [Burrage 1906, 73].

Most of the crew would likely have died that winter if Domagaya hadn't come to their rescue and brought them a concoction made from the evergreen aneda, loaded with vitamin C. The Frenchmen would ultimately strip the bark off of an entire tree for the cure, and the dramatic results prompted Cartier to proclaim it a godsend and a miracle. Eighty-five men would survive the winter.

In February, Chief Donnacona and men from the village set out on their annual hunting expedition. When they returned two months later, they brought back with them several people whom Cartier did not recognize, and the French began to fear an attack. To prevent this, the captain decided to take hostages again. This would guarantee them safe passage down the river, and they would have a new batch of Indigenous captives to describe the great marvels of Canada to François I.

Cartier enticed the Iroquoians aboard his ship by hosting what was described as a celebratory feast in their honor. The Amerindians must have been wary after their previous experience but joined in the purported festivities anyway. As soon as they were on board, Cartier's crew grabbed Donnacona, his sons (again), and seven others and took them captive. Cartier promised them that he would return them unharmed in a year and that they would meet the King of France who would give them "great rewards." The captain also "gave Donnacona, as a great present, two frying pans of copper, eight Hatchets, and other small trifles, ... whereof he seemed to be very glad, who sent them to his wives and children" (Burrage 1906, 83).

After a difficult trip down the St. Lawrence River and an ocean crossing of three weeks, Cartier arrived in Saint-Malo on July 15, 1536, concluding his second, 14-month voyage.

## Fate of Donnacona and the Others

In his second voyage, Cartier had discovered a great river, bordered by rich, fertile lands; however, the explorers had suffered terribly in their long winter at Stadacona, making the king hesitant about supporting Cartier in another mission. Cartier's wish to return was also delayed by the invasion of France by Spain. It would take more than three years for another North American mission to be put together. By this time Donnacona had died, along with eight of the other nine captives. Only one girl survived; her fate is unknown.

The Indigenous group had been well cared for while in France and lived at the king's expense (Trudel 2003). Donnacona was interrogated extensively by monk and historian André Thevet. He was presented to François I, whom he regaled with stories of his homeland, including gold and silver mines, an abundance of spices, and men with wings who could fly. The king bought it all. Donnacona and a couple of others in the group were baptized.

## Cartier's Third Voyage

Eventually, the King was persuaded to support another mission by an influential nobleman, Jean-François de La Rocque de Roberval, who was willing to personally undertake an attempt at settlement. By letters patent, dated January 15, 1540, Roberval was placed at the head of the expedition, while Cartier was given the title of captain-general and chief pilot of the king's ships. Cartier and Roberval were empowered by the king to ransack the prisons to complete their crews and obtain colonists. After a number of agonizing delays, Roberval gave Cartier permission to head out ahead of him with the bulk of the settlers to find the "Kingdom of Saguenay" and its riches. The idea of discovering a Northwest Passage was now forgotten.

On May 23, 1540, Cartier set off with five ships, and three months later he arrived at Stadacona. Here he met again with the Iroquoians, who initially greeted him warmly until they found out that Donnacona and the other hostages had not returned with him. He lied and told the new chief that while Donnacona had died, "the rest stayed there as great Lords, and were married, and would not return into their country" (Burrage 1906, 98).

Cartier could not help but find the Iroquoians' growing discontent and their great numbers at Stadacona disconcerting and decided to sail a few kilometers further upriver to build his settlement on the site of present-day Cap-Rouge, Québec. Here the colonists landed; cattle were set loose, a fortress built, and a garden was planted with seeds of cabbage, turnip, and lettuce. The settlement was named Charlesbourg-Royal. The men also began collecting what they were sure was diamonds and gold, and two ships were sent home on September 2, bearing these minerals.

On September 7, 1541, Cartier traveled with a few Iroquoians in longboats to search for the Kingdom of Saguenay, with its presumed gold and riches. Rapids again prevented him from going farther west than Hochelaga, and by the time he returned to the fort, the Iroquoians had turned hostile and refused to visit or trade with the French. Little information is available about the settlers' fate over the winter of 1541–2, but at least one attack by the Iroquoians killed about 35 of them. What must have been a miserable winter convinced Cartier that he should return home, not having enough manpower to either defend the settlement or properly search for the Kingdom of Saguenay.

Cartier left for France in early June 1542 and inadvertently bumped into Roberval and his ships along the Newfoundland coast, finally en route to Saguenay. Roberval ordered Cartier to accompany him back to Saguenay, but Cartier slipped off under the cover of darkness and continued to France. He was totally convinced that his vessels were filled with gold and diamonds. Unknown to him, the minerals in the two ships previously sent to France had already been found to be worthless.

## Colony Attempt of the Sieur de Roberval

The Sieur de Roberval did eventually set off to restore the colony established by Cartier at Cap-Rouge. En route, Roberval abandoned a relative of his named Marguerite, her lover, and a servant on an island in the

St. Lawrence River called Île des Démons. Apparently, he was shocked at their behavior on board.

> Marguerite gave birth to a child, who died; the young man succumbed too, as did the servant-girl. Marguerite stayed on alone on the island, using her firearms against the wild animals; she managed to survive and was one day picked up by fishermen who took her away to France [La Roque de Roquebrune 2003].

At Stadacona, the Sieur de Roberval attempted to renew relations with the Iroquoians, but at this point they had become outright hostile. The new settlers subsequently suffered a long winter, and about 50 of them died of scurvy—clearly neither Cartier nor the Iroquoians had shared the aneda recipe with them. In the spring, ships arrived from France with fresh supplies, but also letters from François I demanding their return because of the war. Roberval abandoned the fort in 1543.

## *Legacy of Jacques Cartier*

Jacques Cartier was the first European to explore the St. Lawrence Gulf and River. He also discovered Prince Edward Island and built a fort at Stadacona, where Québec City stands today. Although his settlement failed, his discoveries led the way to later European explorations in the sixteenth and seventeenth centuries. The French would eventually colonize the area he described, but it would be decades later before they returned to Charlesbourg-Royal. By this time, the Amerindian settlements of Hochelaga and Stadacona were gone, as were the Iroquoians. They had gone extinct for unknown reasons.

## *Lifeways of the Innu, St. Lawrence Iroquoians, and Wabanaki*

### Innu (also Montagnais-Naskapi)

In New Brunswick, Cartier came upon the Innu (Montagnais-Naskapi). The geographical range of the Innu ranged from northern Labrador to Québec. The early missionaries who encountered them in northern Labrador and Québec called them the "Naskapi"; in the St. Lawrence Valley, they referred to them as the "Montagnais." Anthropologists now recognize these groups as a common culture; Innu is what they call themselves.

The Innu were wide-ranging nomadic hunter-gatherers who moved from place to place when animal populations became scarce in one region and more plentiful in another. They traveled long distances with snowshoes and toboggans in winter and birch bark canoes in summer. They fabricated skin clothing, stone tools, and wooden utensils, often on-site rather than carrying them long distances. Many of these items were decorated with painted or woven designs, "and Innu artifacts, such as the famous 'Naskapi' painted caribou skin coats, are so beautiful they have the place of pride in many museum collections across the world" (Tanner 1999).

For most of the year, the Innu lived in small groups of several families who occupied tents of bark or caribou skin, but in midwinter they often moved into communal structures. Large groups came together at times of plenty on the coast in summer or in the interior where caribou gathered, fish spawned, or waterfowl flocked.

Their diet was based largely on meat. They hunted game animals like caribou in the eastern and northern areas, moose in the west, along with beaver and bear. They fished for eels and fish, hunted seals, and gathered roots, berries, and sap.

> Although they were experts at killing game, they saw this relationship with animals not in terms of violent conquest over their prey, but as one of love and respect. Animals were seen to have much more spiritual power, that hunters would have never been able to kill them were it not that they gave themselves willingly [Tanner 1999].

The caribou were of special importance, and they celebrated a special feast called a "Mokushan" where they ate caribou fat and bone marrow, drummed, and sang songs to the animal spirit.

## St. Lawrence Iroquoians

In Acadia, Cartier came upon the St. Lawrence Iroquoians, who occupied the territory surrounding the St. Lawrence River from the mouth of Lake Ontario to Québec City, and the American states of New York and northernmost Vermont (Warrick 2000). There may have been as many as 25 nations among the St. Lawrence Iroquoians, who numbered anywhere from 8,000 to 10,000 people (Tremblay 2006). These groups shared a common language and similar culture but were not politically united (Pendergast 1997; Gagné 2015). The St. Lawrence Iroquoians were distinct from the other nations in the region, the Wyandot and the five nations of the Haudenosaunee later encountered by Samuel de Champlain.

The St. Lawrence Iroquoians were maize farmers who lived in permanent villages located on the slopes and terraces along the St. Lawrence River. Their villages were palisaded and surrounded by extensive crop fields. An entire village site could cover as much as 100 or 150 acres (Day

1951). Because the Iroquoians did not fertilize their fields, the land rapidly lost its fertility, and every couple of years they were forced to plant on virgin sites farther and farther from their villages. This caused them to relocate their villages every 10 to 20 years. By this time, their lodges had also deteriorated and game in the region had become difficult to find.

The forest was burned to clear new fields, and they were planted using a stick to dig holes and bury the seeds. They grew maize, beans, squash, sunflower, and tobacco. While 75 percent of their sustenance came from agriculture, hunting and fishing also played an important role in their food procurement. The Iroquoians of the region found many of their resources in the rich ecosystems of the estuary, including harp seals, harbor seals, small whales such as the beluga, and possibly porpoises. They also fished for mackerel, sea sturgeon, and other fish species, and harvested shellfish. The men were the hunters, and except for the preparation of the land, horticultural production was an activity of women.

Iroquoians temporarily left their villages and settled on the shores of the estuary during the latter half of the winter. This allowed them to take advantage of the abundant marine resources there (St-Pierre 2016). Iroquoians also periodically traveled far from their home country to hunt and fish, traversing the huge area between Québec and the mouth of the Saguenay River, a distance of about 200 kilometers one way, and as far as the tip of the Gaspé Peninsula, another 700 kilometers distant. They made these expeditions in great numbers—Cartier encountered more than 200 of them in 1534 in some 40 canoes.

They lived in rectangular longhouses that were about 30 meters long by five meters wide and seven meters high. The frame was made of poles driven into the ground and tied together with hemp ropes. The houses were generally covered with cedar or fir bark; inside several hearths ran along a central corridor, with sleeping benches hanging above the ground on each side. There were doors at each end of the building. The people living in these homes were of the same maternal clan.

The Iroquoians were a structured society, with men and women having separate tasks (Gagné 2015). The men manufactured hunting tools, wooden utensils, fishing nets, agricultural implements, and pipes. The women made clothing, leather moccasins, wicker baskets, ceremonial necklaces, and clay vessels used for cooking and storing food. The clay pots were decorated with artistic geometric figures.

## Wabanaki (Etchemin, Mi'kmaq, and Abenaki)

As Cartier moved through the Canadian Maritimes on his first voyage, he had brief encounters with the Mi'kmaq, an eastern Wabanaki group. There were two major groups within the Wabanaki—the Eastern Wabanaki (Etchemin and Mi'kmaq), located from Newfoundland to the Kennebec River Valley, and the Western Wabanaki (Abenaki), found between the Kennebec and Merrimack River Valley (Prins and McBride, 2007). The Eastern Wabanaki depended solely on hunting, fishing, and gathering, while the Western Wabanaki were also horticulturalists. Maize, beans, and squash were grown throughout their territory, although most intensively in its milder southern reaches.

The Wabanaki lived in dispersed bands of extended families for much of the year, coming together during the spring and summer at seasonal encampments along rivers or on the seacoast. They foraged in small extended families that were part of a larger tribal community that numbered between 300 and 500 people. The kin groups lived on their own for most of the year, foraging in their familiar areas, but in the spring they rejoined larger kin groups at food-rich sites. Many hundreds of tribal members and visitors from distant regions would then encamp together.

> Each kin group within the small communities had its own vested interests in certain tracts of forest, stretches of rivers and lakes, peninsulas, seashores, and coastal islands sustaining them.... Successive generations of Indian hunters, fishers, and gatherers periodically returned to these familiar places where they could hunt, fish, and gather for some time, before moving on to another place to set up camp. With kinship ties, including intermarriage, between neighboring families, they would have operated in close association, and their foraging territories probably overlapped [Prins and McBride 2007, 17–18].

The Wabanaki hunted and foraged widely. They used dogs to chase their prey, especially moose, deer, and caribou. They also hunted bears, beavers, otters, gray seal, waterfowl, and other birds.

> They tapped the sweet sap of the maple tree and harvested greens (young ferns or fiddleheads, etc.), wild fruits (strawberries, etc.), nuts (chestnuts, etc.), seeds (wild rice, etc.) and edible roots and tubers (groundnuts, etc.). Etchemin families dug clams in the mudflats. Other shellfish were also eaten, including lobster, some being 20 pounds in weight.... Etchemins used harpoons to take seals, porpoise, and sturgeon, and special three-pronged fish spears to catch salmon, trout and bass. At night, they lured the fish with torches of burning birchbark from their canoes. This way, a man could spear up to 200 fish during one trip. In addition to using nets, hooks and lines, Etchemins caught a variety of fish in weirs made of wooden stakes placed in a shallow stream or small tidal bay [Prins and McBride 2007, 21–22].

Wabanaki crafted their tools, clothes, and implements from available resources. They carved harpoons, needles, awls, and fishing hooks from animal bones. They built seaworthy canoes of birch bark, with a white cedar frame sewn with black spruce root, sealed with spruce gum or pitch, and lined with northern white cedar slats. They used chipped stone to craft arrowheads, knives, scrapers, and heavy woodworking tools. They made ceramic cooking pots from fired clay mixed with crushed rock grit or shells. These pots were decorated with a variety of intricate designs that changed over time. They used sweetgrass to weave baskets. Their clothing was made of animal hides and furs, mostly moose, caribou, beaver, bear, and seal.

The Wabanaki lived in tent-like, birch bark homes called wigwams, which means "home" in Algonquian-based languages. They were cone-shaped, with a hole in the top to let out smoke from an internal fire. The interior was blanketed with large deer, moose, and bear pelts. Animal hides hung over the doorway to keep the elements out.

The Wabanaki leaders were usually chosen from a small group of men belonging to families believed to possess supernatural powers. The *sokom* (sagamore or chieftain) kept his position until he died or the people lost confidence in him. A new tribal leader was elected from among the leading family heads, but most were selected from the same respected family as the deceased chief. The sokom mediated disputes and decided on foraging territories, but all decisions were subject to the consensus of family heads and elders of his community. Most major decisions were made during the springtime gatherings.

## Three

# Fool's Gold

## The Arctic Expeditions of Martin Frobisher, 1576–1578

### Setting the Stage: England Gets into the Game

While Spain and France were sparring for control of southeastern Atlantic America in the first half of the sixteenth century, England was largely content to focus on the North Sea fisheries. England really did not emerge as a sea power until 1552, when Queen Elizabeth began sending the privateers John Hawkins and Francis Drake to seize and plunder Spanish and Portuguese ships off the coast of West Africa and then in the Caribbean.

As England began to flex its sea muscles, influential writers such as Richard Hakluyt (1552–1616) and John Dee (1527–1609) began pressuring Elizabeth to build her own overseas empire. Spain was by then well established in the Americas, and Portugal had global empires in Africa, Asia, and Brazil. To get in on the action, Queen Elizabeth gave her blessing to three major expeditions within a few years of one another. These included Martin Frobisher's search to find the Northwest Passage in 1576, an expedition by Humphrey Gilbert in 1583 to claim Newfoundland, and a mission by Sir Walter Raleigh to settle North Carolina in 1584.

Martin Frobisher would wind up sailing to the Arctic in three expeditions. In his first mission, he would set out in search of the fabled Northwest Passage, but in the other two, he would get waylaid in a failed attempt to find and extract gold ore. His voyages were well documented by George Best, an Elizabethan scientist and explorer, who sailed with him on all three expeditions. For quotes from Best, I have used an 1867 publication of Robert Collinson that contained Best's writings from the first edition of *Hakluyt's Voyages*.

## Frobisher's First Voyage

The principal backer of Frobisher's voyage was Michael Lok, an English merchant. A ship of about 20 tons was built for the mission named the *Gabriel*, and two ships were purchased—the *Michael* of 25 tons, and a pinnace of 10 tons. To man the ships, a crew of 35 was employed. On June 7, 1576, the fleet sailed from Ratcliff with Frobisher as its admiral and pilot, Christopher Hall as captain of the *Gabriel*, and Owen Gryffyn as captain of the *Michael*. Accompanying them was also the bark *Dennis* and several other ships. As they headed down the Thames, the queen waved them farewell as they passed by her castle.

On July 1, they sighted the east coast of Greenland, where they were hit by a massive storm. The events were dramatically depicted by William McFee in his 1928 biography of Frobisher (89–90):

> Now came a period in this voyage which some gauge by which we can measure the sort of men Frobisher and his captains were. Hall, going ahead, reported the Straits full of ice. The fleet sailed in. And it is difficult to decide which did more credit to their country—the cool courage of the commanders or the amazing strength of the ships.
>
> The great masses of ice were on the move, they were setting outward and the southeasterly wind was holding them up. The tides and currents added to the confusion. A ship, sailing in between the bergs, would find her way suddenly closed. The ship following her would be as suddenly nipped and all hands had to fend off. The Dennis, Captain Kendal, one hundred tons, was not quick enough. She received such a blow with a rock of ice that she sank down in sight of the whole fleet, says Best, and Thomas Ellis tells in Hakluyt that the site of this collision "so abashed the whole fleet that we thought verily we should taste of the same sauce." The Dennis shot off a great piece of ordnance, according to the standing orders, and by good luck all the crew were saved. But one section of a house, which was to be erected for the colonists, was in her hold and so was lost.
>
> And then, "as though these hazards were not sufficient for our captains," the wind from the southeast rose to gale force, driving the vessels, in spite of themselves crashing among the bergs which were grinding and toppling on each other. The roar of the wind behind them their way out to the open sea was blocked. "Sundry men with sundry devices sought to save themselves," says Best, and he remarks that this storm was "outrageous," which we are willing to believe.... He tells how some won to open water and took in their sails; how others used a piece of ice to fend off the bergs; how yet others again were encompassed about so straitly they needs must put out balks of timber, ropes, bedding, and so forth overside to act as fenders against the ice....
>
> For some, even without board upon the ice, and some within board upon the sides of their ships, having poles, pikes, pieces of timber, and oars in their hands, stood almost day and night without any rest, bearing off the force, and breaking the sway of the ice with such incredible pain and peril, that it was wonderful to behold....

The three ships got separated, and the pinnace was lost. The captain of the *Michael* became so intimidated by the ice that he turned back, and the *Gabriel* was nearly swamped and wound up on its side. Frobisher kept the ship afloat by ordering the men to cut the mizzenmast to lighten the weight and right the ship. This saved the day, but the ship was full of water, and they had lost many supplies. The crew worked diligently to pump *Gabriel* dry, and they rigged a new mizzenmast.

## *Frobisher Continues On*

Undaunted, Frobisher continued westward, and on July 28 he sighted a barren, rocky headland he named "Queen Elizabeth's Foreland," now known as Resolution Island. From there, Frobisher headed west in a great bay reaching into the heart of Baffin Island, and at its head, Frobisher dispatched a party on a small island he named Hall's, after the master of *Gabriel*. As they departed, he told the group to bring him anything that they found "in token of Christian possession" of the land.

McFee (1928, 48) relates:

> Some of his company brought flowers, some green grass, and one brought a piece of a black stone, much like to a Seacoal in color, which by the weight seemed to be some kind of metal or Mineral. This was a thing of no account, in the judgment of the Captain at the first sight. And yet for novelty, it was kept, in respect of the place from whence it came.

This little rock would later lead to a mad search for gold in Frobisher Bay.

Frobisher then sailed into a great bay, which he assumed was the Northwest Passage that divided Asia on the north from America on the south. Best describes:

> And that land upon his right hand, as he sailed Westward, he judged to be the continent of Asia.... This place he named after his name Frobishers Strait, like as Magellan at the Southwest end of the world, having discovered the passage to the South Sea (where America is divided from the continent of that land, which lay under the South Pole ...) [Collinson 1867, 72–73].

Frobisher traveled about 60 leagues into the bay and named it Frobisher's Strait. Unfortunately, as we now know, it was not the Northwest Passage at all but a dead end inside of Baffin Island, a mistake that would go uncorrected until the middle of the nineteenth century. Charles Hall was the first to sail far enough to reach its end.

At this point, Frobisher decided to visit Hall's Island himself and, for the first time, saw signs that the country was inhabited. As Best tells it:

And being ashore, upon the top of a hill, he perceived a number of small things fleeting in the sea afar off, which he supposed to be porpoises, or seals, or some kind of strange fish: but coming nearer, he discovered them to be men, in small boats made of leather [Collinson 1867, 73].

These were the Inuit of Baffin Island.

## Frobisher and the Inuit

Over the next several days, the two groups traded cautiously with each other, sometimes ashore and sometimes aboard the *Gabriel*. The Inuit seemed familiar with ships such as the *Gabriel*, and they willingly consumed English food, drank wine, and competed in acrobatics with the mariners among the ropes of the ship's rigging. Best describes: "They exchanged coats of seal, and bear skins, and such like, with our men, and received belles, looking glasses, and other toys in recompense thereof again" (Collinson 1867, 73).

One of the Inuit, through signs, agreed to show them the way to the "West Sea" (Collinson 1867, 82), and Frobisher sent him with five seamen back to the shore to prepare for the journey. These five sailors disobeyed their orders to stay in sight of the ship and were never seen again. Frobisher waited three days for their return and then searched the coast in vain for his men or some Inuit who might be captured and ransomed. He did not find any of his men and was able to capture only one poor soul who had come to the ship in his kayak to trade. He was lured by a ringing bell until he was close enough to be pulled from his kayak. Frobisher would take this unfortunate man back to England as proof to Queen Elizabeth that he had reached a far and strange land. Sadly, the captive died shortly after reaching England.

## Frobisher Returns Home

Frobisher then decided it was time to turn homeward, as snow had begun falling on deck and the seas were beginning to freeze around the *Gabriel*. He claimed Baffin Island as a possession of Queen Elizabeth and named it "Meta Incognita." Frobisher then sailed back to England and on October 9 docked in London, where he was well received by the queen.

Soon after his return, Frobisher gave the black stone that had been collected on Hall's Island to his backer Michael Lok, who took pieces of it to three different assessors to determine its worth. All three deemed it worthless as marcasite, a mineral very similar to pyrite, also known as fool's gold (McCoy 2014a). Disappointed but undaunted, Lok solicited one more appraisal: Giovanni Agnello claimed he could extract gold from the mineral via a special process known only to himself.

Lok wrote Queen Elizabeth an account of all these findings, and she decided to invest £1,000 on a second voyage, even with the shaky evidence of gold. In March 1577, the Cathay Company was formed and given a royal charter, with Lok as governor and Frobisher as "high admiral."

## Second Voyage

Frobisher's specific commission for his second voyage was to search for gold ore, and at least for the time being, the search for the Northwest Passage was put on hold (Cooke 2003). On May 31, 1577, Frobisher sailed from Harwich with three ships and about 120 men. He captained Queen Elizabeth's ship the *Ayde*, with George Best as his lieutenant and Charles Jackman as his mate. Edward Fenton captained the *Gabriel*, Gilbert Yorke the *Michael*. Also aboard were a group of miners; the artist John White, who would produce the first pictures of Inuit and later would gain fame as the artist of the Roanoke Colony; and six criminals to be set ashore in Friesland (Greenland) "to civilize the natives" (Morison 1971, 517).

Frobisher's specific orders were:

> (1) to set his sappers and miners to work on mining gold on Hall's Island or elsewhere, (2) in one of the barks, to sail no more than 100 leagues up his Strait, but not so long as to jeopardize returning in the same year, (3) to leave some of his company to winter on the Strait with a pinnace and supplies, and (4) if no more promising ore was forthcoming, to send a flagship home and go onto China with the two barks [Morison 1971, 517].

They arrived at the shore of Greenland on July 4, but ice prevented them from landing. On July 17 they reached the island from which the now famous little black stone had originally been taken. Little additional ore was found there, but on another nearby island (now Kodlunarn Island) they did discover a large quantity. While five miners and some of the crew dug ore and loaded the *Ayde*, Frobisher and a group of 40 men explored the island.

Frobisher and the crew began by building a cairn of stones at the island's highest point to claim the island in a brief ceremony. Frobisher dubbed it Mount Warwick in honor of the Earl of Warwick, one of the investors in the expedition.

As Best describes:

> On Friday the nineteenth of July in the morning early, with his best company of Gentlemen and soldiers, to the number of forty persons, went on

shore.... And leaving his boats here with sufficient guard, passed up into the country about two English miles and recovered the top of a high hill, on the top whereof our men made a column or Cross of stones heaped up of a good height together in good sort, and solemnly sounded a trumpet, and said certain prayers, kneeling about the ancient, and honored the place by the name of Mount Warwicke.... This done, we retired our companies, not seeing nothing here worth further discovery, the country seeming barren and full of ragged mountains, in most parts, covered with snow [Collinson 1867, 129].

## Struggle with the Inuit

The land claim did not go unnoticed by the Inuit. Best further describes:

> Marching towards our boats, we spied a certain number of the country people on the top of Mount Warwicke with a flag, waving us back again and making a great noise, with cries like the mowing of bulls, seemingly desirous of a conference with us ... and hereupon we made signs unto them, holding up two fingers, commanding two men go apart from our companies, whereby they might do the like [Collinson 1867, 129].

Each side sent two unarmed representatives to the center of the mountain to conduct trade. The English representatives were Frobisher and a compatriot, who tried to take one of the Inuit captive in a prearranged decision. However, the man proved to be too slippery to grab and ran away, and the two Inuit recovered their weapons. They then chased the two Englishmen down the mountain to their boats, wounding Frobisher with an arrow in the buttock. A volley from the English guns sent the two fleeing, but a man named Nicolas Conyer charged after them and was able to capture one and bring him back to the boat.

Frobisher and the landing party then rowed to the other side of the island, where they were assaulted by another group of Inuit on the bluffs above them. John White produced a drawing of this incident soon after it occurred.

Frobisher and his party were eventually able to land, located an abandoned village, and destroyed a group of Inuit tents that contained traces of clothes that they believed might have been from the missing five (even though they were 200 kilometers from the place they went missing). They then attacked a nearby settlement, where five or six Inuit were killed and one Englishman was seriously wounded. The English aptly named the location "Bloody Point." They also captured two women and a child. One of the women they described as being so old and ugly that they were sure she must be a witch. They had "her buskins picked off to see if she had cloven feet" (Morison 1971, 523), and they let her go when her feet proved normal. The other woman and the child were taken back to their ship.

Best suggested that the female captive was taken on board for the comfort of their male captive. The two were brought together, surrounded by a circle of Englishmen to see what would happen. Best marveled at their modesty: even though the two were forced to bunk together on the voyage home, they

> did never use as man and wife.... The man would never shift himself, except he had first had the woman depart from her cabin, and they were most shame fast, least any of their private parts should be discovered, either by themselves or any other body [Collinson 1867, 144–45].

All three Inuit died soon after their arrival in England, the man due to broken ribs incurred during his capture that eventually punctured his lungs (Fossett 2001). Before he died, at a reception held by the mayor of Bristol, he showed a group assembled along the River Avon how he used his kayak and spear to hunt ducks. One can only imagine how much pain he must have felt from his broken ribs. An engraving was made of the event that was published all across Europe. The man was called Calichough, the woman Egnock, and her child Nutioc, Inuit words for "man," "woman," and "child," respectively.

## Further Discoveries

A few days after visiting "Bloody Point,"

> the crew discovered on a small island a tomb, wherein the bones of a dead man lay together, and they asked their male captive by signs whether his countryman had eaten his flesh, to which he responded negatively. Here they also found hid under stones a good store of fish and other things of the inhabitants including sleds, bridles, kettles of fish skins, knives of bone and such other like. Their male captive took in his hand one of these country bridles, he caught one of our doggies, and hampered him handsomely therein, as we do our horses, and with a whip in his hand, he taught the dog to draw a sled.... Nearby, they also discovered and beheld to their great marvel, the poor caves and houses of those country people which serve them (as it should seem) for their winter dwellings ... they trench these places with gutters so that the water falling from the hills above them, may slide away without their annoyance.... From the ground upward, they build with whale bones for lack of timber, bending one over another, are handsomely compacted in the top together, and are covered over with seal skins rather than tiles fencing them from the rain [Collinson 1867, 136–38].

Another discovery, which gave them particular delight, was a dead narwhal on the shore with its long unicorn-like horn. As Best described: It was about 12 feet long in total, with

> a horn of two yards long, growing out of the snout or nostrils ... wreathed and straight, like in fashion like a Taper made in wax. The horn was taken back to England and given to Elizabeth, who kept it in her wardrobe, handy for bringing out as an exhibit as a jewel and to stimulate the art of bawdy conversation that she is said to have loved [Collinson 1867, 136].

On August 20, the mining work was done. The miners had gathered 200 tons of supposed gold ore in 20 days while Frobisher and the others were exploring. The men were totally exhausted; many had been injured, their clothes were in tatters, and their mining tools were dulled, but they had filled the ships with ore (McCoy 2014a).

Ice was now forming around their ship at night, signaling that it was time to return home. On August 22, after lighting bonfires and firing volleys into the sky, Frobisher and crew headed back to England.

Portrait of Martin Frobisher from the *Heroologia Anglica* (1620) (Folger Imaging Department / Wikimedia Commons).

## Nature of the Ore

Once home, the ore samples were sent to a number of assessors, who again made estimates on the amount of gold in the ore that varied widely (McCoy 2014a and 2014b). Several reported no sign of gold, while others claimed that it contained up to 10 profitable ounces of gold per hundred pounds. McFee (1928, 77) tells us that those who claimed they found gold were "mountebanks [charlatans], and [that] Frobisher, Lock, and company were ignoramuses who knew not the difference between a professional man who knows what he is talking about and the smooth-tongued promoter."

Michael Lok, in a letter to investors, tried to be balanced and attributed the discrepancies to differences in methods and equipment but still deemed the lot of great value at £40 per ton of ore. His assessment was enough to convince the queen to support a third voyage with more ships so they could collect a much more generous quantity of ore. Incredibly, this expedition was then organized without any ore actually having been processed. The Cathay Company would now be operating at a great deficit.

## Third Voyage

On May 31, 1578, Frobisher, once again in the *Ayde*, led a large fleet of 15 vessels from Harwich. He was directed to bring back 2,000 tons of ore and establish a settlement to gather more. McFee (1928, 80) suggests that this marks "the inception of the first authentic scheme of colonial expansion in the history of North America."

The plan was to leave one hundred miners there with enough supplies for the winter and summer (McCoy, 2014b). Three ships would be left behind in case the colonists needed to return home before the supply ships got back the next year. Unfortunately, this was a flawed strategy as the sea in the area was frozen from late November until July, and the miners could not have left even if they had wanted.

The expedition arrived at Greenland on June 20 and found it to be a forbidding place. As McFee (1928, 65) describes:

> Frisland, or Greenland as we call it now, was a singularly unpromising coast. The shore was practically inaccessible, the visible highland consisted of grim snow-covered ranges, and the fogs came down with terrifying suddenness whenever the Admiral wanted to seek a landing. Frobisher had the natural horror of a shipmaster losing sight of his ship. He gave it up and set forward for Meta Incognita.

From Greenland, the group traveled towards Frobisher's Strait and, according to Best, "met with many great whales."

> One of the ships, named the *Salamander*, struck a great whale "with such a blow, that the ship stood still neither forward nor backward." The whale made a great and ugly noise and cast up his body and tail, and so went underwater, and within two days after, there was found a great whale dead, swimming

above the water, which we supposed was that of the Salamander stroke [Collinson 1867, 234].

The fleet then suffered a period of great difficulty where they were forced to battle ice floes, strong currents, and foul weather. They were driven south into an unknown strait, which Frobisher named the "Mistaken Strait." He was, of course, sure that this was a Northwest Passage but left without further investigation as the fabled passage was outside this voyage's specific mission. It would be determined later that his Mistaken Strait was the Hudson Strait leading into Hudson Bay and not to Cathay. A similar misconception would lead to Henry Hudson's death 30 years later.

Windswept ice floes kept the fleet from its intended destination for about a month, during which time one of the ships carrying most of their building materials was crushed in the ice and another deserted and went back to England. Finally, at the end of July, Frobisher found the strait he was looking for, and the miners were deployed to dig for ore on an island he named the Countess of Warwick.

## A Colony Is Built

Using the building materials they still had on hand, a house was built near the mining site, but the idea of a winter colony was dropped because they had too few remaining materials to build any other structures. The remains of this house are still clearly visible on the summit of Kodlunarn Island. These are the oldest known remains of a European house built in America north of the Caribbean.

As soon as the miners began working at the ore, Best went exploring. He climbed to the top of what became known as Hatton Headland to look at the fleet and set up a cross of stone, "in token of Christian possession." A week later, he and some other officers chased and killed "a great white bear, which adventured and gave a fierce assault upon twenty men being weaponed. And he served them for good meat many days" (McFee 1928, 101).

Within a month after beginning the dig, the ships were fully loaded with bags of ore and were ready for the voyage home. After seeing a massive display of the aurora borealis, which Frobisher took as a warning that they should leave, they all departed on August 31, 1578 (McCoy 2014b).

## Refining Finally Begins

At the end of August, the vessels arrived home and the refiners immediately set out to extract the gold, but none was ever found. Repeated attempts went on until 1583, but there was no longer any room for denial, and the queen and all the investors were forced to accept failure. Litigation followed

> and needing a scapegoat, they focused their anger on poor Michael Lok. In gross unfairness, the gullible investors accused Lok of dishonesty, with Frobisher himself among the accusers. Michael Lok furiously accused Frobisher of bringing back valuable ore on the first voyage but worthless ore on other trips.... Lok became the focus of creditors' efforts to collect, and he was bankrupted, sued, and imprisoned. Lok later claimed to have seen the inside of every jail in London [McCoy 2014b].

Frobisher would continue his naval service in many capacities over the next 16 years but would never return to the Arctic.

## *The Fate of the Lost Five*

The fate of the lost five men wasn't solved until almost 300 years after the Arctic voyages of Frobisher. McFee relates (1928, 106–7):

> Two hundred and eighty-three years later an American naval officer, Captain C.F. Hall, visited Frobisher Bay and landed on Countess of Warwick Island, which was known to the Eskimos as Kodlunarn, or White Man's Island. Hall had never read the narratives of Frobisher's voyages and was without prejudice in hearing the native traditions. Their story was that ages and ages ago, white men had come in a ship and taken away two of their women, who had never returned. In proof of this story of white strangers, they showed the explorer, who lived among them for two years, many relics of the earlier visit. He saw pieces of brick, tiles, and wood. He reports the finding of a piece of iron mineral, 19 lbs. in weight, like a "round loaf of burned bread." It was, in fact, a "bloom" of iron, a relic of the "gold miners" smelting so long ago. He beheld the house of lime and stone Captain Fenton built for the next year's colony. He discovered one of the "mines" of iron pyrites which Frobisher's men had sunk into the hillside, painfully digging out the worthless stuff to carry across the sea. And most wonderful of all, he heard the tale of the five lost men. These men, whose fate had given their commander so many days of anxiety, had spent the winters with their migrating captors. Later, they had returned to the island and found the house, with its store of bells and knives, looking glasses and whistles and pipes, with pictures of men on horseback and such like homely trinkets. It may be that some shipmate had also left a note or scrawl on the lime-washed walls. And then, the Eskimos told Captain Hall, the five men found the buried timbers of the fort, which Best says were thus stored against the next adventure. They dug up those timbers and made a boat with a mast and a sail, and set off for home. But it was too early in the season; the ice was too perilous in the sound, and they were never seen again.

## The Lifeways of the Inuit

The Inuit's range covered Greenland, Arctic Canada, Southeastern Alaska, and part of Chukotka in the northeasternmost region of Russia (McGhee 2001, Pedersen et al. 2010). The term *Eskimo*, long applied to the Inuit, is considered pejorative and likely came from a Mi'kmaq word resembling *Eskimo* that means "the eaters of raw flesh."

The Inuit and their culture were well adapted to an extremely cold, snow- and icebound habitat with few vegetable foods and trees. Caribou, seals, walruses, whales, seabirds, and fish were the staple food sources. They used harpoons to kill seals either on the ice or in water from skin-covered kayaks. Whales were hunted in a larger boat called an *umiak* (*umiaq* or *umiat*). They hunted animals on land in the summer with bows and arrows and used dogsleds for transport.

Their clothing was made of caribou furs, which gave considerable protection from the extreme cold. They wore hooded parkas, pants, mittens, inner footwear, and outer boots, all made of animal hide and fur. The back of a woman's parka had an *amaut* or pouch for carrying a baby. The clothing was decorated with inlays of differing colors, as well as fringes and pendants. Some skins were dyed or bleached.

The people usually moved among islands and bays on a seasonal basis. The Inuit spent the winter in snow-block houses called igloos (*iglus* or *igluvigaqs*) or in semisubterranean houses built of stone or sod with a generally whalebone framework. In summer, they lived in animal skin tents.

Their fundamental social and economic unit was the nuclear family. Large regional groupings of Inuit were separated into winter camps (called "bands") of around 100 people and summer hunting groups of a dozen or fewer.

The Inuit were highly skilled craftsmen, making their utensils, tools, and weapons from natural materials including stone, bone, ivory, antler, and animal hides. They also produced miniature ivory carvings, such as earrings, amulets, combs, and figures.

Face tattooing called *kakiniit* or *tunniit* was common among Inuit women. The patterns consisted of dots, zigzags, shapes, and lines, and had unique meanings to each woman. Face decoration was considered a part of coming into womanhood, and women could not marry until their faces were tattooed. The tattoos were done by other women.

A unique cultural activity of the Inuit was throat singing, performed by two women producing a wide range of sounds from deep within the throat and chest.

#### FOUR

# The Arctic Voyages of John Davis
## 1585–1587

### Setting the Stage: The Next in Line

In the late 1570s, Martin Frobisher failed in his attempt to extract wealth from Arctic Canada, but the passion to explore the North Atlantic and find a Northwest Passage to Cathay still ran high in England. John Davis would be the next to make that quest in three missions between 1585 and 1587. He didn't find that fabled passage, but he did learn much about Greenland and its people. He became widely renowned for his navigational skills and careful charting of the Arctic seas and their weather conditions.

We are fortunate to have firsthand records of all three of his missions. Accounts of the first and third missions were written by John Janes, a merchant who accompanied Davis and served as his clerk and secretary. The second voyage was documented by John Davis himself. These reports were first published in 1589 by Richard Hakluyt in his chief work, *The Principall Navigations, Voiages and Discoveries of the English Nation*, which included reports of all the seagoing voyages that had occurred up until that time. Herein, I quote from a later compilation of Janes's and Davis's chronicles in A.H. Markham's (1880) *The Voyages and Works of John Davis, the Navigator*. I also quote from C.R. Markham's biography (1889) *A Life of John Davis, the Navigator 1550–1605, Discoverer of Davis Straits*.

### Who Was John Davis?

John Davis was born in the parish of Stoke Gabriel in Devon circa 1550 and spent his childhood in Sandridge Barton. It is not known where or how he received his sea training, but it is not surprising that he wound up at sea, as his boyhood friends were the sea dogs Humphrey and Adrian

Gilbert and Walter Raleigh, whose exploits will be described elsewhere. Of their youth together Markham (1889, 7) writes:

> When boys together, Humphrey and Adrian Gilbert, Walter Raleigh, and John Davis must often have made excursions down the river to Dartmouth. In those days the landlocked little harbour was much frequented, and ships were built in the dockyard at Hardness. The boys might sit on the stone steps and parapets of the wharf and listen for hours to the tales of mariners from all parts of the world, till their young hearts thrilled with longing to seek honor and fame on the great deep. The voyages of English ships were being extended in several directions. When the young friends on the Dart were still at school, John Hawkins was visiting the coast of Guinea and the West Indies, while the servants of the Muscovy Company were striving to purchase perpetual fame and renown by wrestling with the icefloes in the Kara Sea. There were old sailors who had made voyages to Guinea and to the White Sea many years before. Dartmouth was a great resort of sailors, and the boys would have had many opportunities to listen to their yarns.

John Dee, the great astronomer and mathematician in Queen Elizabeth's court, was also an early friend of Davis. Dee had been instrumental in convincing Elizabeth to support Frobisher's voyages and would be intimately involved with all English voyages of discovery, instructing pilots in the principles of navigation, preparing maps, and furnishing navigational instruments.

Through his friends, Davis met the queen's principal secretary, Francis Walsingham, who agreed to help finance his attempt to find the Northwest Passage. Other sponsors would be Sir Edward Dyer, the Earl of Warwick, and Mr. William Sanderson (Markham 1889).

## First Voyage

Davis left Dartmouth on June 7, 1585, with two ships, the *Sunshine* (50 tons, 23 crew, including a four-man band) and *Moonshine* (35 tons, 19 crew). Davis captained the *Moonshine* and Janes, a nephew of Sanderson, piloted the *Sunshine*.

The group was held up for several days in Falmouth's harbor due to a strong southwest wind and then was delayed in the Isles of Scilly for another 12 days before, on June 23, they were able to make full sail and head out across the Atlantic Ocean. As they sailed the ocean they hunted for dolphins, which were plentiful, and saw scores of whales. Markham (1889, 38) describes:

> The number of whales seen during the rest of the voyage across the Atlantic would be considered extraordinary now. But in those days the *Balæna*

*biscayensis* had not yet been hunted almost to extinction. Not only were these great whales ... often met with in the Atlantic, but they frequented the coasts of the Bay of Biscay and were hunted in boats from the villages of Biscay and Guipuzcoa [province of Spain]. It is many years since those villages were enriched by the bone and oil of the Biscayensis whales, but they still occur in municipal coats of arms, and the old harpoons, long since disused, still hang on the walls of houses whose owners have been fishermen for generations. In the days of Davis, the Basque sailors throve on the whale-fishery, and great store of whales was seen by those who crossed the Atlantic.

Sadly, by the late 1800s, Atlantic whale populations had already dropped dramatically from the time of Davis.

Janes recalled what happened on July 19, when, after three weeks at sea, the ships approached Greenland: "[We] heard a mighty great roaring of the sea, as if it had bene the brech of some shoare, the ayre being so foggy and full of thick mist, that wee could not see one ship from the other" (Markham 1880, 3). It turned out that the ships were next to a tremendous stream of pack ice; the noise was the grinding of huge pieces of ice together. The next day, the fog lifted, and they saw the rugged mountains of Greenland, with a massive flow of pack ice between them and the shore, preventing their landing. Davis named the area "Land of Desolation" in light of its forbidding appearance (Markham 1980, 4).

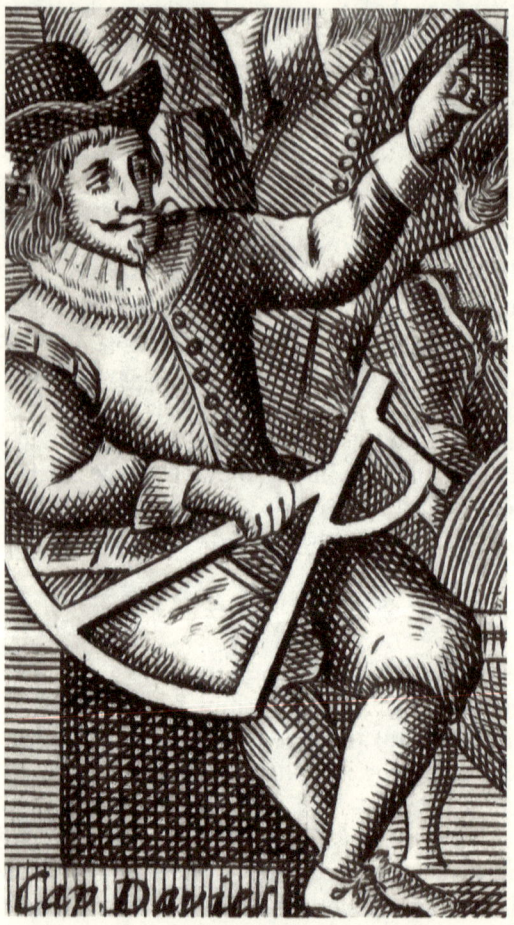

Portrait of "Cap. Davies" (John Davis) holding a late seventeenth-century version of his invention, the Davis quadrant; from the title page of John Seller's *The Coasting Pilot* (Wikimedia Commons).

## Four. The Arctic Voyages of John Davis

Struggling against strong westerly winds, the two ships sailed up the coast of Greenland to the present site of Nuuk. There they had a most pleasing interaction with the local Inuit (Markham 1880, 6). It began with the crew hearing a "lamentable noise" that they thought must be wolves. It turned out to be the Inuit trying to get their attention. In response, the crew went on shore with their band, who began to play while the officers and sailors danced and "allured the Inuit by friendly embraces and signs of courtesy." The sailors then placed some stockings, caps, and gloves on the ground as gifts and danced and sang their way back into their boats and rowed back to the mother ships.

This enticement apparently proved effective, as the next day scores of Inuit came to trade with them. Despite Frobisher's previous altercations with the Inuit, they were still willing to trade with Davis and his crew. Thirty-seven kayaks surrounded the ship and many other Inuit, standing on the shore, gestured that the crew should join them.

> Again the boat went on shore, and perfect confidence was established. Five *kayaks* were purchased and specimens of native clothing; the impression left on the minds of Davis and Janes being that the Eskimos were tractable people, whom it would be easy to civilize [Markham 1889, 41].

On August 1, Davis left Gilbert Sound after exploring among the islands. Traveling northwest across the channel, he spotted land on the other side. Here he anchored under a towering cliff he named Mount Raleigh at a place he called Totnes Road. Janes describes what happened next (Markham 1880, 10):

> Under Mount Raleigh, we espied four white bears at the foot of the mount. We supposing them to bee goates or wolves, manned our boats, and went towards them: but when wee came neere the shore, wee found them to be white beares of monstrous bignesse: we being desirous of fresh victual and the sport, began to assault them, and I being on land one of them came down the hil right against me; my piece was charged with haileshot and a bullet, I discharged my piece and shot him in the necke: hee roared a litle and took the water straight, making smal amount of his hurt. Then we followed him in our boate, and killed him with boare speares, and two more that night.

They left Totnes Road on August 8, coasting along the shore towards Cumberland Gulf. They then sailed for miles into the gulf, which Davis believed must be the Northwest Passage, but on August 20, before they had completed their investigations, the blustery wintry winds convinced them that they had better return or risk spending the winter icebound. Davis turned back before going far enough into the bay to realize that the waterway was not the Northwest Passage, but in fact ended in the center of Baffin Island.

Davis and crew arrived back at Dartmouth on September 30. On his return, Davis wrote a letter to Sir Francis Walsingham, a member of Her Majesty's Privy Council, which enthusiastically boasted about the voyage. It read:

> Right honorable most dutifully craving pardon for this my rash boldness, I am herby, according to my duty, to signify to your honor that the north-west passage is a matter nothing doubtful! but at any time almost to be passed, the sea navigable, the air tolerable, and the waters very deep. I have also found a very great quantity, not in any globe or map described, yielding a sufficient trade of fur and leather, and although this passage hath been supposed very impassible, yet through God's mercy, I am in experience and eye witness to the contrary, yea in this most desperate climate; which, by Gods help, I will very shortly most at large reveal onto your honor so soon as I can possibly take orders for my mariners and shipping. Thus depending on your honors good favor, I most humbly commit you to God this third of October [Markham 1880, xix].

Davis wrote this letter only three days after his return, hoping to induce people to join him in fitting out another expedition to verify that he had discovered the Northwest Passage.

## Second Voyage

The following year, Davis headed out on another voyage to the Arctic Ocean with four ships, largely supported by the merchants of the West Country. The ships were the *Mermaid* of 120 tons, the *Sunshine* of 60, the *Moonshine* of 35, and the *North Star* of 10. The squadron left Dartmouth on May 7, 1586, scooted past Ireland, and then set course for Greenland. On reaching latitude 60° north, Davis sent the *Moonshine* and *North Star* under Captain Pope to explore the east coast of Greenland while he sailed the other two ships toward the west coast.

On May 15, Davis came in sight of the southern extremity of Greenland, but the pack ice again rendered it impossible to land, so Davis named it "Cape Farewell" and made his way along the strait that now bears his name. There he encountered severe gales, and it was not until May 29 that he again sighted the towering mountains of Greenland near Gilbert Sound, which he had seen the previous year. He then took shelter among the islands along the coast and decided to examine the shore.

As Janes tells the story (Markham 1880, 16):

> The ships being within tile sounds, we sent our boats to search for shole water, where we might anchor, which in this place is very hard to find: and as the boat went sounding and searching, the people of the country having spied them, came in their canoes towards them with many shouts and cries: but after they

had spied in the boat, some of our company that was the year before here with us, they presently rowed to the boat, and took hold in the oar, and hung about the boat with such comfortable joy as would require a long discourse to be uttered: they came with the boats to our ships, making signs that they all those that yere before had been with them.

After I perceived their joy ... myself with the merchants and others of the company went ashore, bearing with me twenty knives. I had no sooner landed, but they leaped out of their canoes, and came running to me and the rest, and embraced us with many signs of hearty welcome: at this present, there were eighteen of them, and to each of them, I gave a knife: they offered skins to me for reward, but I made signs that it was not sold, but given them of courtesy: and so dismissed them for that time, with signs that they should return again after certain hours.

Davis was again employing a level of diplomacy rarely displayed by other North American explorers.

The next day the pinnace was landed on an island for assembly, and while the carpenters got to work, they were surrounded by a great number of Inuit, who were again very friendly. Davis records that as many as 100 kayaks came up to the ship at one time: "[The Inuit] very diligent to attend to us, and to help us up the rocks, and likewise down" (Markham 1880, 17). He and his crew could not help but be struck by the innocent and unsuspecting nature of the Inuit and their friendly behavior.

After exploring the island for a while, Davis organized some athletic events. He writes:

> At length, I was desirous to have our men leap with them, which was done; but our men did overleap them. From leaping they went to wrestling. We found them strong and nimble, and to have skill in wrestling, for they cast some of our men that were good wrestlers [Markham 1880, xxii].

The pinnace was launched on July 4. "[We] had forty of the people to help us," Davis reports, "which they did very willingly: this at this time our men again wrestled with them, and found them as before, strong and skillful" (Markham 1880, 18). In one of the crew's early expeditions, a grave was found on one of the islands, where a cross had been laid over the interred bodies. The origin of this grave site is unknown. Markham (1889, 46) suggests "that this could have been a relic of the Norsemen, or [an indication] that the tradition of the use of the cross may have been preserved by the Skraelings from the wreck of the Norse colonies." Skræling is the name the Norse used for the Indigenous people they encountered in Greenland.

The English were almost constantly surrounded wherever they went by Inuit in their kayaks, and thieving started to become a major problem. Davis relates: "They began through our lenity to show their vile nature: they began to cut our cables: they cut away the Moonlight boat from her stern, they cut our cloth ... they stole our oars, a caliver, a spear, a sword and diverse other things." Davis also wrote that "these natives, in spite of the friendship that appeared to animate them, could not divest themselves entirely of their thievish propensities, which at last reached such a height as nearly to cause a rupture of the friendly union that existed between them and the English" (Markham 1880, 19).

One night, the Inuit began firing stones upon a ship with slings, and the boatswain of the *Moonshine* was knocked down by a large rock. Davis finally lost his patience and chased after the perpetrators in their kayaks but without success. The next day his crew did manage to capture one of the ringleaders, whom they hoped to exchange for their anchor. However, this poor soul was carried out to sea when the wind came up and the ships hastily departed. He proved to be congenial company but never got back home, as he died on the return voyage.

As Davis and crew traveled southward of Gilbert Sound on July 17, they met and enormous iceberg.

> Its extent and height were so extraordinary that the pinnace was sent to ascertain whether it was land or really ice. The report that it was indeed one gigantic mass of ice, floating on the sea, with bays and capes, plateaus and towering peaks excited great astonishment [Markham 1889, 42].

Soon, masses of ice began to collect around the ships, while the ropes and sails became frozen and covered with ice, and the air was obscured by fog. This was particularly disheartening to all because the previous year the sea had been free and navigable at the same latitude. Further progress was checked, and the men began to lose hope, telling the captain "that he should regard the safety of his own life and the preservation of his people, and that he should not through over-boldness run the risk of making children fatherless and wives desolate" (Markham 1889, 47–48).

At this point, Davis decided to send the *Mermaid* home with the sick and feeble, while he continued on in the *Moonshine*. Davis sailed westward and made landfall on the opposite side of the strait, near Exeter Sound where he had been before. Then sailing southwest, he entered the Cumberland Gulf again, passed the entrance to Hudson Strait without observing it, and sailed along the coast of Labrador.

Here they fished for cod, which they salted to take home. Fishing required some innovation.

> Davis had been unprovided with fishing gear, had been obliged to make hooks out of bent nails, and to use his sounding lines to fish with; while his small stock of salt only enabled him to bring home about thirty couple of cod. Yet he had had ocular demonstration of the wonderful abundance of fish on the coast of Labrador [Markham 1889, 52].

While they were at anchor, several men were sent on shore to collect some fish that had been laid out on the rocks to cure. Unknown to them, concealed in the woods were several more warlike Mi'kmaq, who sent a murderous round of arrows at the sailors.

> Seeing this unfold from the boat, Davis sailed towards the shore and discharged his muskets at the savages, which scattered them. Unfortunately, two of his men were killed by arrows, two were seriously wounded, and just one escaped with an arrow wound to the arm, by swimming off toward the ship [Markham 1889, 56].

Davis and the crew were then caught up in a furious gale that lasted for three days. This proved to be the tipping point for Davis, and he decided it was time to return home. He left for England on September 11 and arrived home in early October 1586.

The *Sunshine* and *North Star*, after parting from Captain Davis on June 7, headed north according to their instructions and anchored in Iceland on June 9. Here, they discovered another English ship from Ipswich. Captain Pope then headed to the east coast of Greenland, arriving on July 7. They then explored the coastline, following their orders, and arrived at Gilbert Sound on the August 3. The two ships headed home on August 31, but three days into the voyage, they were caught in a severe gale, and the *North Star* was lost. The *Sunshine* arrived safely in the Thames on October 6.

## Third Voyage

Upon his return from the second voyage, Davis almost immediately proceeded to Exeter "to give an account to the West Country merchants and urge them to continue the enterprise. But they had lost heart. Their expectations of large returns were not fulfilled" (Markham 1880, 53). He would have a much better reception in London, where his friend William Sanderson helped him gain sufficient support to outfit a third mission.

On May 19, 1587, Davis went again to the Arctic with three ships: the *Sunshine*, the *Elizabeth*, and a little, disassembled pinnace called the *Ellen*. John Janes sailed along as a merchant for Sanderson and as a friend and confidant of Davis.

On June 14, the crew spied the rugged mountains of Greenland covered by a huge glacier, and on June 16, the vessels anchored in Gilbert Sound. Almost immediately, the local people surrounded them in kayaks, and they traded for seal skins. At this point, Davis decided that both *Sunshine* and *Elizabeth* would be dispatched to the fishery to make the trip profitable, while he would use the pinnace for exploration.

The parts of the pinnace were taken to an island for assembly while an exploration party roamed the environs. While there, they must have grabbed an Inuit captive, as Janes mentions offhandedly that "the master of the *Sunshine* took one of the people, a very lusty young fellow" (Markham 1880, 42).

Four days later, when the pinnace was about to be launched, a group of Inuit landed on the island and tore off the two upper strakes for the iron. Before they could totally destroy the boat, the crew managed to chase them away, and Davis was still able to use it for his explorations.

At midnight on June 21, all the vessels departed from Gilbert Sound, the *Sunshine* and *Elizabeth* off to fish, and the pinnace for discovery. Davis in the *Ellen* proceeded northwards along the coast of Greenland, occasionally bartering with the Inuit in kayaks. He reports:

> The 24th being in 67 degrees and 40 minutes, we had a great store of whales and a kind of sea bird ... this day about six of the clock at night, we spied two of the country people at sea, thinking at the first they had been two great seals, until we saw their oars glistering with the Sun: they came rowing towards us as fast as they could, and when they came within hearing they held up their oars, and cried out, making many signs: and at last they came to us, giving us birds for bracelets, and of them had a dart with a bone in it, or a piece of Unicorn's borne, as I did judge ... when he saw a knife he let it go, being more desirous of the knife then of his dart.
>
> On the 25th in the morning at 7 of the clock, we discovered 30 savages rowing after us ... they brought us salmon, pearls, birds, and caplin, and we gave them pins, needles, bracelets, nails, knives, bells, looking glasses, and other small trifles, and for a knife, a nail or a bracelet ... they would sell their boat, coats, or anything they had, although they were far from the shore. We obtained from them few skins, but they made signs to us that if we would go to the shore, we should have more [Markham 1880, 43-44].

Davis reported on the June 30 that he was at latitude 72°12' north, which was the furthest north reached by him on this voyage. In his book on *The Life of John Davis*, Markham (1889, 58) waxes eloquently:

> A bright blue sea extended to the horizon on the north and west, obstructed by no ice floes, but here and there were a few majestic icebergs, with snowy peaks shooting up into the sky, floated on the bosom of the deep. Near the horizon, in the far distance, these icebergs, distorted by the refraction, were raised up into the most fantastic and beautiful forms imaginable. To the eastward were the granite mountains of Greenland, and beyond them the white line of the mightiest glacier in the world, upheld by the mountain buttresses like huge caryatide & rising immediately above the tiny vessel was the beetling wall of Hope Sanderson, with its summit 850 feet above the sea-level. Its surface is slightly broken by a narrow ledge on which hundreds of thousands of guillemots rear their young; and when disturbed, they fly out in dense clouds, and return after circling many times over the water. At its base, the sea was a sheet of foam and spray. The little

clincher of twenty tons would have looked like a bird flapping its white wings over the water from the summit of the Hope when she came thus to christen the mighty cliff for all time. Insignificant as she appeared amidst that scene of calm magnificence, there were great and swelling hearts on board the *Ellen*, on whom the grandeur of the scene must have made a deep impression.

On July 2, *Ellen* encountered a huge bank of ice, lying north and south, which checked her progress. "This was the famous middle pack, a mass of ice drifting towards the Atlantic, and sometimes extending for 200 miles, its average thickness being eight feet." (Markham 1889, 60). Coasting along the pack in calm, foggy weather, they observed the western coast of Davis Strait and traded with some Inuit in kayaks. On July 19, they sighted Mount Raleigh, which they had discovered on their first voyage, and soon were at the entrance of Cumberland Gulf. Davis decided to make a second examination of this great gulf and sailed along its northern entrance until he reached a group of islands at the end. Proceeding southward,

> they came to a wide opening between 62° and 63° N. latitude, to which Davis gave the name of Lord Lumley's Inlet; and a headland passed on the 31st was called the Earl of Warwick's Foreland. The inlet was clearly Frobisher's Strait, and the land was no other than the Meta Incognita of that navigator [Markham 1889, 61].

Next came the discovery of another great strait, which would come to be called Hudson's Strait. Markham (1889, 61–62) describes it:

> Davis says in his log, we fell into a mighty race, where an island of ice was carried by the force of the current as fast as our barke could sail. We saw the sea falling down into the gulf with a mighty overfall and roaring, with diverse circular motions like whirlpools, in such sort as forcible streams pass through the arches of bridges. Mr Janes, in his journal, says: "We passed by a great gulf, the water whirling and roaring as it were the meeting of tides."

The strong current and ice prevented his going west, so he headed south along the Labrador coast and entered the Labrador fjord that now bears his name (Davis Inlet). To cover a portion of the expedition's cost, he then fished the Hamilton Inlet. From there, having not located the *Sunshine* and *Elizabeth* at their appointed rendezvous, he headed home, arriving safely at Dartmouth on September 15, 1587. Remarkably, Davis, in his tiny, leaky pinnace, had navigated through more than 20° of Arctic waters.

It is unknown when *Sunshine* and *Elizabeth* returned.

## The Legacy of John Davis

Davis was by no means the first European to explore the Arctic. Norsemen had settled Greenland long before his visit, and Cabot had probably been on the Labrador coast almost 100 years earlier. The Portuguese had also likely viewed Hudson Strait in the early 1500s, and Frobisher had very recently collected ores on what he called Meta Incognita. None of these other navigators had the scientific expertise of John Davis, however. Markham (1889, 65) writes: "All the coasts and seas not actually discovered were laid down and mapped afresh and must be considered to have been rediscovered and first brought within the actual knowledge of his generation by him. The great continent of Greenland ... was rediscovered and made known by him."

"He charted long stretches of Greenland, Baffin, and the Labrador coasts and made careful observations of ice conditions, terrain, rock formations, weather, vegetation, and animal life" (Larnder, 2003, n.p.). His original logs have been lost, but his discoveries appear in detail on the great maps of the period by Edward White and on the famous Molyneux globe (1592). He provided one of the earliest descriptions of the Inuit, which was both accurate and much more sympathetic than those of other European explorers of the sixteenth and seventeenth centuries.

Davis would not go back to the Arctic after his third visit, as England's energies were now focused on its struggle with Spain and not exploration. He would write *The Worlde's Hydrographical Description* in 1595 to drum up support for a further search, but to no avail. He would spend the rest of his distinguished career mostly in expeditions to the Indies, and he compiled a treatise on navigation (*The Seaman's Secret*) that became a sailor's bible (Larnder, 2003).

FIVE

# English and French Expeditions to the North Atlantic
## 1578-1621

*Setting the Stage: First Visitors to Newfoundland*

Portuguese sailors from the northern ports of Viana and Aveiro are credited with being the first to explore the Atlantic coast of the Avalon Peninsula (Pope 2009). They were active there until English fishermen from the West County displaced them between 1580 and 1620 and then spread northward towards Bonavista Bay. The Bretons and Normans initially set up camps along Newfoundland's south coast and along the west coast of the Great Northern Peninsula to Chateau in southern Labrador. France came to dominate the Newfoundland fisheries in the sixteenth century due to its geographical proximity and its possession of huge European markets for cod.

At first, the cod fishermen plying the Grand Banks cleaned the cod aboard their ship and stored them between thick layers of salt. But it was not long before they found that cod could be sun-dried on land and that cured cod tasted better and was easier to store. The fishermen began to go ashore each summer to build "fishing rooms" which were makeshift villages with temporary shelters and drying stands for their fish (Pope 2009). By 1539, the French, Portuguese, and English had set up many such outposts on the shores of Newfoundland, the Acadian peninsula, Cape Breton Island, and the St. Lawrence River.

By the 1580s, the number of ships plying the Grand Banks was huge. Anthony Parkhurst counted around Newfoundland in 1578 between 350 and 380 in total—150 French cod-fishing vessels, 100 Spanish, 50 Portuguese, 30 to 50 English, and 20 to 30 Basque whalers (Turgeon 1998). This was probably a great underestimation, as European fishermen were scattered over several thousand miles of coastline over many months of the year. Turgeon (1998) suggests that a more plausible number was a French fleet of about 500 ships in about 1580.

> The Newfoundland fleet—comprising between 350 and 380 vessels crewed by 8,000–10,000 men—could have more than matched Spain's transatlantic commerce with the Americas, which relied on 100 ships at most and 4,000–5,000 men in the 1570s—its best years in the sixteenth century [Turgeon 1998, 590–91].

## *Cries for the Settlement of Newfoundland*

In the mid-1500s, a strong push began in England to colonize Newfoundland. It was spearheaded by the merchant Anthony Parkhurst, who had begun fishing off Newfoundland in 1565 and gotten "a taste for exploration" serving with John Hawkins on a slaving voyage from 1564 to 1565.

Parkhurst made a number of trips to Newfoundland and became completely convinced that the English should colonize it. In a letter to Richard Hakluyt, he raved about the natural resources of the island, including the forests, minerals, flowers, animals, birds, and fish (Quinn 2003a). He suggested that the climate was not unfavorable to settlement, and he did some preliminary trials with English fruit, grain, and vegetable seeds.

Parkhurst was sure that "settlement would bring advantages to the English economy: the exploitation of a product (fish) which need not be paid for expensively in exports, but which would provide cheap food at home; the acquisition of an independent source of naval stores; prospects of iron mining and smelting; the training of seamen; the occupation of surplus population" (Quinn 2003a).

In 1576, Sir Humphrey Gilbert further stoked English interest in North American exploration and settlement when he published the fanciful treatise *A Discourse of a Discovery for a New Passage to Cathay*, in which he provided "evidence" of the Northwest Passage and suggested that a colony "in halfway" could be established next to the "Sierra Nevada," northwest of the continent, and that trade with the natives would be profitable (Quinn 2019). Its publication elicited much excitement among the European sailing community, and Gilbert gained notoriety as an authority on America.

## *Early North American Missions of Gilbert*

On June 11, 1578, Gilbert obtained a patent from the queen to discover and occupy a site that was not already in European hands. He was given permission "to expel any intruders who planted within 600 miles of him," and "he himself could hold land and convey it to others" (Quinn 2019). His objective was North America.

In preparing for his trip, Gilbert received advice from Dr. John Dee, who was particularly interested in finding the Northwest Passage to Asia, and Hakluyt, "who had made sensible suggestions for settling Englishmen in lands between 35° and 40° N" (Quinn 2019). He also knew about the settlement ideas of Parkhurst for Newfoundland. Gilbert likely planned to go first to the Caribbean to plunder Spanish ships and then head north and establish his settlement. It is not known exactly where he planned to land his colony.

Gilbert assembled a fleet of 10 vessels, which were well armed and manned (175 guns, 570 men). Many of the sailors were pirates, and some had even been released from prison, facing execution (Quinn 2019). Gilbert's flagship was *Anne Ager* (or *Anne Aucher*). Another ship in his fleet was the *Falcon*, commanded by his half-brother Sir Walter Raleigh and piloted by the Portuguese Simão Fernandes.

The mission proved to be a disaster. Gilbert set off on November 18, 1578, with only seven of the ships, after three of them had taken off alone to pirate. The remaining seven got only as far as Cork Harbor in Ireland before turning back when the *Falcon* and *Anne Ager* started leaking badly, and their stores were deemed inadequate for the long haul.

The group set off again in February 1579. However, they did not get very far before the fleet was scattered apart by storms, and most returned home over the next six months. The only vessel to travel any distance was Walter Raleigh's *Falcon*, which got as far as the West Indies before returning in May. Gilbert and his family lost most of their personal wealth in the fiasco.

Still undeterred, Gilbert put together a much more modest expedition in 1583. He equipped a tiny eight-ton frigate, *Squirrel*, for the journey and hired Simão Fernandes again as the pilot. They set off on June 11, 1583, and this time did make it to North America and back in three months, but there is no record of where they landed. All that is known is that Gilbert had a recommendation from Dr. John Dee to visit the River of Norumbega (Penobscot Bay), which Verrazzano had visited earlier (Quinn 2019).

## *Sir Gilbert Decides on Newfoundland*

Upon his return, Gilbert was able to quickly organize another expedition to Newfoundland and its burgeoning fisheries. The English appetite for North American exploration was now reaching a fever pitch, fueled by Richard Hakluyt's 1582 publication of *Divers Voyages Touching the Discoverie of America* and *The Principal Navigations, Voyages, Traffiques and Discoveries of the English Nation*. In it, he described all the previous western explorations, including the letters patent granted to John Cabot in 1496, the narrative of Verrazzano's journey in 1524, and a report by Ribaut on his Florida colony in 1562. He also provided a list of types of products found in America and opinions on the colonization of the Americas.

Gilbert acquired supporters by promising them titles to great estates with vast quantities of fertile land in good climates. This offer appealed especially to English Roman Catholic gentlemen, who had refused to conform to the Church of England and were now subject to crippling fines (Quinn 2019). By the spring of 1583, Gilbert was ready to set off. He planned to follow the typical route of the Newfoundland fishing fleet to the Grand Banks, and then head for Cape Breton and search along the southern coast for good colony site (Quinn 2019).

An account of the voyage was published by Captain Edward Hayes in 1589 in Richard Hakluyt's *Principall Navigations*, which was supplemented with other narratives in his *The Third and Last Volume of the Voyages, Navigations, Traffiques, and Discoveries of the English Nation* (London, 1600). Herein quotes are taken from a more modern version of the manuscript published by H.S. Burrage, *Early English and French Voyages, Chiefly from Hakluyt, 1534–1608*.

It is not known whether Hayes was hired to write the journal of the voyage or decided to write it on his own. It is known that he was already an experienced sailor, had engaged in at least one privateering voyage before, was known to Richard Hakluyt, and worked closely with Gilbert in preparing the venture (Quinn 2019).

## *The Voyage*

Gilbert set sail to Newfoundland on June 11, 1583, with a fleet of five vessels: the flagship *General*, captained by himself; the *Delight*, captained by Gilbert's elder brother Sir John; the *Bark Raleigh*, owned and commanded by Walter Raleigh; the *Golden Hind*, captained and owned by Edward Hayes; the *Swallow*, captained by Maurice Brown; and the *Squirrel*, which had made the 1580 voyage and was captained by William Andrewes (Quinn 2019).

Also along was a large group of potential settlers. As Hayes describes:

> We were in number in all 260 men: among whom we had of every faculty, shipwrights, masons, carpenters, smithies, and such like, requisite to such action: also mineral men and refiners. Besides the solace of our people and the

allurement of the savages, we were provided with music in good variety: not omitting the least toys, such as Morris dancers [English folk dance], hobby horses,…. To delight the savage people…. And to that end, we were indifferently furnished of all petty haberdasheries wares to barter with those people [Burrage 1906, 192].

It is interesting to note that the mission was well-equipped for encounters with the Indigenous people, although Hayes makes no mention of any in his later report.

Soon after leaving port, bad luck again assailed Gilbert, as *Raleigh* had to turn back, and the remaining vessels got separated in fog again when they were not far from Newfoundland. Hayes reports:

> We never had a fair day without fog and rain, and winds bad, much to the west-northwest … we were encumbered with much fog and mists in manner palpable, in which we could not keep together, but were disserved, losing the company of the Swallow and Squirrel upon the 30th of July [Burrage 1906, 193].

Fortunately, the four ships were able to reunite in Newfoundland. The *Golden Hind* and the *Swallow* located each other at Conception Bay and traveled together to St. John's, where they found first the *Squirrel* and then, on August 3, the *Delight*.

After regrouping, the four ships tried to enter the port at St. John's but were refused passage. The port admiral, even though he was English, had gotten all the ships in the harbor (Portuguese, Basque, French, and English) organized to deny passage to Gilbert's group. This was done because the *Delight*'s master, Richard Clark, had previously pirated Portuguese ships at St. John's. The blockade did not last long, however, after Gilbert brandished his royal commission.

Upon landing on August 5, Sir Humphrey Gilbert unabashedly took possession of Newfoundland and all of the land 200 leagues to the north and south, approximately 37°35' north to 57°35' north. As Quinn (2019) tells it:

> He proclaimed the land to be the Queen's in perpetuity. He promulgated "laws" to be observed—no public exercise of religion apart from that of the Church of England, no opposition (on pain of punishment for high treason), no disrespect to the queen (without cutting off ears and seizing of ships and goods).

To all these demands the assembled agreed, really having no choice. A wooden pillar was raised with the royal arms attached, and Gilbert issued a certificate to all the ships in the harbor authorizing them to continue fishing.

On August 4, Gilbert went ashore to evaluate the flora and topography of Newfoundland and search for precious metals. His mineral expert from Saxony, Daniel of Buda, collected iron ore and what he thought was silver. In Hayes's account, he described the rich flora and fauna of the region and stressed its mineral potential but acknowledged that the rigorous winters would be a challenge.

> The common opinion is that of in climate and extreme cold that should be in this country, as of some part it must be verified, namely the north, where I grant it is colder than in countries of Europe, which are under the same elevation.... Nevertheless, the cold cannot be so intolerable under the latitude of 46, 47 and 48 that it should be uninhabitable.... Besides, as in the months of June, July, August, and September, the heat is somewhat more than England at those seasons [Burrage 1906, 201–2].

At this point, some of the men lobbied hard to go no further, and so Gilbert sent the *Swallow* home with the sickest and most recalcitrant. Gilbert then headed down the coast to take possession of as much land as possible before his patent expired in June 1584. He traveled down to Cape Race and sent shore parties into Trepassey and Placentia Bays before sailing for Sable Island on August 22.

Gilbert then changed course from west-southwest to east-southeast, and after a windy night, the ships wound up in shoal water on the morning of August 29, and the *Delight* went aground and broke up. Much of its crew was lost, including the Saxon miner, his ore, and everything else on board.

Hayes relates:

> This was a heavy and grievous event, to lose at one blow our chief ship filled with great provisions, gathered together with much travel, care, long time, and difficulty. But more was the loss of our men, which perished to the number almost of a hundred souls. Among them was drowned a learned man, a Hungarian ... who of piety and zeal to good attempts adventured in this action.... Also perished, our Saxon refiner and discoverer of inestimable riches... [and] Captain Maurice Browne, a virtuous, honest and discreet gentleman.... Choosing to die, rather than incur infamy, by forsaking his charge ... by leaving the ship first himself [Burrage 1906, 211–12].

The loss greatly demoralized the survivors. As Hayes observes:

> Those in the frigate were already pinched with spar allowance and want of clothes chiefly; Whereupon they sought the general to return for England, before they all perished.... And to them of the Golden Hinde, they made signs of their distress, pointing to their mouths, and to their clothes thin and ragged. They grew of the same opinion and desire to return home [Burrage 1906, 214].

Gilbert decided on August 31 to return to England. The wind was now in their favor, and they were able to sail to the southeastern tip of the Avalon Peninsula in two days flat and, from there, set out across the Atlantic.

About 900 miles out from Newfoundland, they encountered some very rough seas, and the *Squirrel* was nearly overwhelmed. Captain Hayes pleaded with Gilbert to leave it and switch boats, but Gilbert refused, saying: "I will not forsake my little company going homeward, with whom I have passed so many storms and perils" (Burrage 1906, 218).

On Monday, September 9, the frigate was again "nearly cast away, oppressed by waves, yet at that time recovered," Hayes writes. "Giving signs of joy, the general sitting shaft with a book in hand, cried out unto us in the *Hind*.... We are as near to Heaven by sea as by land" (Burrage 1906, 220).

These words proved to be prophetic, for at midnight the crew of the *Golden Hind* saw the frigate's lights disappear, and, in Hayes's words, "the Frigate was devoured and swallowed up of the Sea" (Burrage 1906, 219).

Now alone, the *Golden Hind* continued on course through stormy seas and reached Falmouth on September 22. Newfoundland was now declared to be English, but at the cost of Gilbert's life, two ships, and 100 members of the crew. No settlement attempt was made.

## *The Voyage of Étienne Bellenger*

The first Frenchman to try to establish a colony in northeast America was Étienne Bellenger. He was a general merchant in Rouen who by 1582 had been on at least two voyages to the Maritimes, visiting Cape Breton for trade and traveling down the coast of Nova Scotia (Quinn 1962, 2003b). In 1583, Bellenger organized a mission to Cape Breton with Michel Costé as captain and pilot. The expenses were covered by Cardinal Charles de Bourbon and Anne de Joyeuse, admiral of France. The original plan was to explore the Maritimes and, at a suitable location, drop off Bellenger and 20 men to establish a colony.

Neither Bellenger nor any of his associates wrote a narrative of this voyage, but he was interviewed soon after his return by Richard Hakluyt, who published two brief notes on the voyage in his *Discourse Concerning Western Planting* of 1584. Hakluyt also wrote a fuller account titled *The relation of master Stephen Bellanger dwelling in Roan ... of his late voiadge of discoverie of two hundreth leagues of coast from Cape Brittone ... west-south-west at the charges of the Cardinall of Borbon this last yere 1583*. This account of the voyage was never published but was found in the papers of a friend of Hakluyt's, Julius Caesar, who was a judge of the Admiralty (Marsh 1962; Quinn 1962).

Bellenger and Costé left Le Havre on January 19, 1583, in the *Chardon* of 50 tons, carrying a small pinnace, and arrived only 20 days later. Bellenger then made a thorough survey of the coast, west-southwestwards from the cape, charting bays and harbors, rocks and islands and sounding shallows and deeps. He explored the coasts southward from Cape Breton, coasted the southern shore of Nova Scotia, and then turned along its north coast into the Bay of Fundy, followed its limits around southern New Brunswick and, in the open sea again, some way along the coast of Maine, before turning homewards to France [Quinn 2003b].

His carefully prepared charts would become a significant part of Jacques de Vaulx's early illustrated work on cosmography, *Les Premieres Euvres de Jacques de Vaulx pillote en la marine.*

Bellenger set on land at least 10 or 12 times during his voyage to search for mineral wealth and trade with the local Innu. On one of his landings, near today's Cape Sable, Bellenger visited a large village of 80 houses, with a population of about 800, and traded some small merchandise for a wide range of skins and pelts, porcupine quills, dyestuffs, and some deer-flesh (Quinn 2003b).

Most of his interactions with the local people were positive, but he had a very negative one about 200 miles west of Cape Breton. As Hakluyt tells it:

> In diverse places, they are gentle and tractable. But those Cape Briton and threescore or fourscore leagues westward are cruel and subtle of nature than the rest. And you are not to them but to stand upon your guard for among them he lost two of his men and his small pinnace which happened through their folly in trusting the savages too far [Marsh 1962, 250].

Quinn (1962, 332) suggests:

> The difference in hostility displayed by the Amerindians may have been due to previous contact with Europeans or it may represent a tribal boundary. If it was the former, it would not be surprising that contact with violent, drunken, fire-armed European fishermen and part-time fur traders should have rendered the Indians at least equally violent and, perhaps more treacherous. But the Micmac did not, universally, have a bad reputation amongst the whites.

It is possible that John Cabot visited Cape Breton in 1497, and European fishermen likely began landing in the territory in the early 1500s. In about 1521–2, the Portuguese João Álvares Fagundes established a fishing colony on the island at what is now known as Ingonish (Morison 1971). It lasted there for a year to 18 months until the settlers were killed or forced to move by the locals. The colony's subsequent fate is unknown.

In late May, Bellenger decided to return home after only four months and abandon his plan to colonize Cape Breton. He likely feared further conflict with the Innu. Bellenger's return may have underlined the potential threats that such a venture might experience from the Amerindians, even though his overall report was favorable (Quinn 2003b).

Regardless, Bellenger's mission was considered a success. He got a good return on his investment, as his trade goods had cost him £4, but he sold the furs he obtained for £88. This success would spur many more French fur trading missions to America.

## Bernard Drake's Newfoundland Expedition

In 1585, the Anglo-Spanish War exploded when Spain began seizing English merchant ships in its ports. In response, Queen Elizabeth's privy council ordered Sir Walter Raleigh to organize an expedition to Newfoundland to seize all Spanish ships in that area and inform all English ships that they should stop selling fish in Spanish and Portuguese ports (Bicheno 2012; Cell 1969). On June 27, 1585, Sir Walter awarded Sir Bernard Drake command of the *Golden Riall* and a fleet of 10 ships to wage that war. Many of these ships were funded by investors hoping to share in the plunder.

Drake arrived at St. John's in mid–August after capturing a Portuguese ship loaded with Brazilian sugar. He immediately ordered all the English fishermen to stop shipping fish to anywhere but England and asked them to join ranks in a concerted effort to intercept, capture, plunder, and destroy all the Spanish and Portuguese fishing ships they could find. These combined forces quickly destroyed Spain's Newfoundland fishing fleet.

By the end of September, Drake had cleared the south coast frequented by Spanish ships and sent several of his ships back to England, escorting his prizes. He then attacked a Spanish whaling and fishing base on the Burin Peninsula, taking all its stores and burning it to the ground.

He linked up with another of Sir Walter's associates, George Raymond in the *Red Lion*, and headed to the Azores, where they captured many more Spanish ships coming from the West Indies loaded with sugar, wine, and ivory, and a French ship carrying gold. All in all, he took possession of more than 20 ships, although many of them were ultimately lost in storms or destroyed in battle.

Through Drake's efforts, great wealth was brought back to England, and England gained complete control of the Avalon Peninsula fisheries.

> Bristol merchants rubbed their hands in glee. Heading to Newfoundland in record numbers, crews from England's West Country began delivering to market thousands of tonnes of lightly salted cod [Pringle 1997, 37].

## Expedition of Marquis de la Roche-Mesgouez

The next French expedition to the North Atlantic was sent out in 1598 by the Marquis de la Roche-Mesgouez, the governor of Brittany.

> The marquis ... received new letters patent from the king ... appointing him lieutenant-general of the territories of Canada, Newfoundland, Labrador, and Norumbega. These letters granted him title to the area and the monopoly of the fur trade, and forbade all others to trade in furs without his consent, on pain of "losing all their ships and merchandise." They further authorized him to recruit hardened criminals for his undertaking [Lanctot 2003b].

La Roche hired Thomas Chefdostel, the master of a boat named *La Catherine* (170 tons) to fish off the coast of Newfoundland and land a group of soldiers and settlers on Sable Island, which La Roche had seen in another fishing trip he had made in 1597 (Tattrie 2014). La Roche agreed to "pay for one-half the cargo of salt at Brouage, one-half the wages of the crew, and the whole of the provisions undertook to embark on board his vessel a company of soldiers and to land them" (Biggar 1901, 5).

When no willing colonists stepped forward to make the trip, La Roche arranged with the Parliament of Rouen to get prisoners to fill out the party. He was given "200 sturdy beggars, male and female" (Biggar 1901, 40) and agreed to pay Chefdostel an additional 600 crowns to transport them. La Roche would ultimately take only about 40 of the criminals, allowing the rest to purchase their freedom from him.

Added to the mission was Captain Jehan Girot of the *François*, who received 100 crowns to join. It was agreed that any furs and goods obtained in trade with the Amerindians would be divided equally between Chefdostel, the owners of the *Catherine*, and La Roche. Any profits from fishing would go to the ships' captains.

When the expedition arrived at Sable Island, La Roche set up his colony on the north coast, on a small waterway he named the Boncœur River. He built living quarters and a storehouse and then headed to the Newfoundland fisheries (Lanctot 2003b).

Biggar (1901, 41) suggests that

> a slight examination of the island convinced him [La Roche] that it was not fit for settlement, but he left them behind anyway. The island was pretty much a barren sandbar that was 300 km distant from the little-known mainland. It barely stood above sea level and big waves crashed hard over it. Little lived.

La Roche hoped to find a more suitable location on the mainland; however, when he attempted to return to Sable Island after his fishing, a storm blew him all the way back to France and he was forced to leave the colony in place.

Upon his return, Henry IV awarded La Roche a grant of one *écu* for each barrel of merchandise passing through the ports of Normandy. La Roche used this subsidy to maintain his little settlement, and each spring he had it resupplied by Chefdostel. The deportees were forced to remain, acquiring what food they could from the locally available fish and game, as well as a small herd of cattle probably landed on the island by the Portuguese Fagundes around 1520. They also cultivated gardens, which supplied them with vegetables (Lanctot 2003b).

In 1602, for some unknown reason, no relief vessels were sent. In the long winter of 1602–3, some of the deportees went on a rampage, killing their two leaders and some of the other settlers. When a relief mission was finally sent in the summer of 1603, only 11 wretched souls were left after a winter of hunger and dissent on the barren reef of sand. Remarkably, when they were returned to France, Henry IV rewarded each with 50 écus for the furs they brought back rather than having them hanged.

La Roche tried to obtain more prisoners to replenish his colony, but the Parliament of Rouen refused, knowing that only a fraction of the original batch had been transported to Sable Island. A frustrated La Roche died three years later.

## Colonization of Newfoundland

When Sir Bernard Drake destroyed Spain's Newfoundland fishing fleet in 1585, England gained complete control of the Avalon Peninsula fisheries. As the seventeenth century progressed, the fishermen and their families began staying in Newfoundland over the winters, at least for a few years, rather than returning to England at the end of each season. Some of them overwintered as caretakers of supplies and properties belonging to the West of England fish merchants. Others actively engaged in hunting and trapping, wood cutting, and boat building. The settlements that were occupied each winter were rarely inhabited for more than a few years by the same people, but some families persisted (Handcock 2000). These permanent residents were called planters and were mostly English. They lived on the shore and operated fishing boats, raised some garden produce, and kept hogs and other livestock.

All the planters depended on fishing and trading ships from the outside for many of their food staples, clothing, and fishing equipment, and they marketed their cod, cod oil, and other produce through these contacts.

> English ships furnished food such as bread and flour, manufactured goods and fishing equipment from home, but they also brought Irish produce such as butter, salted beef and pork, and clothing materials. New Englanders were noted for bringing livestock, bread and flour, but especially tobacco, and vast quantities of West Indian rum and molasses [Handcock 2000].

## *The First Formal English Colony on Newfoundland*

In 1610, the Newfoundland Company, founded by Bristol and London merchants, was awarded a royal charter for the whole Island of Newfoundland with the understanding that its activities would be focused on the Avalon Peninsula. The intent was to make a secure and safe place for the trade of fishing. The settlers were to:

> fortify the settlement ... experiment with farming, cut spars and planks, make salt, potash, and glass, collect samples of ore and, significantly, to fish and trade in cured fish and train oil [oil from whale blubber] ["The Cupids Colony and John Guy" 2008].

John Guy, an alderman of Bristol who had already made two voyages to Newfoundland, was put in charge of the colony (Munn 1934). He brought together 39 settlers, provisions, and livestock, and set sail for Canada on July 5, 1610. They anchored at Cuper's Cove, Newfoundland (now called Cupids).

> Guy and his settlers scrambled ashore to begin settling the raw wilderness. Jumping into work immediately, trees were felled, and a portion of the logs loaded onto the ship for the return trip to England. Cutting other logs into lumber, a storage building, and a residence were completed by early December, just in time to shelter the colonists from the icy winter winds [McLeod 2019].

The colony survived their first winter well, and of the initial 39 men, only four died. The settlers were able to continue exploring their surroundings, clearing the land and building new structures, as there was little snow to hamper their efforts. They constructed a fort, a workhouse to protect them in the bitterest weather, a blacksmith's shop, six small fishing boats, and a 12-ton "bark" with three masts.

Leaving his brother Philip Guy in charge, Governor Guy returned to England in 1611, and came back the next year with 16 young women ready to make the settlement their home. More settlers arrived a year later in 1612, and a sawmill and brewery were built that year. It was now a growing colony, actively engaged in cutting timber and fishing.

Despite this good luck, the colony still struggled. The colonists could grow vegetables, but grain failed due to the short season. They were also not able to harvest enough hay to feed their animals through their first hard winter of 1613, and 22 of the 66 settlers developed scurvy; eight died that winter. The only good news was that a son was born to the wife of Nicholas Guy (probably also a relative of John) on March 17.

The settlement was also harassed by a pirate named Peter Easton, who forced the settlement to pay him for protection against Basque raiders (Hunt 2003a). Easton arrived in Newfoundland in 1612 and began raiding coastal harbors all along the Avalon Peninsula, making Harbour Grace in Conception Bay his headquarters. Easton took two ships and provisions at Harbour Grace and 30 English vessels in the harbor of St. John's and raided numerous French and Portuguese ships at Ferryland. The total value of the booty taken by Easton from the fishing fleets was estimated at £20,400.

## Guy's Expedition to Trinity Bay

In the autumn of 1612, before the colonists' first nasty winter, John Guy made an expedition to Trinity Bay in hopes of establishing trade with the Beothuk (Gilbert 1990; Holly et al. 2010). For the first several days of exploring the bay, Guy and his group saw only unoccupied Beothuk campsites and a few Beothuk at a distance, and it wasn't until November 6 that they finally contacted a small party of them on the shore. The Beothuk were wary but appeared friendly:

> A white wolf's skin was waved and headless arrow shafts were offered to the colonists, accompanied by singing and dancing. The colonists followed suit....

An etching of John Guy's encounter with the Beothuk (Matthaeus Merian, 1628) (Centre for Newfoundland Studies, Memorial University of Newfoundland).

Then the party shared a meal of smoked caribou meat and wild roots. As dusk fell, a prominent member of the Beothuk party gave the colonists the white animal skin that earlier had been presented as a token of peace and took their white flag in exchange [Holly et al. 2010, 32].

When the Beothuk departed, the colonists started to construct a small trading post, but foul weather conditions forced them to depart on November 8. As they were about to leave, they found a number of items including animal furs and shell necklaces, and they left a hatchet, knife, scissors, and sewing needles in their place. They then sailed home, full of optimism about the promise of future profitable trade with the natives. Unfortunately, the colonists' hopes were never realized, subsequent attempts to trade were largely unfulfilled, and the Beothuk actually abandoned the area (Gilbert 2002). "Indifference and avoidance" would characterize Beothuk interactions with the Europeans for the next hundred years (Holly et al. 2010, 32).

## *The Eventual Demise of Cuper's Cove*

In 1613, Guy began quarreling with the company about property that he felt they owed him. He finally left Newfoundland in 1615 for a new career in Bristol, England, as a mayor and then alderman. He died in March 1628 (McLeod 2019).

Guy was replaced by John Mason, who proved to be better at handling the pirates but was not so good at placating the local fisheries, who perceived the colonists as competition. Mason moved to New England in 1621, and the people at the Cupids settlement largely dispersed. When Cupids did not prove as productive as the investors in the Newfoundland Company had hoped, they divided their original grant into lots and regional proprietorships. Several of these organized into colonies, including Sir William Vaughan at Renews, Sir George Calvert at Ferryland, and William Payne and others at St. John's. "When Cupids failed, there were several other colonies established in Newfoundland including Bristol's Hope, Renews, New Cambriol, South Falkland and Avalon. Calvert would become the first permanent settlement in Canada" ("The Cupids Colony and John Guy" 2008).

While the colony at Cuper's Cove proved ephemeral, the fishery itself would grow by leaps and bounds. Sir Richard Whitbourne, in a report to the British government in 1615, stated that 250 vessels were visiting annually, manned by 5,000 men. In 1621, Governor John Mason reported there were 300 vessels and 10,000 men (Munn 1934).

## Six

# L'Acadie

*The French Begin a Fur Trading Empire, 1588–1603*

## Setting the Stage: Beginnings of North American Fur Trading

Fur trading emerged in the second half of the sixteenth century as a means for fishermen to diversify their income. When the fishermen began salting and drying their cod on the Newfoundland coast, they came in increasing contact with the local Indigenous people. The fishermen began trading metal objects for robes made of native-tanned beaver pelts, called *castor gras* by the French. Initially, the robes were used by the fishermen for warmth on the cold Atlantic crossings, but in the second half of the sixteenth century, it was discovered that these pelts could be converted into felt to make hats. A new industry was subsequently born when beaver-felt hats became the rage in Europe.

Fishermen from the province of Normandy in northwestern France were the first to take up trading in North America. Notarial records show the first outfitting for the fur trade after 1550. These traders were bound for what was referred to as "Florida," which then constituted all of eastern North America from Florida to Cape Breton Island. Cod fishermen plied the coast from Newfoundland to Cape Cod, the southern boundary of the cod fisheries.

Basque whalers soon followed the Norman fishermen into fur trading, with 15 ships being outfitted annually in the 1580s. They combined whaling with trading near the mouth of the Saguenay River (Turgeon 1998). Brittany fishermen joined the Basques as fur traders in the late sixteenth century.

Fur trading in the mid–1580s was stimulated by a general expansion in the market for fur, but specifically, the beaver had become the rage due to the popularity of the broad-brimmed felt hat. The downy portion of beaver pelts is far superior to other furs for making felt. The depletion of fur-bearing animals in Western Europe had forced hat makers to look further and further eastward to supply their needs. Russia became the principal source, but the Swedish capture of the port of Narva in 1581 brought a halt to Baltic trade. The fur trade was rerouted by the Dutch through Archangel and the White Sea in 1585, but not before Canadian fur supplies had appeared as an alternative.

The estuary of the St. Lawrence River became a hotbed of French trading activity as it could support both whaling and fur trading. Large numbers of whales migrated there to feed on the rich stores of phytoplankton and zooplankton in the water, and traders "could draw from the south shore of the St. Lawrence for substantial fur resources, from the northern regions via the vast Saguenay-Lac Saint-Jean hydrographic system, and from the Great Lakes region via the St. Lawrence" (Turgeon 1998, 598).

The St. Lawrence fisheries became a powerful attraction along with fur trading, and hundreds of ships arrived annually by midcentury. Three French groups came to be trading in two different regions: Basques and a few Bretons shared the gulf and estuary of the St. Lawrence, and the Normans fished off Cape Breton and the Florida coast (Turgeon 1998). The French traded kettles, harness bells, pendants, axes, knives, swords, beads, and fabric for beaver, marten, and otter coats and moose hides.

## *The Traders of the St. Lawrence Valley*

By 1600, the once populous St. Lawrence Iroquoians discovered by Jacques Cartier in the 1530s were gone. They were extinct. It is unclear what happened to them. Gagné (2015) explains:

> Researchers have different theories or use a combination of factors to explain the departure of these groups from the St Lawrence Valley. It is likely that the main causes were the impact of diseases transmitted by Europeans, wars of conquest initiated by outside groups (the Huron or Five Nations Iroquois: Mohawk, Cayuga, Onondaga, Oneida and Seneca), and the control of trade routes with Europeans. To this day, however, none of these hypotheses has been truly validated.

It was now the Innu who had for centuries migrated in the summer to the St. Lawrence Valley that had become the middleman in the lucrative fur trade. This trade became "their leading source of income, and they did not permit any other traders—Indian or European—to go up the Saguenay at the pain of death. Control of this artery was vital to their prosperity" (Fisher 2008, 137).

Over time vast trade networks would develop between the nations across Ontario and beyond, each protecting their part of the trade routes from outsiders. Champlain would describe two major trading networks, one operating on the Saguenay and the other on the Ottawa River. Each of the Algonquian nations strove to control the trade coming from upriver and to prevent the French from making direct contact with the nations of that region. The first half of the seventeenth century became a period of constant conflict over the control of fur supplies.

There were two characteristics that were key in the development of the fur trade networks. As Trigger (1962, 243) describes:

> First, most, if not all, tribes were anxious to acquire European goods and soon became dependent on them. Secondly, each tribe strove to gain a monopoly over the goods passing back and forth between the French and tribes who lived farther than themselves from the place of trade.

Intertribal warfare subsequently intensified as the inland tribes sought their own monopolies.

## Early Movement of European Trade Goods Across New England

When the English first began exploring the coast of Maine in the early seventeenth century, they were astonished to find that the local people already had European manufactured goods. Bartholomew Gosnold, the first Englishman to land in Maine in 1602, was hailed from a Biscay shallop by a man wearing black serge breeches and a European waistcoat. The source of these materials could only have been Basque and French contacts with Eastern Etchemin and Mi'kmaq along the far-off coasts of Newfoundland, Labrador, and the Gulf of St. Lawrence. So, while the Europeans themselves had had little contact with New England before 1602, except for brief visits from Verrazzano and perhaps the Portuguese João Álvares Fagundes and Esteban Gómez, their manufactured goods had already found their way into the region (Bourque and Whitehead 1985). Incredibly, soon after the first Europeans had touched Atlantic Canada, an extensive Indigenous trade route evolved across Eastern Canada and New England for coveted manufactured goods.

Bourque and Whitehead (1985) propose that there were two routes that European goods followed to get to the Gulf of Maine. In the first, the Wabanaki carried furs and hides up the St. John and Penobscot Rivers and down the Rivière du Loup and Chaudière. The second route was taken by shallop-sailing Amerindians ranging the entire gulf coast bartering

European goods brought from the St. Lawrence. The shallops were of European manufacture, stolen or purchased with furs. By the time this pattern of trade was first observed in 1602 by Gosnold, it may have been in place for decades and probably ranged as far west as Massachusetts Bay. Thus, a massive exchange network existed that extended along the coast from Newfoundland to Cape Cod and stretched inland from the Gulf of Maine to far beyond the St. Lawrence Valley.

The people moving the goods across Nova Scotia to the Gulf of Maine and down to Cape Cod by boat were called "Tarrentines" by the English. The exact nature of this term is disputed, but these Indigenous traders probably represented the Souriquois (Mi'kmaq) of Nova Scotia and their neighboring Etchemin (Passamaquoddy and Maliseet) across the Bay of Fundy.

The Tarrentine trade networks would decline rapidly after Europeans appeared on the coast of New England and began trading directly with the local fur producers. European diseases would also decimate their population, and after a major epidemic in 1617–8, most Tarrentine trade activity ceased.

## *The First French Fur Trade Monopoly*

In 1588, two nephews of Jacques Cartier, Stephan Chaton and Jacques Noël petitioned King Henry III for a monopoly in the northeastern fur trade for 12 years and asked to have 60 convicts released a year to colonize the country and work the mines. Their claim was based on money purportedly owed to their uncle Cartier. They also claimed that "they had already contracted friendly relations with the savages of the country, several of whom had been brought home to France in order to facilitate future intercourse" (Biggar 1901, 34) and that they had discovered copper mines. Henry temporarily granted this request in January 1588; however, it was quickly revoked when other French merchants and fishermen howled that they were already actively trading fur there.

In 1599, Pierre de Chauvin de Tonnetuit made another request to the government for a fur-trade monopoly of 10 years (Biggar 1901; Morley 2003). Chauvin was a wealthy merchant, a captain of an important Huguenot garrison, and already engaged in the fur trade and cod fisheries in the Maritimes. He owned four vessels: the *Don-de-Dieu*, the *Espérance*, the *Bon-Espoir*, and the *Saint-Jean*. His request was accepted by Henry IV on the condition that he deliver to New France 50 colonists a year or 500 in total.

Chauvin gathered a number of settlers in the spring of 1600 and headed to the St. Lawrence River, where Jacques Cartier had traveled in

1535 during his second voyage. On Chauvin's voyage was also François Gravé Du Pont (also called Dupont-Gravé, Gravé Le Pout, Pont-Gravé) as his partner and lieutenant and Pierre Dugua de Monts as a passenger. (Author's note: This name is also spelled as Mons. Much of the research for this book regarding Dugua is from Champlain, who used both Mons and Monts. I have elected to use Champlain's "Monts" spelling, since he seemed to use it more frequently.)

Gravé Du Pont was a merchant who had traded furs with the Innu at Tadoussac and as far downriver as Trois-Rivières every summer since 1578. He would become a key figure in the exploration and development of New France, although few people today recognize him. "Champlain described him as a most honorable man, a good Catholic, a great servant of the King, who worthily and faithfully served his Majesty on many important occasions" (Fisher 2008, 121).

De Monts would also play a seminal role in the foundation of New France, later establishing his own colony in Québec.

Chauvin traveled down the St. Lawrence River to Tadoussac, which he chose as the location for his colony, against the advice of both Gravé Du Pont and de Monts, who favored a site further west. They considered the area to be unsuitable for colonization because of its rugged terrain, poor soil, and bitterly cold winter. Chauvin chose Tadoussac as his destination because it was "strategically situated at the junction of the Saguenay and St. Lawrence rivers, the Indian trading routes to the interior, with a harbor adjacent. Tadoussac had long been a Innu summering place for barter and for half a century a fur-trading and fishing resort for Europeans" (Morley 2003).

Champlain in his later writings would assert that Chauvin never intended to fulfill the conditions of his monopoly "but had taken out a few men merely to throw dust in the eyes of the Government." Biggar (1901, 45) suggested that Chauvin "cared less for the welfare of the colonists than for the gains of the trade."

A house was built for the settlers, "twenty-five feet long by eighteen wide and eight feet high, covered with boards with a fireplace in the middle, encompassed by a wattle palisade and a ditch" (Morley 2003). After it was completed, the rest of the summer was devoted to peltry until autumn, when the ships sailed back to France loaded with a cargo of beaver and other pelts. Defying his agreement to leave 50 colonists behind, Chauvin left "a miserable remnant of sixteen men, huddled together for warmth in the small lug-hut on the bleak rocks at the mouth of the Saguenay" (Biggar 1901, 43).

Chauvin sent only one vessel, the *Esperance*, to the Saguenay the following spring and did not sail himself. By this time, only five of the colonists were still alive, having taken refuge with the Innu. These five returned with this ship in the fall, and no others were left to replace them.

In 1602, Chauvin commanded another expedition from Honfleur to New France, with two ships, the *Don-de-Dieu* and the *Esperance*, but again no colonists. After a summer of trading, he returned in October 1602, apparently having totally abandoned the idea of colonization.

Not surprisingly, Chauvin's patent was now clamorously opposed by the excluded merchants. Henry IV summoned a commission of inquiry on December 28, 1602, receiving as delegates merchants from Rouen and Saint-Malo, and Chauvin himself. An agreement was reached to admit one vessel each from Rouen and Saint-Malo, but before any left, Chauvin died.

## A New Group Is Assembled

Henry next awarded a monopoly to François Aymar de Clermont de Chaste, whom he named lieutenant general of New France. To support his expedition, the Sieur de Chaste formed the Monts Company, which included very wealthy merchants. He gave command to François Gravé Du Pont.

Also added to the voyage was Samuel de Champlain, included as an observer. Unlike Pont-Gravé, Champlain would become quite famous and, for more than 30 years, was the central figure in the exploration and settlement of New France. Champlain assured his fame by producing a detailed treasury of books of his travels, illustrations, and maps. The Champlain biographer W.F. Ganong (1922, 94) suggests that Champlain "narrates with all the authority of a leading participant and the matter-of-fact accuracy of an official report ... and he has neither peer nor competitor." His maps of New England and Acadia consist of three large maps of the general area, 13 maps of important harbors, and drawings of the settlements at Saint Croix and Port Royal.

## Champlain's Background

Before this Gravé Du Pont expedition, Champlain had been groomed as an explorer under the tutelage of King Henry IV himself (Fisher 2008). Champlain came from a little town on the Bay of Biscay, Brouage, known for its salt trade. Born around 1570 and likely baptized Protestant, he was part of a wealthy maritime family. His father was a self-made man who had risen through the ranks from seaman to pilot and then master, merchant, and ship owner. He served in Henry's army during the later stages of the French religious wars in Brittany, starting as a quartermaster responsible for the feeding and care of horses.

In 1599, Champlain served as a secret agent in a remarkable espionage visit to Spanish America, where he traveled as an observer on a French ship accompanying one of the Treasure Fleets and had a one-month overland trip through New Spain. From this voyage, Champlain produced a long report called *Bref Discours* that discussed the strengths and weaknesses of the Spanish empire.

Champlain was particularly fascinated by the Indigenous people of New Spain and devoted a large part of the report to the cruelties they suffered at the hands of the Spanish. He included watercolors of Amerindians burned alive for heresy, Amerindians bludgeoned for not attending Mass, and Amerindians and African slaves being forced to dive for pearls at unsafe depths off the coast of Venezuela. He vowed that when given the chance, he would treat the Indigenous people more humanely.

Etching of Samuel de Champlain from François Pierre Guillaume Guizot's *A Popular History of France from the Earliest Times* (Boston: Dana Estes & Charles E. Lauriat), volume 6, page 190; signed E. Ronjat (Wikimedia Commons).

In appreciation for his report, King Henry awarded Champlain a pension to work on plans to settle North America with other experts in the basement of the Louvre. He studied the history of the earlier, disastrous French settlements of Jean Ribaut and René de Laudonnière, and he visited the Atlantic ports of France to interview fishermen who knew the waters of North America. Champlain became as knowledgeable about American exploration as any man alive but had never visited there. He was about to get his chance.

## The Chaste/Gravé Du Pont Voyage to New France

On March 15, 1603, the Sieur de Chaste dispatched three ships to New France. One, the *Bonne Renommée*, belonging to de Chaste, was commanded by Pont-Gravé, who was to survey the resources of the region and find an auspicious place for settlement; in this, he was aided by Samuel de Champlain (Morley 2003). Champlain must have looked forward to seeing all of the places that Jacques Cartier had described 60 years earlier, and he likely hoped to travel more extensively.

Sailing with the *Renommée* were two smaller ships, *La Françoise*, outfitted by merchants of Rouen, and another ship of unknown name belonging to Jean Sarcel de Prévert of Saint-Milo. No colonists were carried, as the mission was only for trade and discovery. They took with them two Amerindians who had been in France for some time, probably brought over by Chauvin on his last voyage (Otis 1880).

Prévert and the crew of *La Françoise* were sent to trade, while Gravé Du Pont and Champlain were to search for an optimal colonization site. Champlain published an account of the expedition in 1603, titled *Des Sauvages, ou voyage de Samuel Champlain, de Brouage, fait en la France nouvelle l'an mil six cens trois...* ["Concerning the Primitives: Or Travels of Samuel Champlain of Brouage"]. To quote Champlain, I use Biggar's 1922 translation of this manuscript in *The Works of Samuel D. Champlain*, published by The Champlain Society.

The *Bonne Renommée* and her consorts arrived at Tadoussac Harbor at the mouth of the Saguenay River on May 26, 1603, after a long, hard journey through the coastal waters of Newfoundland and North America. They arrived at an incredibly auspicious moment, as an immense gathering of Amerindians had just arrived on the other side of the Saguenay River at St. Matthew's Point, today's Pointe-aux-Alouettes. Champlain estimated there were more than 200 canoes and 1,000 Amerindians.

> Among them were several different groups of Montagnais [Innu], Algonquin Nations from the Ottawa River to the far Northwest and Etchemin [Eastern Wabanaki] from as far south as the Penobscot River, in what is now the state of Maine. They had come together to celebrate a major victory over their common enemy, the Iroquois [Fisher 2008, 130].

Incredibly, Champlain and Pont-Gravé sailed directly across the river and joined in the celebration. Fisher (2008, 130) further describes the affair:

> It was a lively scene: billowing clouds of white smoke rising above the lodges, a swirl of color and movement in the camp, crowds of young braves and beautifully dressed Indian maidens mixing with each other, gangs of children and packs of dogs dashing to and fro. The Indian drums were beating in celebration. More than a hundred fresh Iroquois scalps were on display. Wounded Iroquois captives were tightly bound to stakes, and their torture had already begun.

The Frenchmen marched boldly into the chaos, without any apparent fear and without weapons. Champlain describes the encounter:

Having landed, we proceeded to the cabin of their grand Sagamore named Anadabijou, whom we found with some eighty or a hundred of his companions celebrating a tabagie, that is, a banquet. He received us very cordially, and according to the custom of his country, seated us near himself, with all the savages arranged in rows on both sides of the cabin. One of the savages whom we had taken with us began to make an address speaking of the cordial reception the king had given them, and the good treatment they had received in France, and saying they were affirmed that his Majesty was favorably disposed towards them, and was desirous of peopling their country, and of making peace with their enemies, the Iroquois, or offending forces to conquer them. He also told them of the handsome manors, palaces, and houses they had seen, and of the inhabitants and our mode of living.... Now, after he had finished his address, the grand Sagamore, Anadabijou, who had listened to it attentively, proceeded to take some tobacco, and give it to Sieur du Pont-Gravé of St. Malo, myself, and some other Sagamores, who were near him. After a long smoke, he began to make his address to all (speaking with gravity), stopping at times a little, and then resuming and saying, that they truly ought to be very glad in having his Majesty for a great friend. They all answered with one voice, Ho, ho, ho, that is to say, yes, yes. He, continuing his address, said that he should be very glad to have his Majesty people their land and make war upon their enemies; that there was no nation upon earth to which they were more kindly disposed than to the French: finally he gave them all to understand the advantage and profit they could receive from his Majesty. After he had finished his address, we went out of his cabin, and they began to celebrate their banquet, at which they have elk's meat, which is similar to beef, also that of the bear, seal and beaver, these being their ordinary meats [Biggar 1922, 99–100].

The French and three great tribal groups had come together by accident, but as Fisher (2008, 134) relates:

Here was a moment of high importance in the history of North America. Nobody had planned these events, but both the French and Indian leaders were quick to see an opportunity. The Great Tabagie marked the beginning of an alliance between the founders of New France and three Indian nations. Each entered willingly into the relationship and gained something of value in return. The Indians acquired a potential ally against their mortal enemies, the Iroquois. The French won support for settlement, exploration, and trade. The alliance that formed here would remain strong for many years because it rested on a mutuality of material interest.

Champlain saw the Indigenous peoples as potential partners rather than slaves. In his model, he saw the locals as a conduit for trade, not as a potential labor source. An approach quite unique to the Spanish.

Prévert traded that summer at Île Percée near Chaleur Bay, an arm of the Gulf of St. Lawrence. Guided by a few Innu, he also explored some potential mining sites on the Acadian Peninsula. Sieur Prévert gave to the Amerindians wedges and chisels to extract ore from one of the mines, which they promised to do, and bring it to Sieur Prévert in the following year. There is no record of whether this happened.

Gravé Du Pont and Champlain explored the St. Lawrence as far as the Lachine Rapids. The further along the river they traveled, the more impressed they became with its suitability for settlement.

As they traveled down the river, Champlain interrogated many Amerindians about the course and extent of the St. Lawrence, as well as other adjoining rivers, the location of lakes and falls, and the general features of the country.

After making their way to the Lachine Rapids, they returned to Tadoussac for a few days and then explored the Gaspé and the Acadian Peninsulas. They then reunited with the other ships and headed back to France.

Before leaving, they brought on board six Amerindians—one the son of a sagamore; an Iroquois woman who had been taken in war; and an additional man, woman, and two boys (Otis 1880). Their fates are unrecorded.

## *The Lifeways of the Algonquin, Wyandot, and Iroquois*

### Algonquin

At the time of first contact, about 3,000 Algonquin lived in small bands in western Québec and Ontario, centered on the Ottawa River and its tributaries (Black and Parrott 2018; Clément 1996). The name Algonquin should not be confused with Algonquian or Algonkian, which represents a much larger linguistic and cultural group. However, Algonquin society and culture were very similar to the other Algonquian nations that the French and English encountered along the Eastern Seaboard.

The Algonquin hunted and traded across large territories of the eastern woodlands and subarctic regions. They were largely hunter-gatherers, but in the southernmost region some groups practiced agriculture. Even among the groups who mainly hunted, agricultural products were an important part of their diet. They obtained these crop products through trading or raiding other agricultural societies.

During the summer months, Algonquin bands gathered along the river to fish, hunt, and socialize. During winter, smaller groups spread out into small hunting camps made up of large, related families. They hunted a variety of animals for meat and fur, including deer, beaver, bear, moose, otter, and raccoon. For fishing, they used birch bark canoes. They transported materials by toboggan in winter, and people also used snowshoes to facilitate travel.

The Algonquin lived in communities of related patrilineal clans that followed the male line of descent.

Clans were represented by animal totems such as Crane, Wolf, Bear, Loon and many others. The communities were egalitarian, with leadership provided by respected elders and heads of clans. Intermarriage within a clan was forbidden, even if the parties were from separate communities [Black and Parrott 2018].

Each Algonquin band had its own chief, who depended on political approval from the band's clan leaders.

They lived in wigwams that were conical and could accommodate one or two families. The outer coverings consisted of animal skins, reed mats, or sheets of bark. These coverings were supported by frames of pliable poles inserted into the ground, then tied together at the opposite end. There was a hearth in the middle area of the wigwam, where cooking implements were typically hung.

The Algonquin made beautiful woven baskets, pottery, and beadwork. These crafts were not only functional but also deeply symbolic and often had spiritual meaning. Their clothing was made of animal skin, often decorated with intricate beadwork and designs. Women wore long dresses, while men wore breechcloths and leggings.

## Wyandot (also Wyandotte, Wendat, and Hurons)

The Wyandot lived between Lake Simcoe and the southeastern corner of Georgian Bay in Ontario. In their language, Wyandot meant "Dwellers of the Peninsula" or "Islanders." The French called them Hurons from the French *hure* meaning "boar's head," after their bristly coiffure.

The Wyandot was not a single nation but a confederacy of four or five nations (Trigger 1987). In the fifteenth century, it was initially an alliance between the Attignawantan (People of the Bear) and the Attigneenongnahac (People of the Cord). It was joined in about 1590 by the Arendarhonon (People of the Rock), and then the Tahontaenrat (People of the Deer) around 1610. A fifth group, the Ataronchronon (People of the Marshes or Bog), may have later become full members of the confederacy or become a division of the Attignawantan.

The Wyandot were mostly farmers who supplemented their diet with hunting. Agriculture represented 80 percent of their diet. The women grew corn, beans, and squash, while the men tended tobacco. There were 18 to 25 villages of Wyandot, with up to 3,500 people in each, clustered in an area measuring 35 miles east to west and 20 miles north to south (Trigger 1987). The total population size of the confederation was between 20,000 and 40,000, at a density of 23 people per square kilometer.

Villages were usually set on a slight rise, adjacent to a permanent water supply. Families lived together in longhouses that were about seven meters wide and varied in length depending on family size. The largest houses were 90 meters in length (Heidenreich and Filice 2018). The larger villages were surrounded by the wooden palisade that was typical of all Iroquois cultures. Every 10 to 15 years, the Wyandot would move their villages when the soils became exhausted.

> The Huron villages were clustered close to each other, with their corn fields forming a surrounding belt. These fields were extensive; early in the seventeenth century, it was reported that they covered about seven thousand acres; one early visitor to Huronia, as the region occupied by the Hurons was known, said that "it was easier to get lost in a corn field" than in the surrounding forest [Dickason 1996, 264].

Agricultural products not only fed the Wyandot but also became important trade commodities. The Hurons were at the northern limits for corn production and were at the center of the region's trading networks.

The fundamental socioeconomic group of the Wyandot was the matrilineal-extended family, whose female members all traced a common descent to a mother or grandmother. Individuals belonged to one of eight matrilineal clans—Bear, Deer, Turtle, Beaver, Wolf, Loon/Sturgeon, Hawk, or Fox (Heidenreich and Filice 2018). A child was not allowed to marry a member of their mother's clan but could marry a member of their father's clan.

The villages were ruled by two councils, one for civil affairs and the other for war. All decisions were made by consensus of all men over the age of 30, but old men and chiefs of large families tended to dominate. Wyandot women had little say in councils.

In summer, Wyandot men wore breechcloths and leggings. In winter they added deerskin tunics. Wyandot women wore wraparound skirts with poncho-style blouses or deerskin dresses. They wore moccasins on their feet. Clothing and moccasins were often made of blackened buckskin with red borders. Wyandot men often carried beautifully decorated shoulder purses or pouches, which were sometimes used to carry food or bullets.

Wyandot art objects included clay pots, weaving, and beadwork. They crafted wampum out of white and purple shell beads. Wampum was traded as a kind of currency but was just as important as art. Wampum designs represented a person's family or told a story.

## Iroquois

The Iroquois or Haudenosaunee Confederacy (People of the Longhouse), also referred to as the Five Nations, was composed of five nations at the time of Champlain's visits to North America—the Mohawk, Cayuga, Onondaga, Oneida, and Seneca (east to west). When the Europeans first arrived in North America, the Iroquois were based in central and western New York, ranging north to the St. Lawrence River, east to Montréal, and south into northwestern Pennsylvania. Their total numbers likely did not exceed 12,000 (Williams 1904).

The purpose of the confederacy was to put an end to internal warfare and to strengthen themselves against outside foes.

> An attempt was made to bring all the Iroquois people into the confederacy, but only the Mohawks, Oneidas, Onondagas, Cayugas and Senecas joined.... The feeling against the Iroquois tribes who would not join the confederacy was very bitter. They were regarded as traitors and pursued as relentlessly as were the Algonquins. They were all ultimately subdued or exterminated [Williams 1904, 11].

Champlain, with his Algonquin companions, fought the Mohawk (Kanyen'kehà:ka or Kanien'kehá:ka). The Mohawk occupied the area from Lake Champlain westward along the Mohawk River and northward into the St. Lawrence Valley (Abler 2019; Snow 1994).

The Haudenosaunee Confederacy was an extraordinary democracy.

> Each nation was a distinct republic so far as its own domestic affairs were concerned, but all were bound together in matters of general interest. Each nation was divided into eight clans known as the Wolf, the Bear, the Beaver, the Turtle, the Deer, the Snipe, the Heron and the Hawk. There were in each nation at least eight principal sachems, one for each clan.... All told there were fifty sachems divided among the nations as follows: The Onondagas, fourteen; the Cayugas, ten, the Mohawks and Oneidas, nine each, and the Senecas eight.... The fifty sachems constituted what was known as the Council of the League. They combined the legislative, executive and judicial authority of the nation.
>
> The meetings of the council were held annually, in the autumn at Onondaga. Aside from these regular meetings special meetings might be called at any time or place. The council declared war, made peace, received ambassadors, entered into treaties, and in a word decided all matters of political, military, and religious action. In order to secure favorable action on any it was necessary to have an unanimous vote of all the present. In debate a speaker was never interrupted, and rarely was [there] any heat. Each presented his views in manner he could, usually repeating the substance of all been said by those who preceded him. This habit frequently made their debates tediously long. Important councils would last days [Williams 1904, 15–16].

The Mohawk were agricultural peoples. The men cleared the fields, while the women planted and tended the crops.

> The men hunted for food, spent long seasons in the severe work of trapping and protected their territory from their enemies. All the property of the men

except the arms he used, belonged to the wife.... Owing to warfare and the hard life led by the men, the women were more numerous than the men in all the tribes. In the lodge the Indian was a man of few words. He acknowledged the woman's right to rule there [Williams 1904, 17].

The Iroquois lived in villages in forest clearings. These villages were protected by palisades and surrounded by extensive corn fields. Mohawk villages were relatively large, containing one thousand people or more.

Each village had its own council and a village chief or sachem, chosen by the women. Iroquois society was matrilineal, where descent was traced through the mother rather than the father. Their social organization included division into phratries (kinship groups) and clans.

> The laws governing marriage and descent had an important bearing upon the civil life of the Iroquois. Originally the Wolf, Bear, Beaver and Turtle clans were regarded as brothers, as were also the Deer, Snipe, Heron and Hawk clans. All marriages were between members of the first group with members of the second. Not only was one forbidden to marry one belonging to his clan or group of clans, but he must not marry a member of his own tribe, though belonging to the other group of clans [Williams 1904, 16].

For clothing, men wore a breech cloth of deerskin in summer, while women often went topless and wore a skirt of deerskin. In winter, men wore deerskin leggings and a deerskin shirt and carried a flint arrow hunting bag. Both men and women wore ankle-wrap moccasins.

The Iroquois lived in longhouses that extended hundreds of feet in length, depending on the size of the resident clan. The larger Mohawk villages contained dozens of these longhouses that were occupied year-round.

> Their roofing frames of bent (or perhaps prebent) saplings were lashed atop vertical upright posts. Roofed with elm-bark slabs, a clan totem emblazoned by the doorway, such a structure could be expanded when a new husband married into the building's social unit. Within the building, bunk like compartments lined both sides, with families sharing cooking fires that were spaced down the central corridor and from whose pots any house resident was free to partake [Nabokov 1996, 38].

## Seven

# Pierre Dugua de Monts's Colonies at Saint Croix and Port Royal

## 1603–1606

### Setting the Stage: A Search for a New Sponsor

When Gravé Du Pont and Champlain returned from Acadia, they discovered that Chaste had died. They would need a new sponsor to continue their North American adventures. Champlain began at once to prepare a report of their activities for the king.

Champlain laid before his sovereign Henry IV a map constructed by his own hand of the regions he had just visited, together with a very particular narrative of his voyage.

> Henry IV. manifested a deep interest in Champlain's narrative.... An account of the country, its trees, plants, fruits, and vines, with a description of the native inhabitants, their mode of living, their clothing, food, and its preparation, their banquets, religion, and method of burying their dead, with many other interesting particulars relating to their habits and customs.... He listened to its recital with great apparent satisfaction, and by way of encouragement promised not to abandon the undertaking, but to continue to bestow upon it his royal favor and patronage [Otis 1880, 34–35].

In 1603, King Henry chose Pierre Dugua de Monts (1558–1628) to lead a new expedition to L'Acadie, covering eastern Canada and the northeastern United States. He asked him to set up a settlement from which furs could be obtained from the Indigenous people and appointed him first lieutenant of Acadia and vice admiral (McManamon 2022). His mission was to conquer the land and convert the local Amerindians to Christianity. To finance this expedition, Henry IV gave him a monopoly over all the fur trade in the region.

The Sieur de Monts was born in Royan around 1560, and he belonged to a wealthy family who lived in Saintonge. De Monts was a Huguenot who fought alongside Henry IV during the religious wars against the Catholic League, and for his support he had been awarded a large pension, governorship of the town of Pons, and royal patronage. Before Henry's grant, de Monts had already been to L'Acadie with Champlain in Pierre Chauvin's settlement attempt at Tadoussac.

Until this point, the French had been focused on the St. Lawrence River Valley and Tadoussac. De Monts, however, believed the climate there was too harsh for a year-round colony, and he turned his eyes further south to the Wabanaki (Etchemin and Mi'kmaq) homelands, which were beginning to receive considerable English attention. He would focus on the land surrounding the Bay of Fundy, in particular the Saint Croix River, the Saint John River, and the Annapolis Basin. He and Champlain would subsequently make the first extensive explorations of the coast of Maine and New England.

De Monts put together an expedition force of 120 men and two vessels, one of 120 tons, captained by Sieur de Pont-Gravé, and another, of 150 tons, which he captained himself. On board were also the French nobleman and a senior member of the expedition, Jean de Biencourt de Poutrincourt et de Saint-Just; carpenter/pilot Pierre Angibault, known as "Champdoré"; and Samuel de Champlain as the cartographer and historian.

Champlain would produce a full account of the De Monts expedition in his 1613 publication *The Voyages of the Sieur de Champlain of Saintonge, Captain in Ordinary for the King in the Navy*. Herein, I use Biggar's (1922) publication *The Works of Samuel de Champlain, Vol. 1* for quotations and twentieth-century place names.

## Expedition of Pierre Dugua, the Sieur de Monts

The de Monts expedition set sail from Le Havre in April 1603 and arrived at the coast of Acadia (now Nova Scotia) in May, in a very rapid crossing. Champlain immediately set out to survey the bay in a small skiff. "He sounded its depth, calculated the latitude, measured compass variation, and made a very accurate chart" (Fisher 2008, 161). He also mapped two large Innu (Mi'kmaq) encampments located on both sides of the bay. Champlain noted that a web of Indian paths bore witness to the importance of the place, and an old burial ground testified to its long use.

De Monts, Champdoré, and Champlain made a careful examination of the coast of Acadia for potential settlement sites and landed the crew at a place Champlain named Port au Mouton after a sheep fell overboard and drowned. While the crew established a temporary encampment,

Champlain continued his explorations in a barque of eight tons, accompanied by 11 men. He came upon immense populations of birds and seals, which the explorers dispatched easily, then gorging themselves on the fresh meat.

Traveling with Innu guides they came upon a place they named Port Royal in the Bay of Fundy on the site of modern-day Annapolis Royal, Nova Scotia. As told by Champlain: "We entered into one of the most beautiful harbors I have seen on all these coasts, which could safely hold 2,000 ships." They loved the surrounding land as well as the harbor. Champlain wrote, "From the mouth of the river to the point we reached many prairies or meadows, but these are flooded at high tide, and numbers of small creeks that cross from one side to the other" (Biggar 1922, 256). On shore, they also found traces of copper. They thought about making a permanent settlement there, but the Sieur de Monts decided to continue traveling.

After some further exploration, they built their settlement on a small island (now Muttoneguis Island) in the Saint Croix River, which separates today's Maine and New Brunswick. It caught their eye as a handsome island that would be easy to fortify. Champlain writes:

> The island is covered with firs, birches, maples, and oaks. It is naturally very well situated, with but one place where it is low, for about forty paces, and that easy to fortify. The shores of the mainland are distant on both sides some nine hundred to a thousand paces, so that vessels could only pass along the river at the mercy of the cannon on the island. This place we considered the best we had seen, both on account of its situation, the fine country, and for the intercourse we were expecting with the Indians of these coasts and the interior since we should be in their midst ... this place was named by the Sieur de Monts the island of Saint Croix [Biggar 1922, 271].

On the development of their fort, Champlain continues:

> Each worked so efficiently that in a very short time it was put in a state of defense, though the mosquitoes (which are little flies) gave us great annoyance while at work, and several of our men had their faces so swollen by their bites that they could scarcely see.... After the Sieur de Monts had chosen the site for the storehouse, which was fifty-four feet long, eighteen broad, and twelve feet high, he settled the plan for his own house, which he had built quickly by good workmen. Then he assigned a place to each one, and immediately they began to collect fives and sixes, according to their preferences. After that all set to work to clear the island, to fetch wood, to cut timber, to carry earth, and other things necessary for the construction of the buildings. An oven was also built, and a hand mill for grinding our wheat, which gave much trouble and labor to most of us, since it was a painful task. Afterward, some gardens were made, both on the mainland and on the island itself, wherein many kinds of grain were sown which came up very well, except on the island where the soil

was nothing but sand in which everything was scorched when the sun shone, although great pains were taken to water the plants [Biggar 1922, 275–76].

When the fort was completed, Gravé Du Pont and de Poutrincourt headed back to France to settle some affairs, leaving 79 colonists behind including Pierre Dugua and Champlain.

## *The First Explorations of Coastal Maine*

While the artisans were busy building the settlement at Saint Croix, de Monts sent Champdoré, Champlain, 11 sailors, and two local guides to explore the coast of what is now Maine. It would be the first deep European penetration into this region.

They set out on September 2, 1604, and heading down along the rugged, rocky coast within a few days sighted Mount Desert Island, which Champlain named for the stone mountain peaks bare of trees. He describes Mount Desert Island as

> about four or five leagues in length, of which we were almost lost on a little rock, level with the surface of the water, which made a hole in our pinnace close to the keel. The distance from this island to the mainland on the north is not a hundred paces. It is very high and cleft in places, giving it the appearance of the sea of seven or eight mountains one alongside the other. The tops of them are bare of trees because there is nothing there but rocks. The woods consist only of pines, firs, and birches. I named it Mount Desert Island [Biggar 1922, 282].

On September 6, Champlain had his first major encounter with the Wabanaki of Maine when he came across two local people rowing a canoe. Champlain called them Etchemin, probably a translation of the Indigenous word *Skidijn*, meaning "people." After some initial trepidation, the French traded with them for fish, and the Etchemin showed them the way south to the mouth of the Penobscot River and proceeded with them up the river about 20 miles to the fall line at present-day Bangor, Maine.

Champlain reports that along the riverbank were "neither town nor village, nor any traces that there ever had been any, but only one or two empty Indian wigwams." Champlain repeats what he learned from his guides:

> They come there and to the islands only for a few months in summer during the fishing and hunting season when the game is plentiful. They are a people of no fixed abode, from what I have discovered and learned from themselves; for they pass the winter sometimes in one place and sometimes in another, wheresoever they perceive the hunting of wild animals is the best [Biggar 1922, 292].

The Etchemin followed a migratory foraging subsistence way of life and were only on the coast during the spring and summer seasons.

Near Bangor, Champaign and his party met with another group of Etchemin, including two of their leaders, Bashabez and Cabhis. Each was accompanied by at least 30 followers. As Champlain describes:

> I ordered the crew of our pinnace to draw near the Indians and to hold their weapons in readiness to do their duty in case they perceived any movement of these people against us. [Bashabez], seeing us on shore, bade us sit down, and began with his companions to smoke, as they usually do before beginning their speeches. They made a present of venison and waterfowl [Biggar 1922, 295].

The meeting went smoothly, and strong desires were expressed for cooperation and alliance. Champlain recounts:

> [I told the Etchemin] that the Sieur de Monts had sent me to them, and also their country; that he wished to remain friends with them, and reconcile them with their enemies, the Souriquois [Mi'kmaq] and Canadians [Innu]; moreover, that he desired to settle in their country and show them how to cultivate it so that they might no longer lead so miserable an existence as they were doing; and several other remarks on the same subject.... I made them presents of hatchets, rosaries, caps, knives, and other little knick-knacks; then we separated. The rest of this day and the following night they did nothing but dance, sing, and make merry, awaiting the dawn when we bartered a certain number of beaver skins [Biggar 1922, 295–96].

Thus, the two cultures made their first tentative steps to seek an arrangement that would reward them both. The meeting concluded; Champlain and his men sailed down the river the next day. They explored Penobscot Bay and the mid-coast region a bit more, and then returned to the Saint Croix settlement, arriving there on October 2.

## A Difficult Winter at Saint Croix

Champlain returned to Saint Croix Island at the end of September. Almost immediately snow began to fall and the settlers' preparations for winter were cut short. The river became impassable with treacherous ice floes, and they could no longer cross to the mainland. This left them with a shortage of drinking water and firewood.

Champlain relates:

> Our beverages all froze except the Spanish wine. Cider was given out by the pound. This loss was because the storehouse had no cellar, and the air that entered through the cracks was more severe than that outside. We were obliged to make use of very bad water and to drink melted snow since we had neither

springs nor brooks; for it was not possible to go to the mainland on account of the great cakes of ice carried by the ebb and flow of the tide, which rises three fathoms between low and high water. The labor with the hand mill was very painful, because most of us, having poor quarters and suffering from shortage of fuel which we could not procure on account of the ice, had almost no strength; and, again, we ate only salt meat and vegetables during the winter, which produced poor blood. Such in my opinion was in part the cause of these unfortunate maladies. All these circumstances made the Sieur de Monts and others dissatisfied with the settlement [Biggar 1922, 306-7].

As the winter progressed, the men began to fall prey to scurvy. Champlain's descriptions of this disease are quite graphic:

There was engendered in the mouths of those who had it large pieces of superfluous fungus flesh (which caused great putrefaction), and this increased to such a degree that they could scarcely take anything except in very liquid form. Their teeth barely held in their places and could be drawn out with the fingers without causing pain. The superfluous flesh was often cut away, which caused them to lose much blood from the mouth. Afterwards, they were taken with great pains in the arms and legs, which became swollen and very hard and covered with spots like flea bites; and they could not walk on account of the contraction of the nerves; consequently, they had almost no strength, and suffered intolerable pains. They had also pains in the loins, stomach, and bowels, together with a very bad cough and shortness of breath. In brief, they were in such a state that the majority of the sick could neither get up nor move, nor could they even be held upright without fainting away; so that of seventy-nine of us, thirty-five died, and more than twenty were very near it [Biggar 1922, 303-4].

The selection of Saint Croix Island for a settlement turned out to be a great mistake, as it was too exposed to the extreme winter weather. Champlain writes:

It was difficult to know this country without having wintered there; for on arriving in summer everything is very pleasant on account of the woods, the beautiful landscapes, and the fine fishing for the many kinds of fish we found there.... There are six months of winter in that country [Biggar 1922, 307].

Champlain also notes that the local people suffered greatly during the winter:

During the winter, when the snow is deepest, they go hunting for moose and other animals, on which they live the greater part of the time. If the snow is not deep, they are scarcely rewarded for their pain, since they cannot capture anything except with very great labor, whereby they endure and suffer much. When they do not go hunting, they live on a shellfish called the clam.... When they go hunting, they make use of certain racquets, twice as large as those of our country, which they attach under their feet, and with these they travel over the snow without sinking, both the women and children as well as the men who hunt for the tracks of animals. Having found these, they follow them until they catch sight of the beast, when they shoot at him with their bows, or else kill him with thrusts from swords set in the end of a half-pike. This can be done very easily because these animals are unable to travel in the snow without sinking in. Then the women and children come up and camp there and give themselves up to feasting. Afterward, they go back to see whether they can find other animals, and thus they pass the winter. In March following, there arrived some Indians, shared with us their game, for which we gave them in exchange for bread and other articles. Such is the manner of life of these people in winter, and it seems to me very wretched [Biggar 1922, 308–9].

As spring came, the surviving settlers desperately waited for relief to come from France. When none had appeared by the end of April, "everybody began to have forebodings, fearing least some accident had befallen them" (Biggar 1922, 309). De Monts ordered them to build a pinnace of 15 tons' burden, and another of seven, so they could travel to Gaspé to search for a vessel that could take them back to France.

This proved unnecessary as, on June 15, Gravé Du Pont finally arrived with vessels filled with supplies. Now, rather than flee home, de Monts decided that they should search for a more suitable site for a settlement where the climate would be milder.

## De Monts and Samuel Champlain Explore the Coast of Maine

On June 18, 1605, de Monts set out from Saint Croix Island, accompanied by Champdoré, Champlain, 19 of the healthiest sailors, and two Indigenous guides—Panounias, an Etchemin who spoke the language of northern Maine, and his wife, name unknown, an Abenaki who spoke the language of the south.

The group traveled along the coast of Manan Island and a series of smaller islands and anchored on Great Wass Island. Champlain relates: "On this was a multitude of crows, whereof our crew took a great number, and we named it the Isle of Crows" (Biggar 1922, 312). The French then sailed past Mount Desert Island, anchored at today's Monroe Island overnight, and then headed further southwest into the mouth of the Kennebec River. Here they charted the surrounding islands and channels and then headed upstream. After traveling for some distance, they were met by two canoes of Wabanaki hunting birds. Champlain describes what happened:

> We accosted these Indians through our own, who went towards them with his wife, and she explained to them the reason for our coming. We made friends with them and with the Indians of that river who acted as our guides. And

proceeding farther to see their chief, named Manthoumermer ... we passed some islands, straits and streams which are spread along the course of the river, where we saw some fine meadows [Biggar 1922, 315].

Coasting along Westport Island, they landed at Wiscasset, where Manthoumermer awaited them with 25 or 30 Wabanaki. Champlain writes:

> Drawing near our pinnace he made us a speech, in which he expressed his pleasure at seeing us, and said he desired an alliance with us, and through our mediation to make peace with their enemies. He added that the next day he would send word to two other Indian chiefs who were up country, one called Marchin, and the other Sasinou, chief of the Kennebec River. The Sieur de Monts had biscuits and peas given them, wherewith they were much pleased [Biggar 1922, 316].

The next day they were guided to Merrymeeting Bay, where the Kennebec and Androscoggin Rivers meet. They waited there for a day for Marchin and Sasinou, who did not show. They were then led back down the main Kennebec River to its mouth, where they caught "a great number of fine fish" (Biggar 1922, 320). Their guides subsequently went off hunting and did not return.

De Monts and Champlain then sailed into Casco Bay and spent the night near Portland. They continued the next day along the coast:

> We caught sight of two clouds of smoke which some Indians were making for us, and heading towards them we came to anchor behind a small island close to the mainland [Ram Island]. Here we saw more than eighty Indians, who ran along the shore to observe us, dancing and showing by signs their pleasure thereat. The Sieur de Monts sent two men with our Indian to go and fetch them, and after these had spoken to them for some time and had assured them of our friendship, we left one of our men with them, and they delivered to us one of their companions as a hostage. Meantime the Sieur de Monts paid a visit to an island which is very beautiful on account of what it produces, having fine oaks and nut-trees, with cleared land and abundance of vines which in their season bear fine grapes [Biggar 1922, 323].

They anchored for a while in Saco Bay, of which Champlain made a drawing, and they entered the Saco River. Here Champlain describes that a "large number of Indians came towards" them upon the bank of the river "and began to dance."

> Their chief, whose name was Honemechin, was not then with them; but he arrived about two or three hours later with two canoes, and went circling round and round our pinnace.... These people showed that they were much pleased. Their chief was good-looking, young, and active. We sent some goods on shore to barter with them, but they possessed only their clothes.... The Sieur de Monts had certain articles given to their chief, with which he was

much pleased, and he came on board several times to visit us [Biggar 1922, 325–27].

The following day de Monts and Champlain went on shore and found a series of great agricultural fields that ran along the bank of the river. As Champlain tells it:

> We saw their grain, which is Indian corn. This they grow in gardens, sowing three or four grains in one spot, after which, with the shells of the aforesaid sign, they heap about it a quantity of earth. Then three feet away they sow as much again, and so on in order. Amongst this corn, they plant in each hillock three or four Brazilian beans [*Phaseolus vulgaris*], which come up in different colours. When fully grown these plants twine around the aforementioned corn, which grows to a height of five to six feet; and they keep the ground very free from weeds. We saw there many squashes, pumpkins, and tobacco, which they likewise cultivate! The Indian corn we saw was then two feet in height, and there was also some three feet high. As for the beans, they were beginning to burst into flower, as were likewise the pumpkins and squashes. They plant their corn in May and harvest it in September [Biggar 1922, 327].

What Champlain describes here is the northern reaches of a cropping system being utilized by Indigenous people all across the eastern United States. This system traced back more than a thousand years to southeastern North America, where small-scale agriculture was first conducted by North Americans. At the time of the European conquest, the eastern forests were by no means pristine—all had been disturbed to varying degrees by Amerindian farming activity.

De Monts and Champlain then headed further south to Cape Ann, leaving quite impressed with the coast and people of southern Maine. Champlain writes:

> The fixed abodes, the cultivated fields, and the fine trees led us to the conclusion that the climate here is more temperate and better than that where we wintered, and any of the other places on this coast.... The forests inland are very open, but nevertheless abound in oaks, beeches, ashes, and elms, and in wet places, there are numbers of willows.... This place is very pleasant and as attractive a spot as one can see anywhere. The river, which is bordered by meadows, abounds greatly in fish. At its mouth lies an islet adapted for the construction of a good fortress where one would be safe [Biggar 1922, 330].

## *Interactions in Southern New England*

When the explorers arrived at Cape Ann, they discovered another group of agricultural people. As Champlain records it:

> Near it we caught sight of a canoe in which were five or six Indians, who came towards us, but after approaching our pinnace, went back to dance upon the

beach. The Sieur de Monts sent me ashore to visit them, and to give to each a knife and some biscuit, which caused them to dance better than ever. When this was over, I made them understand as well as I could, that they should show me how the coast trended. After I had drawn for them with a charcoal the bay and the Island Cape, where we then were, they pictured for me with the same charcoal another bay which they represented as very large. Here they placed six pebbles at equal intervals, giving me thereby to understand that each one of these marks represented that number of chiefs and tribes. Next they represented within the said bay a river which we had passed, which is very long and has shoals [Merrimac] [Biggar 1922, 334–36].

These Indians informed us that all those who lived in this region cultivated the land and sowed seeds like the others we had previously seen…. Having gone half a league we perceived upon a rocky point several Indians who ran dancing along the shore towards their companions to inform them of our coming. Having indicated to us the direction of their home, they made signal-smokes to show us the site of their settlement. We came to anchor close to a little island [Thatchers Island], to which we sent our canoe with some knives and biscuits for the Indians, and observed from their numbers that these places are more populous than the others we had seen. Having tarried some two hours to observe these people, whose canoes are built of birch-bark like those of the Canadians, Souriquois, and Etchemin, we raised anchor and with promise of fine weather set sail [Biggar 1922, 336–37].

As they continued south they had many more positive interactions with the locals, until at what they named Port de Mallebarre (Port of Dangerous Shoals, now Nauset Harbor) they drew their ire. De Monts, with nine or 10 others (including Champlain), decided to examine a Nauset settlement, tromping through fields of flowering corn, tobacco, beans, and squash. As they passed through, they helped themselves freely to the bounty without asking permission, surely angering the inhabitants.

On July 23, the French and local Nauset people had a deadly skirmish. Champlain relates:

> Four or five seamen having gone on shore with some kettles to get fresh water, some of the savages, coveting them, watched the time when our men went to the spring, and then seized one out of the hands of a sailor, who was the first to dip, and who had no weapons. One of his companions, starting to run after him, soon returned, as he could not catch him, since he ran much faster than himself. The other savages, of whom there was a large number, seeing our sailors running to our barque, and at the same time shouting to us to fire at them, took to flight. At the time there were some of them in our barque, who threw themselves into the sea, only one of whom we were able to seize. Those on the land who had taken to flight, seeing them swimming, returned straight to the sailor from whom they had taken away the kettle, hurled several arrows at him from behind, and brought him down. Seeing this, they ran at once to him and dispatched him with their knives. Meanwhile, haste was made to go on shore,

and muskets were fired from our barque: mine, bursting in my hands, came near killing me.

The savages, hearing this discharge of firearms, took to flight, and with redoubled speed when they saw that we had landed, for they were afraid when they saw us running after them. There was no likelihood of our catching them, for they are as swift as horses. We brought in the murdered man, and he was buried some hours later. Meanwhile, we kept the prisoner bound by the feet and hands on board of our barque, fearing that he might escape. But Sieur de Monts resolved to let him go, being persuaded that he was not to blame and that he had no previous knowledge of what had transpired.... Some hours later there came some savages to us, to excuse themselves, indicating by signs and demonstrations that it was not they who had committed this malicious act, but others farther off in the interior. We did not wish to harm them, although it was in our power to avenge ourselves [Biggar 1922, 353–54].

This encounter may have signaled a difference in attitude between the Wabanaki in the relatively unsettled north and the Nauset in the more densely settled south. McManamon (2022) tells us:

All of the good harbors from the Saco River, in southern Maine, southwards ... had Indian settlements in the choice locations around them. These southern Indians were permanent residents of these locations and horticulturalists. Vacant land in these locations might have been scarce, mainly fallow land set aside for subsequent use when their fertility was replenished. Such land would not have been available for new settlers to set up trading colonies or residences.

Also, Champlain did not have a translator at Mallebarre, making communication difficult.

## *De Monts and Champlain Return to Saint Croix Island*

At this point, the explorers had spent more than five weeks on their mission, and their provisions had become critically low. They were also being met with hostility by the Nauset. De Monts decided that it was time to return to the island of Saint Croix before their supplies ran out.

On June 25, they left Nauset Harbor and traveled northeast until they were well clear of the coast. They then swung to the north to Saco Bay, where they met with Marchin, the chief they had hoped to see previously at Kennebec Lake. Biggar (1922) places their meeting site at present-day Prouts Neck in Scarborough, Maine, and their anchorage between Bluff and Stratten Islands. De Monts gave Marchin many presents, which pleased him, and in return he gave them a young Etchemin boy whom he had captured in war. De Monts and Champlain then "set out from this place in mutual good fellowship" (Biggar 1922, 364).

They then sailed northeast back to Kennebec, where they arrived on June 29. Here they hoped to meet Sasinou, whom they had missed before, but he again did not show. They did, however, meet another chief named Anassou, whom they bartered with and befriended. He told them about another ship that had recently visited the region and whose crew had murdered five Wabanaki. As will be described later, this was the English explorer George Waymouth, who had abducted but had not killed the five off the coast of Monhegan Island.

The de Monts party then traveled briskly along the coast of Maine back to Saint Croix Island.

## A Move to Port Royal

Upon his return to Saint Croix, de Monts decided to move the colony to the much more benevolent Port Royal, which had attracted them many months ago. Champlain records:

> Sieur de Monts determined to change his location and make another settlement, to avoid the severe cold and the bad winter which we had had in the Island of St. Croix. As we had not, up to that time, found any suitable harbor, and, because of the short time we had for building houses in which to establish ourselves, we fitted out two barques, and loaded them with the frame-work taken from the houses of St. Croix, to transport it to Port Royal, twenty-five leagues distant, where we thought the climate was much more temperate and agreeable. Gravé and I set out for that place; and, having arrived, we looked for a site favorable for our residence, under shelter from the northwest wind, which we dreaded, having been very much harassed by it. After searching carefully in all directions, we found no place more suitable and better situated than one slightly elevated, about which there are some marshes and good springs of water [Biggar, 1922, 367].

As Biggar (1901, 59) describes it:

> Since the possibility of passing a second winter at Ste. Croix could not be considered for a moment, it was finally decided to transport the colony to the beautiful harbor of Port Royal across the Bay of Fundy. Although in the same latitude as St. Croix, it offered many advantages not possessed by that place, and ... in the meanwhile, the search for a more southern site could be steadily pushed on. When this decision was arrived, all the buildings, provisions, people, stores, and animals were transported across the Bay of Fundy. Here the buildings were again set up, not scattered about as at Ste. Croix, but in the form of a large square to protect the colonists against winter and the Indians.

The move to Port Royal went well. Gravé, Champlain, and 45 men would stay the winter, while de Monts and Poutrincourt would return to

France. Gravé Du Pont was asked to be the colony's commander. The settlers were blessed with a much milder winter than before, and although scurvy again proved to be a problem, the colony lost only five of its residents to the disease this time. Water and game were readily available, and the local people came to the settlement to trade fresh meat for French bread. The Frenchman became great friends with two local chiefs, Secoudon and Messamouet. Messamouet was an Etchemin and Secoudon a Souriquois (Mi'kmaq). Both were Tarrentine traders.

When spring arrived, Gravé Du Pont had a pinnace fitted for another voyage of discovery along the coast of New England. With Champdoré at the helm, they set out on March 16 but crashed on Manan Island and, after making repairs, returned to Port Royal. On April 9, they set out again and suffered another crash, this time destroying the boat. They were saved by the local chief, Secoudon, and his companions. Champdoré was blamed for this accident and put in chains.

By this time, the colonists were becoming quite concerned that no relief vessels had come from France. When none had appeared by June 15, Pont-Gravé decided they must build another pinnace to travel to Cape Breton or Gaspé to find a ship to take them back to France. Champdoré, as an expert carpenter, was released to build it, and on July 17, they departed, leaving two men to take care of the goods remaining in the colony. Messamouet pledged to take good care of the two.

It was another momentous journey, with Champdoré again playing a central role (De Costa 1891). As Champlain relates:

> We came to anchor in Long Island strait, where during the night our cable broke, and we were in danger of being lost because of the great tidal currents which dash against numerous rocky points that lie within and at the outlet of this place: but by the efforts of all, this was avoided, and we managed that time to escape. On the twenty-first of the month, between Long Island and Cape Fourchu, there arose a heavy squall that broke our rudder-irons and placed us in such a predicament that we did not know what to do, for the fury of the sea did not permit us to land, since the breakers ran mountains high along the coast.... As we were thinking what could be done for our safety, Champdoré, who had again been handcuffed, said to some of us that if Pont Grave were willing, he would find a means of steering our pinnace.... Champdoré was accordingly set free for the second time; and thereupon, taking a rope and cutting it, he very cleverly mended the rudder, and made it act as well as ever it had done. In this way he makes amends for the mistakes he had committed on the first pinnace, which was lost; and through the entreaties we made for him to Pont-Gravé, who had some reluctance in coming to this decision, he was freed from the accusation against him [Biggar 1922, 385–86].

The group finally arrived at Cape Breton, where they learned that a relief vessel was on the way to the colony. They turned back and, on July 22, found Sieur de Poutrincourt at Port Royal with 50 men, including his son Biencourt and Marc Lescarbot. Lescarbot was a French author, poet, and lawyer who would become famous for his *Histoire de la Nouvelle-France* (1609), based on his experiences in Acadia and his research on other French missions to North America.

As soon as the new and old groups of settlers were united, they got busy improving the colony for the next year. Champlain relates:

> The next day the Sieur de Poutrincourt proceeded to explain what ought to be done, and with the approval of everyone decided to remain at Port Royal for this year, since nothing had been discovered since the Sieur de Monts' voyage and the four months which remained before winter were not sufficient to seek a new site and make another settlement ... during this time we should merely discover some more commodious situation for our abode. Upon this decision, the Sieur de Poutrincourt at once dispatched some laborers to cultivate the land at a spot he considered suitable.... There he had wheat, rye, hemp, and several other seeds sown to ascertain how they would thrive [Biggar 1922, 389–390].

## *Poutrincourt and Champlain Go on Another Voyage of Discovery*

On August 29, Poutrincourt and Champlain started on another excursion along the coast of New England, piloted by Champdoré. Bad weather initially sent them back to Port Royal, but they got off for good on September 5. They briefly stopped at Saint Croix, where they picked up Secoudon and Messamouet, who wanted to travel with them to Saco "to alliance with those of that country by offering them sundry presents" (Biggar 1922, 394). The two sagamores traveled in their own shallop.

The group left Saint Croix on September 12, paused for a while in Casco Bay, and arrived at Saco on September 21. Champlain relates:

> On the 21st we reached Saco, where we saw Onemechin, chief of that river, and Marchin, who had finished harvesting their corn.... In this place, Sieur de Poutrincourt rescued a prisoner from Onemechin, to whom Messamouet made presents of kettles, axes, knives, and other articles. Onemechin made return in Indian corn, squashes, and Brazilian beans; but these did not altogether satisfy Messamouet, who departed much displeased because he had not been suitably repaid for what he had given them, and to make war upon them before long; for these people give only with the idea of receiving something, except to persons who have done them some signal service, such as aiding them in their wars [Biggar 1922, 396].

Lescarbot recorded in his history that Messamouet gave a speech that "occupied about an hour and was delivered with much vehemence and earnestness, and with such gestures of body and arm as befit a good orator" (Biggar 1922, 396).

The Frenchmen then proceeded to Cape Ann and then Gloucester Harbor. Secoudon continued with them, while Messamouet returned to Nova Scotia. At Gloucester Harbor, the Sieur de Poutrincourt landed with eight or 10 of the company and had a friendly interaction with a large group of Nauset. The Frenchmen found this location particularly appealing and named it Le Beau-port (Beautiful Port). They found much of the area to be cleared for farming, and it had many fine meadows that they thought could support cattle, along with plenty of water for their vessels. Biggar (1922, 401) suggests:

> It was the only place upon the entire coast of New England which seemed to them worthy of comparison with Port Royal as a possible site for future permanent settlement. The possibility of removal from Port Royal to this place was actually under discussion.

The group sailed to Cape Cod and Mallebarre. As on the previous visit of the Sieur de Monts and Champlain, their interactions with the locals started out well but ended very badly. Champlain describes what happened on one outing after a couple of weeks of peaceful exploring:

> We observed that the Indians were taking down their wigwams and were sending into the woods their wives, children and provisions, and other necessaries of life. This made us suspect some evil design, and that they wished to attack our people who were working onshore [Biggar 1922, 416].

This premonition proved to be quite true, as a few days later a small party of Frenchmen on shore were attacked. As told by Champlain:

> The Indians, to the number of four hundred, came quietly over a little hill, and shot such a salvo of arrows at them as to give them no chance of recovery before they were struck dead. Fleeing as fast as they could towards our pinnace, and crying out, "Help, help, they are killing us," some of them fell dead in the water, while the rest were all pierced with arrows, of whom one died a short time afterward. These Indians made a desperate row, with war-whoops which it was terrible to hear [Biggar 1922, 421].

A group of French attempted a counteroffensive, but the Amerindians fled inland and all that could be done was bury the dead bodies near a cross. After the French left, the Amerindians returned, pulled down the cross, dug up the bodies, and then fled back into the woods. Lescarbot describes the scene:

> This rascally crew came back to the place of their murderous deed, uprooted the Cross, dug up one of the dead, took off his shirt, and put it on, holding up the spoils which they had carried off; and with all this they also turned

their backs to the long-boat and made mock at us by taking sand in their two hands and casting it between their buttocks, yelping the while like wolves. This mightily enraged our men, who spared not to fire on them with cannon; but the distance was very great, and the savages had already learned the trick of throwing themselves to earth when they saw the match applied so that we could not tell whether they had been hurt or not [Biggar 1922, 423].

On October 16, Poutrincourt decided to set sail, but the group didn't get very far due to contrary winds before returning to Mallebarre Harbor. Forced to stay put, they now decided that it was time to exact revenge for the recent ambush. Champlain explains:

[The plan was to] seize a few Indians of this place, to take them to our settlement and make them grind corn at a hand mill as a punishment for the murderous assault committed upon five or six of our men ... [But to do this they would have] to resort to stratagem ... when they should come to make friends with us again, we should coax them, by showing them beads and other trifles, and should reassure them repeatedly; then we should take the shallop well-armed, and the stoutest and strongest men we had, each with a chain of beads and a match and should set these men on shore, where ... we were to coax them with soft words to draw them into the shallop; and, should they be unwilling to enter, each of our men as he approached was to choose his man, and throwing the beads about his neck should at the same moment put a cord around the man to drag him on board by force [Biggar 1922, 478–79].

Champlain then states that "this was very well carried out, as arranged," though he gives no details. We can only assume that this stratagem did not go well, as later in his account he speaks of four or five sick and wounded compatriots and there is never a mention of captives. Lescarbot reported that "overhaste frustrated the design to capture the Indians, though six or seven of them were hacked and hewed in pieces" (Biggar 1922, 478).

Finally, on October 28, 1606, Poutrincourt and crew decided it was time to return to Port Royal. Their trip would not be an easy one, as they would suffer several misfortunes at sea. Most notably, the rudder of their ship would be damaged when their shallop surged at the end of its tow line and smashed into the rudder. They only made it back because Champdoré managed another miraculous repair at sea.

## *Winter of 1606–1607 at Port Royale*

The group fared well in the winter of 1606–7. Champlain organized the first social club in North America, the Ordre de Bon-Temps (Order of Good Cheer), to maintain spirits and keep them occupied. Members took turns providing fresh game and leading a ceremonial procession to the table. It was also during this winter that the first theater event in Canadian history took place—Marc Lescarbot's *Le Théâtre de Neptune*. When spring came, Poutrincourt set his men to work once more to till and hoe the ground and plant new seed. Plants from the seed that had been sowed the previous fall were now growing nicely. Great numbers of fish were coming up the river to spawn, and overall, the future looked very bright for the colony.

All seemed to promise well when suddenly a ship arrived to inform Poutrincourt that de Monts's monopoly, initially granted for 10 years, had been revoked during the winter. Everybody would have to return to France. The costs of the colony had risen so much that support for it could no longer be justified. Maintaining a monopoly and excluding other traders had proven to be impossible.

As MacBeath (2003) describes:

> The final accounting showed that during its three years of activity, revenues were high, but costs were even higher. De Monts's loss alone was said to be 10,000 livres. The chief reason for the failure was the volume of the illicit trade

Marc Lescarbot's *Le Théâtre de Neptune*, the first play performed in Canada at the French settlement of Port Royal in 1606; C.W. Jeffries (Bibliothèque et Archives Canada, no d'acc 1972-26-83 / Wikimedia Commons).

in furs. In 1604 alone, for example, at least eight vessels had been seized for trading with the Indians without a license, and many times that number had not been apprehended.

Those who traded illegally were free of the burden imposed on the de Monts company to support a colony.

Thus ended de Monts's attempt to settle New France with a resounding thud.

## *Tarrentine Wars*

On Champlain's return from his third voyage to New England, near Great Wass Island in Down East Maine, a group of Etchemin "told Secoudon, that [a local chief named] Iouaniscou and his companions had killed some other Indians and carried off some women as prisoners, and that near Mount Desert island they had put these to death" (Biggar 1922, 436). In the autumn of 1606, the murders of Iouaniscou were revenged by the killing of the Mi'kmaq Panounias, who had guided Champlain the previous summer. He was killed by Mawooshen warriors in the Penobscot Bay area. The Mawooshen was the confederation of western Etchemin and Abenaki living between the Kennebec and Cape Neddick who banded together in defense from the Tarrentine.

After Panounias's death, the Mi'kmaq Chief Ouagimou of Passamaquoddy Bay asked Bashabez, the grand chief of Mawooshen, for Panounias's body. He agreed, and the body was delivered by Ouagimou, wrapped in moose hide, to a Mi'kmaq encampment near Port Royal. Membertou, Panounias's father-in-law, welcomed Ouagimou and presented ritual gifts of mourning to Panounias's relatives. Panounias was then buried on an island near Cape Sable.

> During the ceremony, the Indian named Membertou made a speech to his companions upon the death of the deceased, inciting each to take vengeance for the wickedness and treachery committed by the subjects of Bashabez, and to make war on them as soon as possible. All promised him to do so in the spring [Biggar, 1922, 445].

In July 1607, Membertou with 400 warriors attacked the village of Chouacoet, near Saco, Maine, killing 20 people including two sagamores, Onmechin and Marchin.

> Membertou was unarmed when he appeared before the Abenakis, feigned the wish to negotiate, and then, as Lescarbot describes in *La Defaite des sauvages*, "suddenly he and his men seized the weapons he had set out" and attacked. Many Abenaki chiefs died, whereas Membertou's party incurred not a single loss [Béreau 2020].

Membertou's force was composed of Mi'kmaq from his and Messamouet bands, along with Mi'kmaq from the Saint John River under Chief Secoudon and from Passamaquoddy Bay under Chief Ouagimou (Prins and McBride 2007).

This raid began what has been called the Tarrentine or Mi'kmaq Wars, where Tarrentine warriors began raiding and pillaging Mawooshen villages. These wars culminated with the killing of the Mawooshen grand chief Bashabez in 1615. This was followed by the great plague ("Great Dying") of 1616–9, where a staggering number of Etchemin, Mi'kmaq, and Abenaki perished. Even with this mass dying, the Mi'kmaq raids against the Mawooshen continued until as late as 1631.

## The Great Mi'kmaq Sagamore "Henri" Membertou

Membertou was a Mi'kmaq sagamore who lived in the vicinity of Port Royal and was well known to Champlain and the French settlers there. He was considered a great leader by all who knew him, both as a war chief and spiritual leader. Stéphanie Béreau (2003) suggests:

> Membertou was [according to Biard] "the greatest sagamo, the most closely followed, & the most feared." He was a master of repartee, a skill he did not hesitate to use against the French.... Champlain, for his part, accorded him the "reputation of being the most wicked and treacherous of anyone in his nation's history." As Lescarbot wrote in his *Histoire*, Membertou considered himself the equal of the French king and his lieutenants.

Membertou was baptized on June 24, 1610, along with 20 of his immediate family, becoming the first Amerindians to be baptized by the French.

## The Lifeways of the Nauset and Wampanoag

The Nauset lived in Cape Cod, east of Bass River next to lands occupied by their closely related neighbors, the Wampanoag. Although the Nauset were a distinct nation, they were part of the Wampanoag Confederacy and shared with them many similar aspects of their culture.

The Wampanoag controlled at least 24 recorded nations, and in 1600 there were about 15,000 Wampanoag in about 40 permanent villages in northern Rhode Island and southeastern coastal Massachusetts and its offshore islands (now known as Martha's Vineyard and Nantucket) (Weinstein-Farson, 1989). There were about 1,500 Nauset in Cape Cod.

The Wampanoag and their allies were primarily farmers, growing maize, beans, squash, gourds, and tobacco, but they also hunted, fished, and gathered fruits, seeds, and the roots of wild plants (Mark 2021a). Like other Amerindian farmers, they followed a seasonal schedule. They prepared and planted their fields in the spring and summer and subsisted largely on clams, herring, and other fish. Their crops were harvested in the early fall, and the late fall and winter was devoted to hunting deer, bears, and occasionally moose.

Fishing was second to farming as a source of sustenance. Fish could be harvested all year long from rivers and the ocean. The Wampanoag made heavy dugout canoes by hollowing out logs of large trees. Shellfish were also available throughout the year, including oysters, scallops, soft-shelled crabs, and quahogs. Lobsters were used as bait. The Wampanoag fished with spears, lines with bone hooks, nets of woven plant fibers, weirs, and stakes that were driven across rivers.

Foraging by women and children was an important source of food all year. A wide variety of berries could be gathered, including strawberries, raspberries, huckleberries, and currants. They also gathered wild leeks and onions and dug groundnuts. In the fall they gathered acorns and chestnuts.

In the winter, everyone moved inland to hunting camps in family groups of 10 to 20 and lived in oval-shaped longhouses surrounded by palisades. During seasonal migrations, the Wampanoag lived in wigwams, a.k.a. wetus or wikkums, which are also known as birch bark houses. The word *wetu* means "house" (Mark 2021a).

The Wampanoag were ruled by hereditary "sachems," who had councils of esteemed men to advise them. The sachems settled disputes, granted land to individuals for farming, and dealt with outsiders. The extent of their power was very dependent on popular support. If the people were unhappy with their leadership, they would desert their villages and move to another.

### Eight

# English Expeditions to New England
## 1602–1605

## Setting the Stage: English Search for Wealth

The English had failed in the late sixteenth century to settle Roanoke, but the passion still burned brightly in many hearts to find wealth in North America and establish a foothold. As the French were anchoring a lucrative fur trading network in the St. Lawrence Valley, several English explorers began to search New England in earnest for potential profits and possible places to settle. These English voyages yielded much new information on the geography, habitat, and Indigenous people of coastal New England, but no great wealth was uncovered, except for the abundant cod. As Quinn and Quinn (1983, 3) tell it:

> The short-term result of the 1602–5 voyages was not a settlement but the establishment of a seasonal fishery in the Gulf of Maine. The fur trade offered a genuine opportunity in those years and further north it was making considerable fortunes for the French, but southern New England, even the shores and rivers of the central Maine coast, was not the best place for it.... Fur trading could be developed in New England and was to be a considerable resource later, but it could be best carried on after, not before, settlements of a permanent nature had been established, in complete distinction from the St. Lawrence Valley where the trade needed very few men and was maintained for a generation by a mere handful of resident Frenchmen. But furs (with the hope of mineral gains) were what the voyagers of 1602–8 hoped to make their fortunes.

Three major English expeditions would set out for the Gulf of Maine and New England between 1602 and 1605: Bartholomew Gosnold, who briefly settled on Cuttyhunk Island near Cape Cod in 1602; Martin Pring, who harvested sassafras at the mouth of the Pamet River near Cape Cod in 1603; and George Waymouth, who explored Monhegan Island off the coast of Maine in 1605.

All three of these expeditions were well chronicled in accounts published by eyewitnesses. The voyage of Gosnold was recorded by Gabriel Archer (*The Relation of Captaine Gosnols Voyage to the North Part of Virginia*—1625) and John Brereton (*A Briefe Relation of the Description of Elizabeth's Ile, and some others towards the North Part of Virginie*—1602). Waymouth's journey was covered by James Rosier (*A True Relation of the most prosperous voyage made this present year by Captaine George Waymouth*-1605). Martin Pring left record of his own voyage (*A Voyage set out from the Citie of Bristoll—1603*). Herein, I quote Archer and Brereton from David B. and Alison M. Quinn's (1983) *The English New England Voyages 1602-1608* and Rosier and Pring from Henry S. Burrage's (1906) *Early English and French Voyages Chiefly from Hakluyt 1534-1608*.

## *The Colonial Enterprise in the Sixteenth and Seventeenth Centuries*

In the Elizabethan Age, exploration and colonization was a private endeavor. The Crown did not cover the costs but instead granted monopolies to an individual or corporation, giving them the right to exploit a particular area in North America. Thus, the enterprises were profit-driven, and an explorer would need to find a backing group and generate profits for them. There was considerable risk associated with such ventures. In fact, Sir Walter Raleigh lost 40,000 pounds in his failed attempt to find the Roanoke Colony, and he spent much more trying to find the lost settlers.

In the mid–1580s, a colonial plan began to circulate in England. It suggested that any new colonization efforts should be initiated in northern Virginia (New England) instead of the lower latitudes. Here the climate was more congenial to the English and would support an agriculture like theirs. Along the coast of New England, there were also huge populations of cod, which could support small settlements whose profit could be gradually expanded over time via fur trading and farming. Northern Newfoundland was now considered too cold to support settlement even though it also had huge schools of cod.

The colonial plan and the rationale for it first appeared in a treatise written by Edward Hayes to Lord Burghley in 1587. Edward Hayes was the captain who returned from Gilbert's mission to Newfoundland in 1585, and Lord Burghley was Queen Elizabeth's chief advisor during most of her reign. The expeditions of Gosnold, Pring, and Waymouth would fall completely in line with this rationale.

## The Expedition of Bartholomew Gosnold

Bartholomew Gosnold would lead the first English attempt to colonize New England, a little over a decade after Raleigh's failed Roanoke attempts. As David and Alison Quinn relate (1983, 4–5):

> Gosnold in 1602 hoped to find the happy and beautiful bay with its many islands where Verrazzano found rest and Indian friendship in 1524.... There he expected to set up a small English trading post, selling English cloth and trinkets (with knives the most valuable object Europeans had to offer the Indian peoples) in return for furs, medicinal roots, and plants, dyes and such like—and of course minerals if they could be found.

Gosnold was born in 1561 into an East Anglian manorial family that owned Otley Hall, about eight miles northwest of Suffolk. Gosnold attended Jesus College, Cambridge, and then studied law at the Middle Temple in London. Somewhere along the way, he got the bug to explore and settle in New England. That desire may have come from Richard Hakluyt, the famous geographer, who lectured at Middle Temple. As previously mentioned, Hakluyt published two widely read books on earlier English explorations in North America and was a champion of English colonization of the Atlantic coast of North America.

Gosnold got his first taste at sea when his Uncle Robert got him onto the Essex/Raleigh Expedition to the Azores in 1597. This mission was to occupy the islands and intercept the Spanish treasure fleet. It was led by Sir Robert Devereux, Earl of Essex (general-in-chief); Sir Thomas Howard, Earl of Suffolk (vice-admiral); and Sir Walter Raleigh (rear-admiral). The Essex/Raleigh campaign was largely a failure, but it gave Gosnold invaluable training.

After his return to England, Gosnold decided he would put together his own expedition to colonize North America. He ignored the fact that Sir Walter Raleigh still owned the royal charter authorizing him to explore, colonize, and rule unoccupied North American territory. Gosnold was initially backed by Robert Devereux, Earl of Essex, but his plan got stalled when the earl was beheaded in 1601 for conspiring against Queen Elizabeth. Gosnold regrouped and obtained the support of Henry Wriothesley, third Earl of Southampton, although he too was imprisoned for a while as part of the Essex plot.

On March 26, 1602, Gosnold's expedition finally departed Falmouth on the ship *Concord*, carrying 20 gentlemen colonists and a dozen crew members. The *Concord* was a small, uncomfortable ship that had a keel length of only 39 feet and a breadth of 17½ feet. It leaked badly. Instead of making a circuitous route to North America by the Canary Islands as other explorers had done, Gosnold traveled due west and was the first to travel a direct route to New England. In only seven weeks, he made landfall at what is now Cape Elizabeth, near Portland, Maine. While exploring the area, he encountered a Mi'kmaq who was wearing black serge breeches and a European waistcoat.

As described by Archer:

> There came towards us a Biscay shallop with sails and oars, having eight people in it, whom we supposed at first to be Christians distressed, but approaching us near, we perceived them to be savages. These coming within call hailed us and we answered. Then, after signs of peace and a long speech by one of them, they came boldly aboard us, all naked, having about their shoulders certain loose deerskins, and near their waists sealskins tied fast to Irish trousers. One that seemed to be their commander wore a waistcoat of black, a pair of breeches, cloth stockings, shoes, a hat, and a band ... they spoke diverse Christian words and seemed to understand much more than we [Quinn and Quinn 1983, 117].

Gosnold's encounter with a European-dressed Mi'kmaq was a clear affirmation of how extensive the contact between the Europeans and Indigenous people had become by 1600. Quinn and Quinn (1983, 9) suggest:

> Clearly there was much more coastal trade along the northeastern seaboard in the sixteenth century than was formerly realised, and it is evident that the Micmac took a considerable part in this right down the coast to Cape Cod Bay using, by the time the English arrived, stolen French or Spanish Basque shallops to carry on much of their commerce (while they also carried south war parties from time to time with which to attack the Eastern Abenaki or their southern neighbours).

In May 1602, Gosnold continued southward in search of an appropriate site for settlement. He navigated around a peninsula he named Cape Cod, after the large number of fish swimming in the surrounding waters. In his chronicle, Brereton declares:

> I am persuaded that in the months of March, April, and May, there is upon this coast, better fishing, and in as plenty, as in Newfoundland: for the schools of mackerel, herrings, cod, and other fish, that we daily saw as we went and came from the shore, were wonderful and besides, the places where we took these cods (and might in a few days have laden our ship) were but in seven fantoms water: where in Newfoundland they fish in forty or fifty fantoms water [Quinn and Quinn 1983, 147].

The captain went ashore at Cape Cod and made contact with the Nauset people. Archer remembers:

> A young Indian came here to the captain, armed with bow and arrows, and had plates of copper hanging at his ears. He showed a willingness to help us in our occasions [Quinn and Quinn 1983, 120].

As the group sailed on, the Nauset approached them several more times in canoes wanting to trade. Brereton recorded:

> We spent time in trading with them for furs, which are beavers ... martins, otters, wild-cat skins, very large and deep fur, black foxes, Connie skins, of the color of our hares, but somewhat less, deer skins, very large, seal skins, and other beasts' skins to us unknown. They have also a great store of copper, some very red, and some a paler color ... very workmanly made [Quinn and Quinn 1983, 155].

This accumulation of so many dressed skins, Quinn and Quinn (1983, 154) suggest, "shows extensive preparation for the market, strengthening the impression that the Massachusetts and Narraganset Bay Indians were well accustomed to commerce in fur and skins."

Gosnold sailed on and encountered a large island he named Martha's Vineyard in memory of his first child and the large population of wild grapes that covered the land. In Brereton's report, he spent many pages describing the lush flora and fauna of the island.

At Martha's Vineyard, Gosnold encountered for the first time the local Wampanoag, who proved friendly like the Nauset, bringing the English cooked fish, deerskins, and tobacco. Gosnold decided to continue moving, however. He sailed to Gay Head, spent the night in Vineyard Sound, and traveled on to Buzzard's Bay. He finally selected the small island of Cuttyhunk, west of Martha's Vineyard, for his settlement, and he built a small fort there on an island in the middle of a large freshwater lake. They made a flat-bottomed boat to transport them across the lake. The island was called Poocuohhunkkunnah by the Wampanoag, meaning "Point of departure" or "Land's End."

The colonists found fertile land and plenty of sassafras to harvest, which would bring them a high profit in England. In the early 1600s, sassafras was believed to be a wonder drug that could cure just about anything, including syphilis; slow old age; help as a pain reliever; remove kidney stones; and prevent colds. It became so popular that by the mid–1600s it was America's number two export to Europe, second only to Virginia tobacco.

As the summer progressed, Gosnold and the locals traded actively and had mostly congenial interactions. Archer relates what happened in early June:

> There came onto us ashore from the main fifty savages, stout and lusty men with their bows and arrows, amongst them seemed to be one of authority, because the rest made inclining respect for him.... These Indians in a hasty manner came towards us, so as we thought it fit to make a stand at an angle between the sea and fresh water, I moored myself towards him seven or eight steps, and clapt my hands first on the sides of my head, then on my breast, and

after presented my musket with a threatening countenance, thereby to signal onto him, either a choice of peace or war, whereupon he made signs of peace, I stepped forward and embraced him, his company then sat down in manner like grey-hounds upon their heels with whom my company fell a bartering....

Our captain gave him a straw hat and a pair of knives, the hat after a while he wore, but the knives he held with great marveling, being very bright and sharp, this our courtesy made them all in love with us. They came back the next day and they sat with us and did eat of our bacaleure [sun-dried cod] and mustard, but the mustard nipping them in their noses they could not endure: it was sport to behold their faces made being bitten therewith [Quinn and Quinn 1983, 134].

A group of six or seven Amerindians remained with Gosnold's men, keeping them company every day in the woods. Archer reported: "[They] helped us to cut and carry our sassafras and some lay aboard our ships. These people, as they are exceedingly courteous, gentle of disposition, and well-conditioned, excel others we have seen" (Quinn and Quinn 1983, 156).

As the summer progressed, the colonists began to lose their enthusiasm for settlement, realizing their supplies were likely too short to last the winter. They also had an unexplained skirmish where a party of two Englishmen hunting for shellfish were set upon by four locals who shot one in the side with an arrow. This incident made it clear to them just how vulnerable their little settlement was to the moods of the local people.

The original plan was for the colonists to split into two groups, one sailing back to England with their harvested bounty and the other staying through the winter. After a sharp dispute as to who would go and who would stay, Gosnold gave in to a majority vote, and after only a month on the island, everyone sailed back to England, carrying a profitable cargo of cedar wood, sassafras, furs, and a stolen Wampanoag canoe.

Soon after their return, Sir Walter Raleigh found out about Gosnold's mission and laid claim to the cargo (Levermore 1912). The two rapidly made peace, however. Gosnold had many powerful friends like Wriothesley, the Earl of Southampton, and Raleigh came to see the success of the mission as a good advertisement for future ventures that he would control. Raleigh even allowed Brereton to dedicate his publication to him, implying that the endeavor was sanctioned by Raleigh.

The colony of Gosnold's would be ephemeral, but its story would live long after. *The Tempest* of William Shakespeare was based on Gosnold's 1602 voyage, with Prospero's island being drawn from the descriptions of Martha's Vineyard (Huntley 2023). Wriothesley was not only a primary backer of Gosnold's mission, he was also an important supporter of Shakespeare.

Gosnold would go on to be one of the key organizers of the successful settlement of Jamestown in 1607. He is now mostly forgotten but deserves much greater recognition. Dana Huntley (2023) calls Gosnold "a man who perhaps more than any other single individual is responsible for the establishment of British North America, a man whom history ought to have recognized in one sense as at least the Founding Grandfather of these fair colonies."

## The Expedition of Martin Pring

Impressed by the success of Captain Gosnold's 1602 voyage, a group of investors from Bristol banded together the following year to send 23-year-old Martin Pring on an expedition to New England. He was charged with bringing home sassafras and any other commercial products he might uncover. The sponsors consisted of the mayor, the alderman, several merchants, and the famous historian Richard Hakluyt. Taking no chances, the group obtained a proper license from Sir Walter Raleigh. Why the group picked Pring is unclear—there is very little known about his career before this mission.

Two ships made the journey—the *Speedwell*, a 60-ton vessel commanded by Pring with a crew of 30, and the *Discoverer*, a 26-ton vessel with 13 men captained by William Browne and Robert Salterne. They arrived at Penobscot Bay, Maine, in June 1603 and then sailed south to the Piscataqua River, where they disembarked and found very little sassafras. They then continued further south and anchored at the Pamet River on Cape Cod, where they discovered a dense population of sassafras. Here they set up camp and built a fort under the watchful eyes of the Nauset people, who had interacted with Gosnold the year before.

Pring writes in his account of the voyage:

> At our going on shore, upon view of the people and sight of the place, we thought it convenient to make a small barricade to keep diligent watch and ward in, for the advertisement and succor of our men, while they should work in the Woods. During our abode on shore, the people of the country came to our men sometimes ten, twenty, forty, or three score, and at one time one hundred and twenty at once. We used them kindly and gave them diverse sorts of our meanest merchandise. They did eat peas and beans with our men.
> We had a youth in our company that could play upon a Gittern, in whose homely music they took great delight, and would give him many things, as Tobacco, Tobacco-pipes, Snakes skins of six foot long, which they use for Girdles, Fawn skins, and such like, and danced twenty in a Ring, and the Gittern in the midst of them, using many Savage gestures, singing lo, la, lo, la, la, lo: him that first brake the ring, the rest would knock and cry out upon [Burrage 1906, 347].

Not all the early encounters with the locals were friendly, however, for Pring and his crew enjoyed tormenting the locals with their two mastiffs:

> We carried with us from Bristol two excellent Mastiffs, of whom the Indians were more afraid, then of twenty of our men.... And when we would be rid of the Savages company, we would let loose the Mastiffs, and suddenly with outcry's they would flee away [Burrage 1906, 348].

Pring described the Nauset with some admiration but also trepidation:

> These people in color are inclined to a swart, tawny, or Chestnut color, not by nature but accidentally, and due wear their hair braided in four parts, and trussed up about their heads with a small knot behind in which hair of theirs they stick many feathers and toys for bravery and pleasure. They cover their privities only with a piece of leather drawn betwixt their twists and fastened to their girdles behind and before: where unto they hang their bags of Tobacco. They seem to be somewhat jealous of their women, for we saw not past two of them, who wear aprons of leather skins before them down to the knees, and a bearskin like an Irish Mantle over one shoulder. The men are of stature somewhat taller than our ordinary people, strong, swift, well proportioned, and given to treachery, as in the end, we perceived [Burrage 1906, 348].

Pring marveled at the rich flora and fauna of the coast of Cape Cod:

> As for trees the country yielded sassafras a plant of sovereign virtue for the French Pox, and as some of late have learnedly written good against the plague and many other maladies; vines, cedars, oaks, ashes, beeches, birch trees, cherry trees bearing fruit whereof we did eat, witch hazels, ... walnut-trees, maples, ... and a kind of tree bearing fruit like a small red pea-plum.... We found also low trees bearing fair cherries. There was likewise a white kind of plum which were grown to its perfect ripeness. With diverse other sorts of trees to us unknown.
>
> The beasts here are stags, fallow deer in abundance, bears, wolves, foxes, lusemes, and (some say) tigers, porcupines, and dogs with sharp and long noses, with many other sorts of wild beasts, whose cases and furs being here after purchased by exchange may yield no small gain to us. Since we are certainly informed, the Frenchmen brought from Canada the value of thirty thousand crowns in the year 1604. Almost in beaver and otter skins only. The most usual fowl are eagles, vultures, hawks, cranes, herons, crows, gulls, and great store of other river and sea-fowls. And as the land is full of Gods good blessings, so is the sea replenished with great abundance of excellent fish, cods sufficient to load many ships, which we found upon the coast in the month of June, seals to make oil with all, mullets, mackerels, herrings, crabs, lobsters, oysters and mussels with ragged pearls in them [Burrage 1906, 349–50].

Pring also raved about the agricultural potential of New England:

> Having spent three weeks upon the coast before we came to this place where we meant to stay ... we dug up the earth with shovels, and sowed wheat, barley,

oats, peas, and sundry sorts of garden seeds, which ... although they were late sown, came up very well, giving certain testimony of the goodness of the climate and of the soil. And it seemed that oat, hemp, flax, rapeseed, and such like which require a rich and fat ground, would prosper excellently in these parts. For in diverse places, we found grass above knee-deep [Burrage 1906, 349].

By the end of July, the crew had finished loading the *Discoverer* "with as much Sassafrass as ... thought sufficient," and Pring sent it home.

The crew then began filling the hold of the *Speedwell*. A couple of days after they had begun, they were surprised by a massive attack by the Nauset. Several men in their barricade were confronted by "about seven score savages armed with their bows and arrows" (Burrage 1906, 350), and their ship was also surrounded by a large force of warriors. The men in the barricade were lucky to have the two mastiffs, who cleared a path through the Nauset back to the ship. Somehow, these men got on board, and under a likely hail of arrows, Pring decided to flee and immediately set sail for England. As they left, the Nauset set the woods on fire, and "they came down to the shore in great number, very near two hundred by ...[the Englishmen's] estimation" (Burrage 1906, 351).

Similar to Gosnold's chroniclers, Pring didn't record what they had done to wear out their welcome. The attack may have been a last-ditch effort by the Nauset to get as much from the English as they could before they left. It is also possible that they were reacting to the abduction of some of their brethren, or maybe they were just sick and tired of being taunted by those mastiffs. We will never know.

## *The Expedition of George Waymouth*

In 1605, Captain George Waymouth was sent from England by prominent Catholics to search for fishing grounds and possible settlement sites along the coast of Maine. He also was explicitly directed to bring back to England a couple of Indigenous people to interrogate about the people and environs of New England and serve as future pilots and guides.

Very little is known about George Waymouth's youth, except that he was born in Cockington, Devon, and was a student of shipbuilding and mathematics (Dunbabin 2003). Waymouth was chosen for this mission because of his previous North Atlantic experience. In 1602, he had gotten as far as the Hudson Strait in a search for the fabled Northwest Passage to China in a trip sponsored by the East India Company.

Waymouth and crew sailed from England on March 31 on the ship *Archangel* and landed near Monhegan Island off the coast of Maine on May 17. Rosier marveled at the island's resources:

**Captain George Waymouth sails into Penobscot Bay in Maine; image from Thomas Wentworth Higginson's *A Book of American Explorers* (Lee and Shepherd, 1877), page 220 (Wikimedia Commons).**

> This land is woody, grown with fir, birch, oak, and beech.... On the verge grow gooseberries, strawberries, wild peas, and wild rose bushes. The water issued forth down the rocky cliffs in many places: and many ducks breed upon the shore and rocks. While we were at the shore, our men aboard with a few hooks got about thirty great cods and haddock, which gave us a taste of the great plenty of fish which we found afterward wheresoever we went upon the coast [Burrage 1906, 393].

Eleven days after the *Archangel* first moored, the crew first encountered the local Wabanaki people (Etchemin). Rosier describes what unfolded when, on May 30, 1605, the ship anchored in Muscongus Bay:

> This day, about four o clock in the afternoon, we in the ship spied three canoes coming towards us, which went to the land adjoining, where they went ashore, and very quickly made a fire, about which they stood beholding our ship: to whom we made signs with our hands and hats, waffling onto them to come onto us, because we had not seen any of the people yet. They sent one Canoe with three men, one of which, when they came near us, spoke in his language very loud and very boldly: seeming as though he would know why we were there, and by pointing with his oars towards the sea, we conjectured he meant we should be gone. But when we showed them knives and their use, by cutting of sticks and other trifles, as combs and glasses, they came close aboard our ship, as desirous to entertain our friends. To these, we gave such things as we perceived they liked when we showed them the use: bracelets, rings, peacock feathers, which they stuck in their hair, and tobacco pipes.
>
> After their departure to their company on the shore, presently came forth

in another Canoe: to whom we gave as to the former, using them with as much kindness as we could. ... They seemed all very civil and merry: showing tokens of much thankfulness, for those things we gave them. We found them then (as after) a people of exceeding good intention, quick understanding, and ready capacity [Burrage 1906, 367–68].

Over the next several days they placed two crosses along the St. Georges River, had many encounters with the Etchemin and encouraged their trust through trade.

Our Captain had two of them at supper with us in his cabin to see their demeanor, who behaved themselves very civilly, neither laughing nor talking all the time, and at supper fed not like men of rude education, neither would they eat or drink more than seemed to content nature; they desired peas to carry a shore to their women, which we gave them, with fish and bread, and lent them pewter dishes, which they carefully brought again [Burrage 1906, 402].

At this point, Waymouth decided the time was ripe to kidnap some of the Etchemin. Rosier justified this move:

We began to join them in the rank of other Savages, who have been by travelers in most discoveries found very treacherous; never attempting mischief, until by some remissness, fit opportunity afforded them certain ability to execute the same. Wherefore after good advice taken, we determined so soon as we could to take some of them, least (being suspicious we had discovered their plots) they should absent themselves from us [Burrage 1906, 407].

Prins and McBride (2007, 74) suggest:

The English captain in charge of the operations had carefully selected these Etchemin captives for their "ready capacity" to serve colonial entrepreneurial interests. Captain Weymouth more or less followed an established routine, as when North Carolina coastal Algonquian tribesmen Manteo and Wanchese were taken to England in 1584 and then used as guides and interpreters for the expedition to establish Sir Walter Raleigh's short-lived English colony at Roanoke Island the following year. And even earlier (1534), Jacques Cartier had taken two young Iroquoians, Domagaya and Taignoagny at the mouth of the St. Lawrence River, for the same purpose.

On the next day, they abducted five Etchemin, three by duplicity and two by force. Rosier records the events as follows:

About eight a clock this day we went on shore with our boats, to fetch aboard water and wood, our Captain leaving word with the gunner in the ship, by discharging a musket, to give notice if they spied any canoes coming ... there were two canoes, and in each of them were three savages; of which two came aboard, while the others stayed in their canoes about the ship; and because we could not entice them aboard, we gave them a can of peas and bread, which they carried to the shore to eat. But one of them brought back our can presently and stayed aboard with the other two; for he being young, of a ready capacity, and one we most desired to bring with us into England, had received exceeding kind usage at our hands, and was therefore much delighted in our company [Burrage 1906, 378].

These three were prevented from leaving the ship, presumably by putting them in the hold.

Further measures were taken to capture the other two that had left:

We manned the light horseman with 7 or 8 men, one standing before carried our box of merchandise a platter of peas, but before we were landed, one of them (being too suspiciously fearful of his own good) withdrew himself unto the wood. The other two met us on the shore side, to receive the peas, with whom we went up the cliff to their fire and sat down with them, and while we were discussing how to catch the third man who was gone, I opened the box, and showed them trifles to exchange, thinking thereby to have banished fear from the other, and drawn him to return: but when we could not, we used little delay, but suddenly laid hands upon them. And it was as much as five or six of us could do to get them into the light horseman. For they were strong and so naked as our best hold was by their long hair on their heads, and we would have been very loath to have done them any hurt ... being a matter of great importance for the full accompaniment of our voyage. Thus, we shipped five savages, two canoes, with all their bows and arrows [Burrage 1906, 378–79].

Rosier gives the names of the captives as Tahánedo, Amoret, Skicowaros, Maneddo, and Saffacomoit. Later writers would use a series of other spellings of the names, the most common being Tahánedo, Amooret, Skidwarres, Manido, and Assacomet.

It turned out that by chance, Waymouth had abducted captives much more important than they had at first realized. Tahánedo was a sagamore of the region and a close relative of Bashabez, the paramount chief of the whole Etchemin-Abenaki Federation. Bashabez tried frantically to get the captives back, sending canoes filled with fur and tobacco for trade, but the Englishmen were unmoved. "This we perceived to be only a mere device to get possession of our men to ransom all those which he had taken," Rosier suggested (Burrage 1906, 385).

Waymouth now headed back to England with his human cargo below deck. As the ship disappeared into the distance, the Wabanaki assumed their compatriots had been killed. Not long after Waymouth left, Samuel de Champlain on one of his coastal Maine voyages met a native trader on Monhegan, who told him about what he thought were killings.

On board, Rosier was charged with restoring good relations with the captive five and pumping them for information about New England. Eventually the abductees proved to be cooperative, as Rosier describes:

Although at the time when we surprised them, they made their best resistance, not knowing our purpose, nor what we were, nor how we meant to use them;

yet after perceiving by their kind usage we intended them no harm, "they have never since seemed discontented with us" and he called them "very tractable, loving, and willing by their best means to satisfy us in anything we demanded of them, by words or signs for their understanding...." We have brought them to understand some English, and we understand much of their language; so as we are able to ask them many things [Rosier quoted in Burrage 1906, 391].

They also told him that their homeland, the territory of Bashabez, was called Mawooshen.

Upon his return, Waymouth presented his "guests" to Lord Chief Justice John Popham and Sir Ferdinando Gorges, commander of the Fort at Plymouth, and the two readily agreed to house them. Popham and Gorges had become interested in colonizing New England and were keen to obtain information from the "Mawooshen Five."

James Ring Adams (2015) in his engaging article "Alien Abductions" relates:

> Gorges left a record that he greatly enjoyed the company of his house guests. He praised them "for great civility far from the rudeness of our common people" and talked with them at length about their homeland. "And the longer I conversed with them, the better hope they gave me of those parts where they did inhabit, was proper for our uses."

Gorges learned about the important rivers that ran into the land, the flora and fauna, the key leaders and the major alliances. All the Mawooshen Five would be sent on missions to Maine by Gorges and Popham in 1606. Assacomet would also be sent to Martha's Vineyard in 1614 (Chapter 14).

## NINE

# Samuel de Champlain and the Founding of Québec
### 1608–1635

## Setting the Stage: A Change in Scenery

After the return of the colonists from Port Royal, de Monts considered long and hard his involvement with the fur trade of New France. However, on the advice of Champlain, he decided to pursue another monopoly but transfer his interest to the St. Lawrence and Québec, the area explored by Cartier decades before.

> With a factory at the narrows in the St. Lawrence called Quebec, his agents would be able not only to establish fresh trading connections with the savages to the west, but also by means of the alliance thus formed be enabled to push on their investigation into the geography of those regions and, possibly, even to discover the long-sought passage to the East [Biggar 1901, 66].

De Monts petitioned the King and was granted a fresh monopoly for one year. Delighted, he then reassociated with some of his old partners, and three vessels were sent off in 1608. Two of them—the *Lévrier* captained by Gravé Du Pont and the *Don-de-Dieu* under the command of Champlain—made their way to Tadoussac on the St. Lawrence, while the third, under the charge of Champdoré, returned to the old quarters at Port Royal. Gravé Du Pont and Champdoré were sent to trade, and Champlain was asked to explore the St. Lawrence River and establish a colony.

As with all his voyages, Champlain produced a detailed narrative of this expedition. Herein, I use W.L. Grant's (1907) *Voyages of Samuel de Champlain 1604–1618* for quotations.

## First Arrivals

At Port Royal, Champdoré found "everything untouched.... With the Indians of the neighbourhood, who were greatly delighted at his return, Champdoré was soon able to carry on a brisk trade, while at Ste. Croix and along the coast to the south, he secured a further supply of good furs" (Biggar 1901, 66).

Champdoré

> sailed up the Saint John River for a distance of 50 leagues, went to Chouacoet (Saco Bay, Maine), reconciled the Armouchiquois and the Micmacs who had been at war the previous summer, and had them formally conclude peace. He returned to France in the autumn and reported upon the wondrous beauty of the wheat that Jean de Biencourt de Poutrincourt had sown the previous year [Trudel 2003].

Gravé Du Pont was the first to arrive at Tadoussac, and immediately he had a nasty encounter with a group of Basque ships, who fired on the *Lévrier*, severely wounding him. When Champlain arrived in Tadoussac on June 3, he was met by a shallop with the pilot of Pont-Gravé and a Basque, who informed him of what had happened. Champlain visited the bedside of Gravé Du Pont, and they decided that it would be better to negotiate than fight. A truce was struck, when it turned out that the Basques were much more interested in whales than furs.

## Champlain Builds a New Settlement

Champlain then headed down the St. Lawrence in a barque with supplies to build a fort. Champlain writes of his arrival in Québec:

> I arrived there on the third of July, when I searched for a place suitable for our settlement; but I could find none more convenient or better suited than the point of Quebec, so called by the savages, which was covered with nut trees [Grant 1907, 131].

Champlain ordered his men to cut down the nut trees to build their habitations.

A few days after Champlain's arrival in Québec, one of his men, Jean Duval, plotted to kill him and take over the settlement to give it to the Basques or Spaniards then at Tadoussac. Duval's plot was thwarted when one of his coconspirators decided to fess up to Champlain's pilot. Champlain had Duval and three coconspirators seized by enticing them with bottles of wine to gather on a barque. Duval was strangled and hung in Québec and his head was put on the end of a pike and displayed in a "most conspicuous place" in Champlain's fort (Grant 1907, 136). The others were sent back to France and put in the hands of the Sieur de Monts to decide their justice.

Near his settlement, Champlain found the place where Jacques Cartier had wintered. As Champlain describes:

> There are still, a league up the river, remains of what seems to have been a chimney, the foundation of which has been found, and indications of there having been ditches surrounding their dwelling, which was small. We found, also, large pieces of hewn, worm-eaten timber, and some three or four cannon-balls [Grant 1907, 137].

Gravé Du Pont set off for France on September 18 with the three conspirators, and Champlain continued work on his quarters. These, Champlain described as

> composed of three buildings of two stories. Each one was three fathoms long, and two and a half wide. The store house was six fathoms long and three wide, with a fine cellar six feet deep. I had a gallery made all around our buildings, on the outside, at the second story, which proved very convenient. There were also ditches, fifteen feet wide and six deep. On the outer side of the ditches, I constructed several spurs, which enclosed a part of the dwelling, at the points where we placed our cannon. Before the habitation there is a place four fathoms wide and six or seven long, looking out [Grant 1907, 136].

## *Another Cold, Hungry Winter*

Champlain and his men once again suffered a terrible, cold winter. When spring arrived, only eight out of their original party were remaining, and half of these were ailing. They had also seen much evidence of hunger and death among the local people, as Champlain relates:

> Meanwhile, a large number of savages were encamped in cabins near us, engaged in fishing for eels, which begin to come about the 15th of September, and go away on the 15th of October. During this time, all the savages subsist on this food, and dry enough of it for the winter to last until the month of February, when there are about two and a half, or at most three, feet of snow; and, when their eels and other things which they dry have been prepared, they go to hunt the beaver until the beginning of January. At their departure for this purpose, they entrusted to us all their eels and other things, until their return, which was on the 15th of December. But they did not have great success in the beaver-hunt, as the amount of water was too great, the rivers having overrun their banks, as they told us. I returned to them all their supplies, which lasted them only until the 20th of January. When their supply of eels gave out, they hunted the elk and such other wild beasts as they could find until spring....
> These people suffer so much from lack of food that they are sometimes obliged

to live on certain shell-fish, and eat their dogs and the skins with which they clothe themselves against the cold [Grant 1907, 141].

Relief finally came to Champlain's group on June 5 when a shallop arrived bringing the news that Gravé Du Pont had returned to Tadoussac. Champlain immediately embarked to Tadoussac to confer with Pont-Gravé. It was decided that Champlain would explore the interior with the help of the local people and Gravé Du Pont should stay at Tadoussac to trade and arrange the affairs of their settlement. Champlain then returned to Québec and "had a shallop fitted out with all that was necessary for making explorations in the country of the Iroquois," where he was to go with his allies the Innu Montagnais (Grant 1907, 149).

## A Battle in the Interior

Champlain set out with nine soldiers and soon met up with a group of two or three hundred Amerindians who were on their way to Québec to "explore the territory of the Iroquois, with whom they were in deadly hostility, sparing nothing belonging to their enemies" (Grant 1907, 151). Champlain explained his mission to them, and they agreed to accompany him, hoping for vengeance against their bitter rivals, the Mohawk of the Iroquois Federation. The group first headed back to Québec, where Gravé Du Pont had arrived with reinforcements and supplies, and then Champlain, 12 Frenchman, and the Amerindians embarked into the interior. They passed Trois-Rivières at the confluence of the Saint-Maurice and St. Lawrence Rivers and explored the Richelieu River. Champlain became the first European to observe and map Lake Champlain. At this point, having had no encounters with the Haudenosaunee, most of the men headed back, leaving behind only Champlain, two other Frenchmen, and 60 Amerindians.

On July 29, somewhere around Ticonderoga and Crown Point, Champlain and his party encountered a group of several hundred Haudenosaunee ready for battle. As Champlain tells it:

> As soon as we had landed, they began to run for some two hundred paces towards their enemies, who stood firmly, not having as yet noticed my companions, who went into the woods with some savages. Our men began to call me with loud cries; and, in order to give me a passage-way, they opened in two parts, and put me at their head, where I marched some twenty paces in advance of the rest until I was within about thirty paces of the enemy, who at once noticed me, and, halting, gazed at me, as I did also at them. When I saw them making a move to fire at us, I rested my musket against my cheek and aimed directly at one of the three chiefs. With the same shot, two fell to the

ground; and one of their men was so wounded that he died sometime after. I had loaded my musket with four balls. When our side saw this shot so favorable for them, they began to raise such loud cries that one could not have heard it thunder. Meanwhile, the arrows flew on both sides. The Iroquois were greatly astonished that two men had been so quickly killed, although they were equipped with armor woven from cotton thread, and with wood which was proof against their arrows. This caused great alarm among them. As I was loading again, one of my companions fired a shot from the woods, which astonished them anew to such a degree that, seeing their chiefs dead, they lost courage, and took to flight, abandoning their camp and fort, and fleeing into the woods, whither I pursued them, killing still more of them. Our savages also killed several of them and took ten or twelve prisoners. The remainder escaped with the wounded. Fifteen or sixteen were wounded on our side with arrow shots, but they were soon healed [Grant 1907, 165].

After gaining victory, the Amerindians feasted sumptuously on Indian corn and meal left by their enemies. They danced and sang for hours. The party then began the long trek back to Ontario. Along the way, the Innu brutally tortured one of their prisoners, whom they eventually let Champlain put out of his misery with a single shot.

Champlain described what happened when they arrived back at the settlement:

Samuel de Champlain's battle between the Iroquois and Algonquian near the southern tip of Lake Champlain on July 30, 1609; from Francis Parkman's *Historic handbook of the northern tour. Lakes George and Champlain; Niagara; Montreal; Quebec* (1885), page 8 (Library of Congress / Wikimedia Commons).

[I] gave them some bread and peas; also some beads, which they asked me for, in order to ornament the heads of their enemies, for the purpose of merry-making upon their return. The next day, I went with them in their canoes as far as Tadoussac, in order to witness their ceremonies. On approaching the shore, they each took a stick, to the end of which they hung the heads of their enemies, who had been killed, together with some beads, all of them singing. When they were through with this, the women undressed themselves, so as to be in a state of entire nudity, when they jumped into the water and swam to the prows of the canoes to take the heads of their enemies, which were on the ends of long poles before their boats: then they hung them about their necks, as if it had been some costly chain, singing and dancing meanwhile. Some days after, they presented me with one of these heads, as if it were something very precious; and also with a pair of arms taken from their enemies, to keep and show to the king. This, for the sake of gratifying them, I promised to do [Grant 1907, 168].

## Amerindian Relations in 1609

This battle would be the beginning of a new era of French activities in northeastern North America. Champlain would lead a concerted effort to dominate the trade, by forming alliances with the Wyandot-Hurons, Algonquin, and Innu against the Iroquois (Mohawk) people of New France. Relationships between these groups had greatly fluctuated since the visits of Cartier 70 years before. As Biggar (1901, 70–71) describes:

When Cartier visited the St. Lawrence in 1535 he found the Montagnais [Innu] Indians occupying the north shore of the St. Lawrence almost up to the narrows called Quebec. From that point to the Ottawa dwelt the Algonquins, the conquerors of the Montagnais, while beyond Ottawa and still bordering the St. Lawrence lay the country of the Hurons, who acted as the allies of the Algonquins in their wars with the Iroquois. This great nation of the Iroquois, to which the Hurons also belonged, although the two branches were now at war, occupied the territory south of the St. Lawrence and southeast of Lake Ontario. The St. Lawrence was thus the dividing line between the two forces, and though marauding parties crossed it from the north and from the south it was not infrequently itself the scene of their battles.

During the course of the sixteenth century, or between the visit of Cartier and that of Gravé Du Pont and Champlain in 1603, the Iroquois power consolidated itself, and by this increased strength was at length able to drive its enemies far from St. Lawrence. The Hurons took refuge in the peninsula between the Georgian Bay and Lake Huron. They still however kept up intercourse with the Algonquins, who had been likewise obliged after the destruction of their towns to retire to the Upper Ottawa, through the chain of lakes connecting the Ottawa River with the Georgian Bay. In fact, until the middle of the seventeenth century, this was the only route used for going to and from the Huron country to Quebec. The Montagnais [Innu] no longer dared to show themselves on the St. Lawrence west of Quebec and were confined for the most part to the region about Tadoussac. The Etchemin, who had sometimes joined the alliance against the Iroquois, inhabited the shores of the Bay of Fundy.

The European traders at Tadoussac and in the Bay of Fundy had initially been in contact with the Innu and the Etchemin. The Innu traded the goods they got from the French with the nations of Lake St. John and the upper Saguenay.

## *Third Voyage of Champlain to New France*

On August 8, 1610, Champlain returned to France, bragging to the king about his successes and extolling the virtues of Québec as a center for the fur trade. He also got married at the age of 40 on December 27 to Hélène Boullé, aged 12, who brought a large dowry and a royal connection. As part of the marriage agreement, they would wait two years to consummate the marriage.

In the spring of 1610, Champlain returned to New France and continued the war against the Iroquois, meeting up with his tribal allies at Trois-Rivières and traveling to present-day Sorel-Tracy, Québec. At the battle scene, Champlain and his French companions

> heard the yells and cries on both sides, as they jeered at each other, and were skirmishing slightly while awaiting us. As soon as the savages perceived us, they began to shout, so that one could not have heard it thunder. I gave orders to my companions to follow me steadily, and not to leave me on any account. I approached the barricade of the enemy, to reconnoiter it. It was constructed of large trees placed one upon another, and of a circular shape, the usual form of their fortifications. All the Montagnais and Algonquins approached the barricade likewise. Then we commenced firing numerous musket shots through the brushwood since we could not see them, as they could us. I was wounded while firing my first shot at the side of their barricade by an arrow, which pierced the end of my ear and entered my neck. I seized the arrow and tore it from my neck…. Yet my wound did not prevent me from doing my duty: our savages also, on their part, as well as the enemy, did their duty, so that you could see the arrows fly on all sides as thick as hail….
>
> The Iroquois were astonished at the noise of our muskets, and especially that the balls penetrated better than their arrows. They were so frightened at the effect produced that, seeing several of their companions fall wounded and dead, they threw themselves on the ground whenever they heard a discharge, supposing that the shots were sure….
>
> As our ammunition began to fail, I said to all the savages that it was necessary to break down their barricades and capture them by storm; and that, in

order to accomplish this, they must take their shields, cover themselves with them, and thus approach so near as to be able to fasten stout ropes to the posts that supported the barricades and pull them down by main strength....

All this they did very promptly. But, when I saw that the entrance was quite practicable, I gave orders not to fire anymore, which they obeyed. At the same instant, some twenty or thirty, both of savages and of our own men, entered sword in hand, without finding much resistance. Immediately, all who were unharmed took to flight. But they did not proceed far; for they were brought down by those around the barricade, and those who escaped were drowned in the river. We captured some fifteen prisoners, the rest being killed by musket shots, arrows, and the sword....

This, then, is the victory obtained by God's grace, for gaining which they gave us much praise. The savages scalped the dead, and took the heads as a trophy of victory, according to their custom. They returned with fifty wounded Montagnais and Algonquins and three dead, singing and leading their prisoners with them [Grant 1907, 180–84].

Most of the prisoners would be grievously tortured to death. However, Champlain asked for an Iroquois prisoner, which they gave to him. Champlain remarked:

For what I did for him was not a little; for I saved him from many tortures which he must have suffered in company with his fellow prisoners, whose nails they tore out, also cutting off their fingers, and burning them in several places [Grant 1907, 185].

Before the group dispersed, a young man named Étienne Brûlé who had survived the first two winters in Québec asked if he could stay with the Algonquin and learn their language. Champlain and Gravé Du Pont concurred, but the Algonquin were initially nervous, fearing some accident might happen to him, causing the French to make war on them. Champlain was finally able to convince them to take Brulé, but they insisted that in return he take a young man in his place to go to France. Promises were then made all around to meet at the end of June.

Brûlé would be the first of later many French fur traders who lived with the Indigenous people, learning their survival skills and their pathways of travel, canoeing the rivers and portaging the falls. Brûlé was probably the first European to see Lake Erie and Lake Superior.

Champlain then headed briefly to France and, in the spring of 1611, returned and sailed up the St. Lawrence River, making it as far as Montréal. Along the way he found the remains of Hochelaga, which was a flourishing village when visited by Jacques Cartier 76 years earlier in 1535. Champlain observed:

Near Place Royale there is a little river, extending some distance into the interior, along the entire length of which there are more than sixty acres of land cleared up and like meadows, where grain can be sown and gardens made. Formerly savages tilled these lands, but they abandoned them on account of their wars, in which they were constantly engaged [Grant 1907, 203].

On June 13, as planned:

> two hundred Sauvages Hurons, together with the captains, Ochateguin, Iroquet, and Tregouaroti, brother of our savage, brought back my servant. We were greatly pleased to see them. I went to meet them in a canoe with our savage. As they were approaching slowly and in order, our men prepared to salute them, with a discharge of arquebuses, muskets, and small pieces. When they were near at hand, they all set to shouting together, and one of the chiefs gave orders that they should make their harangue, in which they greatly praised us, commending us as truthful, inasmuch as I had kept the promise to meet them at this Fall [Grant 1907, 207–8].

Champlain gives no details on the experiences of the two, but both the Frenchman and Amerindian were apparently happy and healthy.

On June 18, Champlain and party left Trois-Rivières and began the long journey back home. On July 23, they arrived at Tadoussac, and then embarked for France on August 11, arriving at La Rochelle on September 16. They left the factory in Québec with 15 agents, leaving in charge a Captain Chauvin, Sieur de la Pierre.

Upon arriving home, Champlain states:

> I proceeded to visit Sieur de Monts, at Pons 2 in Saintonge, to inform him of all that had occurred during the expedition, and of the promise which the Ochateguins and Algonquins had made me, on condition that we would assist them in their wars, as I had agreed. Sieur de Monts, after listening to it all, determined to go to the Court to arrange the matter. I started before him to go there also. But on the way I was unfortunately detained by the falling of a horse upon me, which came near killing me. This fall detained me some time; but as soon as I had sufficiently recovered from its effects I set out again to complete my journey and meet Sieur de Monts at Fontainebleau, who, upon his return to Paris, had a conference with his associates [Grant 1907, 221].

De Monts found that his former associates the Sieurs Colier and le Gendre of Rouen were unwilling to continue in their previous association, as there was no longer a "commission forbidding any others from going to the new discoveries and trading with the inhabitants of the country" (Grant 1907, 221). Frustrated, de Monts decided to give up and left Champlain to find a new arrangement. Champlain subsequently persuaded Louis XIII to intervene, and he named Charles de Bourbon, Comte de Soissons, to be the lieutenant-general of New France. Charles de Bourbon then chose Samuel de Champlain to be his representative in Québec.

Owing to a fall from his horse, Champlain was unable to go to the St Lawrence in 1612. Little is known of what took place that summer there, but it was reported that more than two hundred Algonquin and Hurons came down the rapids again that year and were met by many traders, who were now forgoing Tadoussac and pressing directly on to Québec. Biggar (1901, 85) reports:

> The non-appearance of Champlain was a great disappointment to his Indian friends, with whom he had hitherto always kept his word. A false report of his death, spread by the rival traders, only induced the Indians to declare that if this were the case, they would never return to the rapids. They knew that the others only sought immediate gain; Champlain alone was generous enough to help them in their wars.

On September 26, 1613, Champlain returned to Québec and traveled down the Ottawa River to restore trade in that region. He also planned to search for a "great sea in the north" (Lake Nipissing), which had been described by a fur trader named Nicolas de Vignau, who claimed he "had seen the sea, the wreck and ruins of an English vessel, together with eighty scalps which the savages had in their possession and a young English boy whom they held as prisoner" (Grant 1907, 251). While Champlain was skeptical, this story seemed at least plausible, as Vignau had spent the winter of 1611–2 living with the Kichesipirini people on Morrison Island in the Ottawa River, and Champlain had heard of an English expedition that might have been in the region. Champlain does not name this English leader, but this was about the time of Henry Hudson's ill-fated voyage into Hudson Bay (Chapter 15).

In a long, hard trip by canoe accompanied by Vignau, Champlain was able to make contact with the Kichesipirini and their chief, Tessouat. The chief laughed at Vignau's story, and he was forced to retract it. "The wretched man was ordered not to return to the French posts and disappears from the pages of history" (Trigger 1971, 93).

Champlain still wanted to travel to Lake Nipissing, but the Kichesipirini refused to take him further north. They suggested that the route was too difficult and the Nipissing people inhospitable. Champlain reports what the Kichesipirini told him about the Nipissing:

> That the people there were sorcerers, that they had caused the death of many of their own tribe by charms and poisoning, on which account they were not their friends: moreover they said that, as it regards war, I was not to think of them, as they were little-hearted. unfriendly [Grant 1907, 248].

Most probably, Tessouat wanted to prevent Champlain from making alliances with other nations whose trade was now passing through their hands. A frustrated Champlain was forced to return downriver.

In 1615, Champlain traveled up the Ottawa River despite the dire warnings of the Kichesipirini, but this time interacted with the Hurons and not the Nipissing. This would be his last great voyage of exploration. As Biggar (1901, 99) tells it:

> Champlain with Father Joseph and twelve other Frenchmen spent the winter of 1615–16 among the Hurons in their homes on the peninsula between Georgian Bay and Lake Huron. The journey thither by way of the Ottawa River, Lake Nipissing and Georgian Bay proved very long and very difficult to the white men. To Champlain the pleasure of exploring these regions made him oblivious of the difficulties of the route. On reaching the Huron country he not only seized every opportunity of examining it in all directions, but he carefully inquired of all strangers the nature of the regions further to the west.

During the expedition, he and 10 Frenchmen accompanied 300 Hurons on an attack of a stockaded village of the Iroquois near Lake Geneva. In what Champlain believed was a premature attack, the assault failed, and they had to flee. Champlain was wounded twice by arrows in his knee and leg.

Champlain then had to spend a winter in a Huron village when his escorts refused to guide him back to Québec. During his stay, he accompanied them on a great deer hunt, where he got lost chasing a bird and wandered for three days living off the land and sleeping under trees. He described what happened when he finally found his companions:

> [They] had about given up all hopes of seeing me again. They begged me not to stray off from them anymore, or never to forget to carry with me my compass, and they added: If you had not come, and we had not succeeded in finding you, we should never have gone again to the French, for fear of their accusing us of having killed you. After this, he was very careful of me when I went hunting, always giving me a savage companion, who knew how to find again the place from which he started so well that it was something very remarkable [Grant 1907, 300].

In his tenure with the Hurons, Champlain also mediated a violent quarrel that broke out between them and a group of Algonquin in the valley of the Petite-Nation River.

Champlain left the country of the Hurons on May 22, 1616, having never seen the "Great Sea in the North." He sailed back to France on July 2.

## From Explorer to Governor

In 1618, Champlain proposed to the French Chamber of Commerce that 300 families and 300 soldiers establish an agricultural and commercial settlement on the St. Lawrence in Québec. Champlain believed that within four years, the colony could attain self-sufficiency from its fisheries, forests, mines, fur resources, and farms, with only a modest investment of the chamber or the king. More importantly, conversion to the

Catholic church could redeem countless Amerindian souls. King Louis XIII approved the plan.

Champlain went back to New France in 1620, spent the rest of his life focused on the administration of the territory, and never again explored new regions. He was now about 50 years old and may not have been as energetic as he had been previously. From this point in time, priests and traders served as his emissaries to distant nations, while he remained in Québec.

> He came to view himself as a colonizer and a vice-regal official, rather than as the employee of a trading company.... No longer young, Champlain must have seen his future closely linked to that of his colony, which he was anxious to see developed as quickly as possible [Trigger 1971, 94].

Over the last 15 years of Champlain's life, he helped transform Québec from a trading colony to a full-fledged city. He continued to work on relations with the Amerindians, imposing a chief of his choice on the locals and negotiating a peace treaty with the Iroquois. He was forced to surrender the colony to the English in 1629 but was able to return as lieutenant general of New France in 1633. Champlain had a stroke in October 1635 and died two months later.

## Ten

# The Virginia Companies and the First Two Attempts to Settle Maine

## 1607–1608

### Setting the Stage—James I Charters the Virginia Companies

Despite his initial setback in settling Cape Cod in 1602, Gosnold remained passionate about the possibilities of English colonization in North America. Hakluyt actively promoted his colonization dreams and helped petition the new King James I for a patent to support the endeavor. The French efforts to gain a foothold in Acadia added fuel to the fire, as Champlain and others pushed to build their fur trading network.

The king proved agreeable and in 1606 chartered the Virginia Companies of London and Plymouth to settle the eastern coast of North America. At that time, the name "Virginia" represented the entire coast from Spanish Florida to Maine and Acadia. The London Company had the responsibility for colonizing the east coast of America between latitudes 34° and 41° north, while the Plymouth Company's responsibility fell between 38° and 45° north. The overlapping area was granted to both companies on the condition that the two would not establish a settlement within 100 miles (160 kilometers) of each other.

Associated with the London Company were Gosnold, Sir Thomas Gates and Sir George Somers (privateers), Richard Hakluyt (the famous geographer), and Edward Maria Wingfield (soldier and member of Parliament). Gosnold would become its prime mover and with Wingfield's help was able to recruit 40 participants to support its first expedition. Six of these were related to Gosnold, including Wingfield, who was his cousin, his brother Anthony Gosnold, and another cousin by the same name.

The primary partners of the Plymouth Company were Sir Ferdinando Gorges (superintendent of the Plymouth fortifications), Sir George Popham (the lord chief justice of England), Thomas Hanham (Esquire), Raleigh Gilbert (nephew of Sir Walter Raleigh), and William Parker (privateer and mayor of Plymouth). The most important driver for this petition was John Popham, who likely wrote the first draft. The primary force behind the subsequent colonization attempts would be Sir Ferdinando Gorges.

## Sir Ferdinando Gorges's Dream

In the seventeenth century, the passion to settle northern New England burned the brightest in the heart of Sir Ferdinando Gorges. As described by Henry Burrage (1923, 3–4) Gorges was

> educated for a military career, he is early mentioned as serving in an English army on the European continent, where for gallantry in battle before Rouen, in Normandy, in 1591, he was knighted by the earl of Essex. Late in 1595, returning to England, he received, through the influence of the earl of Essex, an appointment as superintendent of fortifications in the process of erection at Plymouth, and still later he was placed in command of these important coast defenses. When at length Essex was on trial as the head of a conspiracy against Queen Elizabeth, Gorges, with others, was involved and sent to prison; but he seems to have acted prudently in the affair, and after the accession of James, that soon followed, Gorges was set at liberty and restored to military duty.
>
> Therefore, it was that he was still in command of the fort at Plymouth, when, in the summer of 1605, Captain George Waymouth returned from his memorable voyage to our coast, bringing with him not only a most interesting story with reference to his discoveries here but also five Indians of the country, whom he had seized on his vessel just before leaving the coast. Three of these Indians Gorges kept, sending the other two to Chief Justice Popham, evidently believing that these red men of the new world would awaken in the chief justice the same deep personal interest in American colonization that they had awakened in him.
>
> "The longer I conversed with them," he said later, "the better hope they gave me of those parts where they did inhabit as proper for our uses, especially when I found what goodly rivers, stately islands, and safe harbors those parts abounded with, being the special marks I leveled at as the only want our nation met with in all their navigations along that coast; and having kept them full three years, I made them able to set me down what great rivers ran up into the land, what men of note were seated on them, what power they were of, how allied, what enemies they had." This was a memorable experience with Gorges; and, referring to it in his old age, he said, it "must be acknowledged the means under God of putting on foot and giving life to all our plantations."

As Gorges's knowledge about America grew, a grand idea began to form in his mind—he would establish an English realm in America. Being a man of only modest means, he formed an alliance with Sir John Popham, the wealthy lord chief justice of England, essentially England's top judge. Together they would become the core of the Plymouth Company.

## The First Mission of the Plymouth Company

Soon after the Virginia patent was awarded, Gorges and his close friend Popham set about raising funds and recruiting men to settle in America. Neither intended to go himself. Popham was in his mid–70s and not well, and Gorges suffered terribly from seasickness. They selected Popham's nephew, George Popham, to be the president of the colony, assisted by Raleigh Gilbert, son of the earlier adventurer Sir Humphrey Gilbert.

The first Plymouth Company ship, *Richard*, set sail in August 1606, commanded by Captain Henry Challons and piloted by John Stoneman, with the Waymouth abductees Assacomet and Manido on board to act as ambassadors and interpreters.

Challons was instructed by Gorges

> to take a northerly course as high as the latitude of Cape Breton until the mainland was sighted, and that then he was to sail southward, following the coast until, from the Indians who were with him, he was told that he had reached that part of the American coast [Burrage 1914, 57].

Challons was supposed to meet up with Captain Thomas Hanham, Sir John Popham's 30-year-old grandson, on the coast of Maine. Hanham's navigator was Martin Pring, who was given the Waymouth abductees Tahánedo and possibly Amooret to serve as his guides.

Unfortunately, Challons ignored Gorges's orders and sailed first to the West Indies, where they were taken prisoner by a Spanish fleet somewhere off the coast of Puerto Rico and enslaved. Challons and Stoneman would not get free until late 1608. Manido probably died while in Spanish hands. Assacomet was eventually ransomed and moved back in with Gorges in Plymouth. After several more years, he would get back to Maine in 1614 when Gorges put him on a boat commanded by Nicholas Hobson that explored Martha's Vineyard and the Maine coast.

Apparently, things went much better for Hanham with Tahánedo and his crew, although no written report exists. They successfully explored the rivers and harbors of the Gulf of Maine, including the lower Kennebec. Tahánedo was allowed to rejoin his Etchemin band in the Pemaquid and Muscongus Bay area in reward for his services.

Burrage (1914, 60–61) reports:

Probably Pring sailed from Bristol, and the voyage, as may be inferred from Challons' instructions, and what Gorges says concerning it, was a direct one to the American coast. St. George's harbor, the Pentecost harbor of Weymouth's anchorage in 1605, was doubtless the place of rendezvous agreed upon by Challons and Pring. Not to meet Challons there, or in the vicinity, was a matter of surprise and disappointment to those who followed him and expected to find the work of added exploration already well advanced. There may have been some little loss of time in searching for the co-operating vessel, but the favorable season for accomplishing satisfactory work was drawing to a close, and Hanham and Pring soon entered upon the task assigned to them. The coast was carefully examined, and the explorations made by Waymouth the year before were considerably extended. Especially was the attention given to that part of the coast lying west of the territory of Waymouth's discoveries. The Sagadahoc, now the Kennebec, was found to be a larger and more important river than that which evoked so much admiration from the explorers on the Archangel. It also afforded much larger trade facilities with the Indians and on this account offered advantages for a settlement that ought not to be overlooked. Accordingly, the location of the river and directions with reference to its entrance were carefully noted. Indeed, all facts necessary in planning for the establishment of a colony in the explored territory were sought and made available for use on the vessel's return.

Gorges implies that Pring was obliged to cut short his work of exploration by the approach of winter, and such seems to have been the fact. The vessel that bore the expedition hither left England about the first of October, and if ten weeks are allowed for the voyage and subsequent examination of the coast, Hanham and Pring could not have set out on their return much before the close of the year. Their arrival in England was on an unknown date. It was a winter voyage, and there were doubtless storms and delays. But the port was at length reached—Bristol probably and Popham and those who were interested in the voyage were at once made acquainted with its encouraging results.

They would make their next trip to Maine in May 1607.

## *Gorges Attempts to Colonize Maine*

The 76-year-old Sir John Popham died in 1607, but Gorges decided to continue forward. Based on Pring's maps and glowing recommendations about the coast of Maine, Sir John's nephew George Popham was appointed commander of a new expedition to settle there. He would sail on the flyboat *The Gift of God* with Waymouth abductee Skidwarres as his guide. A much larger ship, the *Mary and John*, would travel beside him carrying 120 colonists and their equipment. The all-male operation included soldiers, carpenters, merchants, and farmers. This vessel would be commanded by Raleigh Gilbert, younger brother to Bartholomew Gilbert, who had been part of the 1602 expedition to the Maine coast. The expedition's goal was to establish a colony at the mouth of the Kennebec River.

The most complete account of the experiences of the Popham colony can be found in *The Historie of Travaile into Virginia Britannia*, written by Jamestown settler William Strachey in 1612 but not published until 1849 by the Hakluyt Society. Apparently, the Virginia Company of London decided not to publish it because of its criticisms of colonial leadership, and they feared it would compare unfavorably with John Smith's history, published the same year (Burrage 1914). Other accounts include a brief report in 1614 in *Purchas His Pilgrimage*, followed by a short statement in 1622 in *A Briefe Relation of the Discovery and Plantation of New England*, and in 1624, Captain John Smith included a short record in his *General History of Virginia*. In 1875, another journal of the colony was found that once belonged to Sir Ferdinando Gorges in the library of Lambeth Palace, London. This narrative was likely written by James Davis, one of Gilbert's officers, and apparently was used by Strachey in his account.

## Skidwarres Guides the Colonists to Mawooshen

The two ships left Plymouth Harbor on May 31, 1607, crossing the Atlantic by way of the Azores and then steering north to Nova Scotia. They briefly anchored at an island near La Hève, where they were approached by a Basque shallop loaded with eight Mi'kmaq men and a boy. This group was initially afraid to board but returned the next day in another Basque boat ready to trade beaver skins for knives and beads.

The ships then sailed around Cape Sable and across Penobscot Bay and anchored between Monhegan Island and the St. George River. This was the place where Skidwarres and the other four Etchemin had been kidnapped by George Waymouth two summers before. Then, according to Strachey (1849, 168–70):

> They weighed anchor [at St. George Island] thereby to ride in more safely, howsoever the wind should happen to blow, howbeit before they put from the island they found a cross set up, one of the same which Captain George Waymouth in his discovery for all after occasions left upon this island [1605]. Having sailed westward they brought the highland before being spoken of to be north. About midnight Captain Gilbert caused his ship's boat to be manned with 14 persons and the Indian called Skidwarres and rowed to westward [across Muscongus Bay to New Harbor], from their ship to the River of Pemaquid which they found to be 4 leagues [12 miles] distant from their ship

where she rode. The Indian brought them to the [Western Etchemin encampment], where they found 100 men, women, and children and their chief commander or sagamo, amongst them named [Tahánedo], who had been brought likewise into England by Captain Waymouth and returned thither by Captain Hanam [Thomas Hanham, a nephew of George Popham] setting forth for these parts [in 1606]....

At their first coming the Indians betook them to their arms, their bows and arrows, but after [Tahánedo] had talked to Skidwarres and perceived that they were Englishmen, he caused them to lay aside their bows and arrows, and he himself came unto them and embraced them and made them much welcome, and after 2 hours interchangeably thus spent, they returned aboard again.

Herald Prins and Bunny McBride (2007, 84) suggest:

One can only imagine what Tahánedo told Skidwarres.... Surely, both expressed wariness about the possibility of another English kidnapping attempt. And they probably discussed mixed feelings about English plans to establish a stronghold in the heartland of their Mawooshen confederacy. That said, they may have recognized the possibility that with well-armed English neighbors, they could gain direct access to European trade goods and weapons, and perhaps even protection against Tarrentines raiding their corn-growing southern friends. At any rate, Skidwarres was all too happy to be back home and preferred to keep his distance from the newly arrived English colonists.

On August 9, most of the company landed on the island where the cross stood and named it St. George Island. They then received a sermon from their preacher, Mr. Seymour, and at its completion returned on board.

Strachey (1849, 170) describes what happened the next day:

Captain Popham manned his shallop and Captain Gilbert his ship's boat with 50 persons in both and departed for the River of Pemaquid, carrying with them Skidwarres. Arriving in the mouth of the river there came forth [Tahánedo] with all his company of Indians with their bows and arrows in their hands, they being before his dwelling houses would not willingly have all our people come on shore, being fearful of us. To give them satisfaction the captains with some 8 or 10 of the chiefs landed, but after a little parley together they allowed all to come ashore. Nevertheless, after one hour they all suddenly withdrew themselves into the woods, nor was Skidwarres desirous to return aboard. Our people were loath to offer any violence to him by drawing him by force, suffered him to stay behind, promising to return unto them the day following, but he did not. After his departure, our people embarked and rowed to the further side of the river and there remained on the shore for the night.

## *The English Build Their Fort*

The colonists then landed at the entrance of the lower Kennebec and began working on a fortified settlement near the modern-day town of

Phippsburg, which they named Fort St. George in honor of the colony's president, George Popham. It was to be a star-shaped bastion enclosing a chapel, homes, a bakery, a storehouse, a market, and other structures. The colonists also built a ship from local timber and sails and iron they had brought from England. The 50-foot pinnace, which they christened the *Virginia of Sagadahoc*, was the first English vessel constructed in North America. Later that season, the *Mary and John* sailed back to England, leaving *the Gift of God* behind.

The building of the fort was, of course, of great interest to the Wabanaki in the region. Prins and McBride (2007, 84) tell us:

> Since the English were building their fortified settlement at the coastal center of the Mawooshen Confederacy, at the boundary between Abenakis and Etchemins, we should not be surprised that various allied chieftains of the region came to inspect the place in person. One of the chieftains was Sasanoa, an Abenaki village headman from the lower Androscoggin River whose son had been killed by Tarrentine raiders earlier that summer. Apparently, he and others hoped that the English would become their allies: As commander of the English colony, Sir George Popham was "earnestly entreated by Sassenow, Aberemet, and others the principal sagamores (as they call their great lords) to go to the [Bashabez], who it seems was their king, and held a state agreeable, expecting that all strangers should have their address to him, not he [the Bashabez] to them."

Popham never did send a delegation to visit Bashabez, which must have been an insult. However, Bashabez did later send his son to trade with Popham, so it seems that, in spite of this, relations between the two peoples were at least initially cordial.

While the fort was being built, Captain Gilbert explored the rivers and islands of the surrounding area. As told by Strachey (1849, 173):

> Captain Gilbert departed in the shallop upon discovery to the westward and sailed all day by many gallant islands. The wind at night coming contrary, they came to anchor that night under a headline, by the Indians called Semiamis [Cape Elizabeth]; the land exceeding good and fertile, as appeared by the trees growing thereon being goodly and great, most oak and walnut, with spacious passages between, and no rubbish under, and a place most fit to fortify.... They departed from this headland Semiamis, in the height of 43½ degrees, and rowed along the shore to the westward, for that the wind was against them, and which blew so hard that they reached no farther than an island two leagues off, where, whilst they anchored, two canoes passed by them but would not come near them.
>
> They returned homewards before the wind, sailing by many goodly and gallant islands; for betwixt the said headland and Semiamis, and the River of Sachadehoc [Kennebunk], is a very great bay [Casco Bay] in which there lay so many islands and so thick and near together, that can hardly be discerned the number, yet may any ship pass betwixt, the greatest part of them having seldom less water than eight or ten fathoms about them. These islands are all

overgrown with woods, such as oak, walnut, pine, spruce trees, hazelnuts, sarsaparilla, and hurts in abundance, only they found no sassafras at all in the country, and this night they arrived at the fort again.

In late September, Captain Gilbert and a small crew sailed a shallop up the Kennebec River for some exploration of the interior woodlands. They arrived at an island

> and in the first of the night there called certain [Amerindians] on the further side of the river unto them in broken English ... [and] in the morning there came a canoe unto them and in her a sagamo and four [Amerindians], some of those which spoke to them the night before.... The sagamo called his name Sebenoa and told us how he was lord of the river Sachadehoc. Gilbert and his men then visited an Indian village with "nearly fifty able men very strong and tall, [armed] with bows and arrows" [Strachey 1849, 175–76].

Prins and McBride (2007, 86) suggest:

> This may have been Chief Sebenoa's village. Possibly, some of these Kennebec Indians had learned some "broken English" from Taháne do or Amooret, who had returned to Mawooshen the previous year. Or, they may have picked some words up from English fishermen just beginning to come to the Maine coast.

In early October, Tahánedo and Skidwarres returned to Sagadahoc to visit the English at Fort St. George. Again, according to Strachey (1849, 178):

> There came a canoe unto some of the people of the fort as they were fishing on the sand, in which was Skidwarres who bide them tell their president that Tahánedo, with the Basshabae's [Bashabez] brother, and others, were on the side of the river and the next day would come and visit him. There came 2 canoes to the fort, in which were [Tahánedo] and his wife, and Skidwarres, and the Basshabaes brother, and one other called Amenquin, a Sagamo; all whom the president feasted and entertained with all kindness, both that day and the next, which being Sunday, the president carried them with him to the place of public prayers, which they were at both morning and evening, attending it with great reverence and silence. Two days later, these Etchemins departed all except Amenquin, the Sagamo, who would stay amongst our people a longer time. Upon the departure of the others, the president gave unto every one of them copper beads, or knives, which contented them not a little, as also delivered a present unto Basshabae's brother, and another for his wife, giving him to understand, that he would come unto his court in the river of Penobscot and see him very shortly bringing many such like of his country commodities with him.

## *The Colony Soon Abandoned*

Busy working on the fortress, the colonists did not plant any crops, owing in part to their late arrival, and "they were forced to live off what they could hunt, fish, forage, as well as the hospitality of the natives" (Mark 2021c). However, food started to run low in December 1607, and the colonists decided to send the *Gift of God* to the Azores for enough supplies to keep them alive through the winter. To trade, they sent 30 long, white pine trees that could be used as ship masts.

The winter proved to be bitterly cold and icy, and the colonists struggled mightily. Remarkably, all the colonists made it through the winter except for their leader George Popham, who was replaced by his second-in-command, headstrong Raleigh Gilbert. The first colonists of the Plymouth Company in Maine would fare much better than those of the London Company at Jamestown, where only 38 of the original 100 survived the first year.

Gilbert proved to be less diplomatic than his predecessor, and rather than welcome the Amerindian neighbors, Strachey (1849, 87) suggests, "they drove the Indians away without ceremony; they beat, maltreated and misused them outrageously without restraint." Many of the colonists were convicts released from prison. At one point, the Wabanaki were lured into the fort for trade, only to be blown to smithereens by the colonists' cannon. The locals retaliated by grabbing and stabbing to death 11 colonists who were off fishing on a skiff.

In the spring of 1608, the *Mary and John* returned from England with more supplies and word that Raleigh Gilbert's brother John had died, leaving him a wealthy estate in Devonshire. He decided to return home, taking back with him all the colonists. They were tired of the hunger, cold, and the worsening relationship with the Wabanaki. After only a year, the colony was abandoned, and Skidwarres and Taháneedo were able to live out the rest of their lives among their own people.

The failure of the colony must have been a terrible blow to Sir Ferdinando. Adding to his overall dismay must also have been the fact that another Virginia Company group that had left for America a few months after Gorges's group had been successful, establishing a colony at Jamestown in 1607 that survived (Chapter 11).

As Gorges wrote in an essay titled "A brief relation of the discovery and plantation of New England, 1620" (Burrage 1923, 142):

> The arrival of these people here in England was a wonderful discouragement to all the first undertakers, in so much as there was no more speech of settling any other plantation in those parts for a long time after, only Sir Francis Popham having the ships and provision, which remained of the company, and supplying what was necessary for his purpose, sent divers times to the coasts for trade and fishing; of whose loss or gains himself is best able to give account.

However unsatisfying, this would not be the end of Gorges's efforts in Maine and North America. As will be described (Chapter 14), in 1614 he sent John Smith on a fishing, trading, and whaling expedition off the coast of New England that had mixed success but did result in the publication of the first map giving an accurate contour of the coast of Maine and Massachusetts Bay. Also in 1614, he supported a failed mission to Cape Cod in search of gold, masterminded by his Amerindian captive Epenow. In 1617, he supported another mission of Smith's to New England that never got out of port. In 1622, Gorges requested a grant for a huge parcel of land in New England, which he received and named the Province of Maine (Butman, n.d.). From then until his death in 1647, Gorges spent most of his money trying to develop an English colony in Maine. Unfortunately, he never set eyes on Maine or developed his dream of a royal realm in the New World. When Gorges died, the province of Maine passed to his grandson, also Ferdinando, who in 1677 sold its rights to the Massachusetts Bay Colony for £1,250.

## Eleven

# The Founding of Jamestown by the London Company
## 1606–1608

### Setting the Stage: The First Colonists of Virginia

The London Company's investors saw the settlement of Virginia as an opportunity to make a profit and relieve overpopulation in England. Spain had richly profited off her colonies in the Caribbean and South America, and the stakeholders in the Virginia Company expected similar results. Hoping to learn from the Roanoke disaster, the company hoped to create an autonomous and self-sustaining colony with its own governing council, which could respond rapidly to any issues that might arise. The dream was that the settlers would put down permanent roots and not just seek short-term fortune.

On December 20, 1606, three ships of the London Company set off for Virginia carrying 105 English men and boys. The little fleet included *Godspeed*, *Susan Constant*, and *Discovery*. Captain Christopher Newport was placed in command, and Bartholomew Gosnold served as vice admiral. They landed in Virginia on April 26, 1607.

This group of colonists left England about five months before Gorges's group took off for Maine, making them the third English settlement attempt after those of Raleigh in Roanoke (1584) and Gosnold in Cape Cod (1602). Two excellent eyewitness reports of the early settlement of Jamestown are George Percy's *Observations gathered out of a Discourse of the Plantation of the Southerne Colonie in Virginia* (1610) and John Smith's *A true relation of such occurrences and accidents of noate as hath happened in Virginia* (1608). For quotations from these, I have used Lyon Gardiner Tyler's (1907) compilation *Narratives of Early Virginia, 1606–1625*. In both these accounts, I have modernized spelling.

Like the colonists who would soon go to Maine, the Virginia colonists had no concept of what it would take to establish a successful settlement. Some of them were former soldiers, privateers, or skilled craftsmen, but most were laborers with no skills. Many were the younger sons of nobles, who, because of primogeniture, would not inherit estates. Most of these were gentlemen, who were inherently lazy and not used to manual labor. They were adventurers, not farmers.

> Almost all of the new colonists were under the impression they need to do very little upon arrival besides picking up the large deposits of gold that they believed were to be found all over the land, free for the taking [Mark 2021a].

The Virginia Company had promised the colonists food, tools, transportation, and clothes in exchange for seven years of indentured servitude. There were to be regular supply ships traveling back and forth, carrying goods and people. The colony was not intended to be completely self-sufficient in the beginning but was to establish trade with the Indigenous people and rely on English supplies during the early lean times.

## The Journey from England

Their journey was a difficult one. Their ships were not initially built to accommodate travelers, and they had to adjust themselves to the inconveniences of a freighter. Turning a freighter into a passenger vessel meant major discomfort for all aboard. When the travelers were below deck, they were crammed in a room, shoulder to shoulder, each having floor space of two by seven feet with a ceiling of five feet. It was dark, wet, smelly, and cold, and there was no privacy. You and all around you were sick from the rocking seas.

The food on the ship consisted of salted and dried beef and pork, biscuits made of both brown and white flour, with oatmeal for porridge. The only vegetable they had was dried peas cooked into a thick soup. Upon arrival, most were sick in varying degrees with scurvy.

The Virginia colonists encountered several storms along the way, and the crew was constantly bickering. They did not sail directly across the Atlantic but instead sailed to the Caribbean to restock supplies before turning northward to Virginia.

## The Landing in Virginia

On April 26, 1607, they anchored their ships at a place they named Cape Henry at the mouth of the Chesapeake Bay and landed a small party of 30 upon the shore. Here they planted a wooden cross in the sand to signal that the Protestant Christians had arrived in the New World. They then crept along the shore to explore the area.

As told by George Percy, in his chronicle of the Jamestown colony:

> The six and twentieth day of April, about four o'clock in the morning, we descried the Land of Virginia. The same day we entered into the Bay of Chesupioc [Chesapeake] directly, without any let or hindrance. There we landed and discovered [explored] a little way, but we could find nothing worth the speaking of, but fair meadows and goodly tall trees, with such freshwaters running through the woods, as I was almost ravished at the first sight thereof [Tyler 1907, 9–10].

When they were about to return to their boat later in the day, they were attacked by a group of local Powhatan. Percy continues:

> At night, when we were going aboard, there came the savages creeping upon all fours, from the hills like bears, with their bows in their mouths, charged us very desperately in the faces, hurt Captain Gabrill Archer in both his hands and a sailor in two places of the body very dangerous. After they had spent their arrows, and felt the sharpness of our shot, they retired into the Woods with a great noise, and so left us [Tyler 1907, 10].

Thus began a pattern of interaction between the English and Amerindians that would play out repeatedly over the next century. The Amerindians would shift back and forth between helping the colonists and attacking them, while the English would waver between bartering fairly for food and outright stealing it. As the English kept pushing onto more and more land, the Indigenous people would try to impede their expansion with raids and ambushes, which would be met in kind by the colonists. Finally, matters would reach a tipping point and one of the two parties would make a full-scale attack on the other's settlements, killing dozens to hundreds, stealing food reserves, and burning homes to the ground. This cycle went on, back and forth, until Amerindian numbers fell to the point that they could no longer adequately defend themselves against the ever-growing population of colonists, and they were banished from their lands.

Initially, the Powhatan and their chief, Wahunsenacawh (also called Powhatan by the English), were ambivalent toward the English, flipping back and forth between ordering raids and providing the inept colonists with food and supplies. Wahunsenacawh was not overly concerned about the English at first because their numbers were few and they were struggling mightily with disease and starvation. They also had no women, so they could not procreate.

In fact, the English would be dependent upon the Indians for about a decade and a half, until the number of settlers increased in the late 1620s.

Until then, the Algonquians were superior in terms of warriors, hunters, fishermen, and knowledge of how to survive in the coastal environment. The English survived only because Wahunsenacawh refrained from outright assault on the fort. He also had hopes that the English would become his allies against the Spanish and other hostile Europeans, and he saw value in having access to European weapons and trade goods, especially iron tools. He thought he could control the English much like he had other nations in the region and mistakenly believed he could bring them into his paramount chieftaincy.

## *The Search for a Settlement Site*

On April 28 the colonists launched a shallop to explore what they called the James River to find a better-protected landing that was uninhabited. They sought an upriver settlement location, which would minimize the chance of a Spanish or pirate attack. The English were well aware of what had happened to the French more than 50 years earlier when they had established a colony on the coast of Florida, making it easy for the Spaniards to find and destroy it.

As Percy describes their first day of exploration:

The Captain and some gentlemen went in her [the shallop] and explored up the Bay. We found a river on the southside running into the main[land]; we entered it and found it very shallow water, not for any boats to swim. We went further into the bay and saw a plain plot of ground where we went on land, and found the place five miles in compass, without either bush or tree. We saw nothing there but a canoe, which was made from the whole tree, which was five and forty feet long by the rule. Upon this plot of ground, we got a good store of mussels and oysters, which lay on the ground as thick as stones. We opened some and found in many of them pearls.

We marched some three or four miles further into the woods, where we saw great smokes of fire. We marched to those smokes and found that the savages had been there burning down the grass, as we thought either to make their plantation there, or else to give signs to bring their forces together, and so to give us battle [Tyler 1907, 10–11].

Two days later, they had their first friendly encounter with the Powhatan:

We came with our ships to Cape Comfort; where we saw five savages running on the shore. Presently the Captain caused the shallop to be manned; so rowing to the shore, the Captain called to them in sign of friendship, but they were at first very timorous until they saw the Captain lay his hand on his heart; upon that they laid down their bows and arrows, and came very boldly to us, making signs to come ashore to their town, which is called by the savages Kecoughtan ["great town," commanded by a son of Wahunsenacawh]. We coasted to their town, rowing over a river running into the main[land], where these savages swam over with their bows and arrows in their mouths.

When we came over to the other side, there were many other savages who directed us to their town, where we were entertained by them very kindly. When we came first a Land they made a doleful noise, laying their faces to the ground, scratching the earth with their nails. We did think they had been at their Idolatry. When they had ended their ceremonies, they went into their houses and brought out mats and laid them upon the ground: the chief of them sat all in a rank; the meanest sort brought us such dainties as they had, and of their bread which they make of their maize or guinea wheat. They would not suffer us to eat unless we sat down, which we did on a mat right against them. After we were well satisfied they gave us their tobacco, which they took in a pipe made artificially of the earth as ours are, but far bigger, with the bowl fashioned together with a piece of fine copper. After they had feasted us, they showed us, in welcome, their manner of dancing, which was in this fashion. One of the savages standing in the midst singing, beating one hand against another, all the rest dancing about him, shouting, howling, and stamping against the ground, with many antic tricks and faces, making noise like so many wolves or devils [Tyler 1907, 11–12].

On May 13, 1607, after several more positive interactions with the Powhatan, they landed on the northeast bank of the river and began building their settlement, which they named Jamestown. The area they picked was in a swampy region some 40 miles (64 kilometers) inland from the Atlantic Ocean. They selected this site as they deemed it was defensible against an Amerindian attack from the mainland and it was far enough from the coast to allow for ample warning of the approach of Spanish warships. It was also uninhabited, although there was a negative reason for this, as the locals felt this site was too swampy for agriculture. It also had too many mosquitoes and the water was too brackish to drink. These issues would eventually push the colonists further upriver.

It did not take very long for the local Paspihae tribe of the Powhatan to come and visit them at their settlement. Again, the interactions were mostly positive. Percy relates:

The first night of our landing, about midnight, there came some savages sailing close to our quarter. Presently there was an alarm given; upon that the savages ran away, and we [were] not troubled anymore by them that night. Not long after there came two Savages that seemed to be commanders, bravely dressed, with crowns of colored hair upon their heads, they came as messengers from the Weroance [chief] of Paspihae [Paspahegh tribe of Powhatan Confederacy], telling us that their Weroance was coming and would be merry with us with a fat deer.

On the eighteenth day, the Weroance of Paspihae came himself to our quarter, with one hundred savages armed, who guarded him in a very warlike manner with bows and arrows, thinking at that time to execute their villainy. Paspihae made great signs to us to lay our arms away. But we would not trust him so far. He seeing he could not have a convenient time to work his will, at length made signs that he would give us as much land as we would desire to take. As the savages were in a throng in the Fort, one of them stole a hatchet from one of our company, which spied him doing the deed: whereupon he took it from him by force, and also struck him over the arm. Presently another savage seeing that, came fiercely at our man with a wooden sword, thinking to beat out his brains. The Weroance of Paspihae saw us take to our arms, went suddenly away with all his company in great anger [Tyler 1907, 15].

On May 21, 1607, Newport, Smith, and 22 others set off to explore the James River. As Smith relates in his *True Relation*:

Captain Newport and myself with diverse others, set forward to discover the River, some fifty or sixty miles, finding it in some places broader, and in some narrower, the Country (for the most part) on each side plain high ground, with many fresh Springs, the people in all places kindly intreating us dancing and feasting us with strawberries, mulberries, bread, fish, and other their Country provisions whereof, we had plenty: for which Captain Newport kindly requited their least favors with bells, pins, needles, blades, or glasses, which so contented them that his liberality made them follow us from place to place, and ever kindly to respect us ... four or five savages came unto us which described unto us the course of the River, and after in our journey, they often met us, trading with us for such provision as we had, and arriving at Arsatecke, he whom we supposed to be the chief King of all the rest, most kindly entertained us, giving us in a guide to go with us up the River to Powhatan, of which place their great Emperor taketh his name, where he that they honored for King used us kindly [Tyler 1907, 33].

To their horror, when they returned, they discovered that the colony had been attacked. As Smith further describes (Tyler 1907, 36):

We heard that 400 Indians the day before, had assaulted the fort and surprised it, had not God (beyond all their expectations) by means of the ships, at whom they shot with their ordinances and muskets, caused them to retire. They had entered the fort with our own men, which were then busied in setting corn, their arms being then in packing cases and few ready but certain gentlemen of their own, in which conflict, most of the counsel was hurt, a boy slain and thirteen or fourteen more hurt. With all speed we palisaded our Fort: for six or seven days we had alarums by ambuscades, and four or five cruelly wounded by being abroad: the Indians losses we know not, but as they report three were slain and diverse hurt.

On June 15, they finished their fort. Percy describes it as

triangle wise, having three bulwarks, at every corner, like a half-moon, and four or five pieces of artillery mounted in them. We had made ourselves sufficiently strong for these savages [Tyler 1907, 19].

On June 22, 1607, Newport sailed back to London with the *Susan Constant* and *Godspeed*, leaving the settlers according to Percy "very bare and scanty of victuals, furthermore in wars and in danger of the Savages" (Tyler 1907, 20). Thus would begin a saga where the colonists would become almost totally dependent on trade with the local Powhatan, due to the infrequent delivery of supplies from England. The Powhatan themselves had little food to spare, as they were greatly stressed by a severe drought between 1606 and 1612. The colony would be kept barely alive by three resupply missions led by Captain Newport in 1608 and 1609, but it wasn't until a fourth mission under Lord Thomas West in 1610 that the colony would achieve a reasonable level of food security.

## Early Leadership Changes

In their voyage across the ocean, the colonists carried with them sealed directions from the Virginia Company to be opened upon arrival. In them, they found that their first leader was supposed to be Captain John Smith, who for some unknown offense had spent most of the trip across the ocean in the brig. In fact, he was scheduled to be executed until his friend Gosnold and a chaplain intervened. The colonists had grown so tired of his behavior that they initially refused to seat him on the council and elected Edward Maria Wingfield as their first president. Smith was tasked with exploring the region and bartering for food from the Powhatan.

As summer progressed and the temperature and humidity rose, many of the colonists became ill with yellow fever and some died. Gosnold was among these, dying on August 22, 1607, at the age of 36. As George Percy recorded:

> The two and twentieth day of August, there died Captain Bartholomew Gosnold one of our council, he was honorably buried, having all the ordnance in the fort shot off with many volleys of small shot [Tyler 1907, 20].

Gosnold's passing greatly saddened the surviving settlers, who had come to see him as the de facto leader of their community.

As the summer went on "the colonists who were unaccustomed to hard labor, became increasingly unhappy with the diminishing food supplies, ongoing Indian attacks, oppressively hot weather, and Wingfield's harsh disciplinary regimen" (Zacek 2021). The first council president, Wingfield, was deposed on September 10, 1607, on trumped-up charges and was replaced by John Ratcliffe. Wingfield was accused of being a Spanish sympathizer and atheist, but in fact, had been made a scapegoat by the colonists because of their growing hunger and sickness. When he was sent back to England, he was able to easily clear his name.

Ratcliffe also fell quickly out of favor as council president for being overgenerous in trade with the natives and dictating that the now sick and dying men build a governor's house. He resigned or was removed in July 1608 and was succeeded by Matthew Scrivener.

## First Expeditions of Smith

John Smith would make several exploratory voyages of the Chesapeake in the summer and winter of 1607. His primary goal was to trade for maize to sustain the colonists. Smith describes one such trip in September:

> As at this time were most of our chiefest men either sick or discontented, the rest being in such despair, as they would rather starve and rot with idleness, than be persuaded to do anything for their own relief without constraint: our victuals being now within eighteen days spent, and the Indians trade decreasing, I was sent to the mouth of the river, to Kegquouhtan an Indian town, to trade for corn, and try the river for fish, but our fishing we could not effect by reason of the stormy weather. The Indians thinking us nearly famished, with careless kindness, offered us little pieces of bread and small handfuls of beans or wheat, for a hatchet or a piece of copper: In like manner I entertained their kindness, and offered them like commodities, but the children, or any that showed extraordinary kindness. I liberally contented with free gifts; such trifles as well contented them. Finding this cold comfort, I anchored before the town, and the next day returned to trade, but God (the absolute disposer of all hearts) altered their conceits, for now, they were no less desirous of our commodities than we of their corn: undercover to fetch fresh water, I sent a man to discover the town, their corn, and force, to try their intent, in that, they desired me up to their houses: which well understanding, with four shot I visited them. With fish, oysters, bread, and deer, they kindly traded with me and my men, being no less in doubt of my intent, then I of theirs; for well I might with twenty men have freighted a ship with corn.
> 
> The town contained eighteen houses, pleasantly seated upon three acres of ground, upon a plain, half environed with a great Bay of the great River, the other party with a bay of the other River falling into the great bay, with a little Ile fit for a Castle in the mouth thereof, the town adjoining to the Maine by a neck of Land of sixty yards. With sixteen bushels of Corn I returned towards our Fort: by the way, I encountered with two Canoes of Indians, who came aboard me, being the inhabitants of Waroskoyack, a kingdom on the south side of the river, which is in breadth 5 miles and 20 miles or nearer from the mouth: With these I traded, who having but their hunting provision, requested me to return to their town, where I should load my boat with corn: and with near thirty bushels I returned to the fort, the very name whereof gave great comfort to our despairing company [Tyler 1907, 37–38].

In December, while leading an expedition up the Chickahominy River west of Jamestown, Smith and his men were taken captive by a large

Powhatan hunting party and were paraded on a long trek through several Powhatan villages, ultimately being brought before Wahunsenacawh.

In his memoirs, John Smith tells the story that Wahunsenacawh sentenced him to death in an elaborate ceremony for killing two Indians, but was spared after the impassioned request of Matoaka (Pocahontas), his 12-year-old daughter. Most historians question whether Smith was in fact facing death, as Wahunsenacawh would have seen him as a valuable conduit of trade for European arms. He may actually have been ceremoniously adopting him into the nation. Regardless of the circumstances of Smith's deliverance, Pocahontas would come to serve as a liaison between the Amerindians and the English colonists, helping to create an uneasy alliance between them, at least for a while.

## First-Year Sufferings

Jamestown barely hung on in that first year. By 1608, only 38 of the original 100 colonists were still alive. Percy relates:

> Our men were destroyed with cruel diseases as swellings, fluxes, burning fevers, and by wars, and some departed suddenly, but for the most part, they died of mere famine. There were never Englishmen left in a foreign country in such misery as we were in this new discovered Virginia. We watched every three nights lying on the bare cold ground what weather soever came warded all the next day, which brought our men to be most feeble wretches, food was but a small can of barley sod in water to five men a day, our drink cold water is taken out of the river, which was at a flood very salt, at a low tide full of slime and filth, which was the destruction of many of our men. Thus, we lived for the space of five months in this miserable distress, not having five able men to man our bulwarks upon any occasion. If it had not pleased God to have put a terror in the savages' hearts, we had all perished by these vile and cruel pagans, being in that weak estate as we were; our men night and day groaning in every corner of the fort most pitiful to hear, if there were any conscience in men, it would make their hearts to bleed to hear the pitiful murmurings & out-cries of our sick men without relief every night and day for the space of six weeks, some departing out of the world, many times three or four in a night, in the morning their bodies trailed out of their cabins like dogs to be buried: in this sort, I did see the mortality of diverse of our people [Tyler 1907, 21–22].

At this desperate point the Powhatan came to their mercy. Percy continues:

> It pleased God, after a while, to send those people which were our mortal enemies to relieve us with victuals, as bread, corne, fish, and flesh in great plenty, which was the setting up of our feeble men, otherwise we had all perished [Tyler 1907, 22].

Eleven. The Founding of Jamestown by the London Company    149

Wahunsenacawh (Powhatan) in counsel when Captain Smith was delivered to him as a prisoner in 1607; this image was cropped from John Smith's map of Virginia and used in various publications (Wikimedia Commons).

The first resupply fleet captained by Newport finally arrived at the colony on January 2, 1608. It brought much-needed food and supplies but also carried an additional 120 men (settlers and crew). One can only imagine their shock when they saw the condition of the colony and its survivors. The settlement's dismal state was further exasperated when a few days later the fort caught fire, destroying most of the existing buildings, food, and supplies.

Newport returned to England with Ratcliffe at the end of winter on April 10, 1608, carrying a sample of what he and the colonists were sure was gold. When he arrived back in England in May, he found out that the "gold" was again iron pyrite, commonly known as "fool's gold." The colonists would never find such easy riches. The commodity that eventually made them wealthy would be tobacco, but that discovery was about a decade away.

## *The Lifeways of the Powhatan*

When the English arrived in Virginia, there were more than 30 different Indigenous peoples spread across the mid–Atlantic and southern New England states. Wahunsenacawh's empire of 15,000–21,000 people stretched from modern-day Virginia through North Carolina. Other important Algonquian people were the Pequot and Mohegan (Connecticut), Narragansett (Rhode Island), Nipmuc (central Massachusetts and adjacent parts of Connecticut and Rhode Island), Woronoco (Connecticut and southern Vermont), Wampanoag (southeastern Massachusetts, eastern Rhode Island, and the islands of Martha's Vineyard and Nantucket—Chapter 6), and Pennacook (Massachusetts, New Hampshire, and southern Maine). Many of these societies paid tribute to Wahunsenacawh in return for peace and protection from other groups outside the confederation, notably the Iroquois.

When the first colonists arrived, the Powhatan had been living in the area for over 12,000 years. They considered Tsenacommacah to be their ancestral home, "given to them by their gods, Ahone, the Creator, and Oke, the helper who participated in the people's daily life. The land was intimately linked to these deities and the rituals enacted asking for help or thanking them needed to be performed at certain places within this territory" (Mark 2021b).

The Powhatan were mostly sedentary with permanent settlements, but during the winter followed the migration of various hunted animals (Rountree 1990; Day 1951). They lived in villages, which might contain only a few individuals to as many as 200 or more; the number of houses ranged from a few to 50 or more and could be distributed across a wide area, some covering as much as 100 acres. The borders of each province were established and recognized, and its members did not encroach upon the lands of their neighbors.

Common dwellings were formed in an oblong rectangle, 25 to 50 feet in length and about 20 feet in width. The framework was a line of poles that were bent over and lashed to opposite ones to form a series of arches. The structures were covered with bark or mats made of long rushes; some had bark walls and matted roofs. Each house contained just one room with a fireplace in the center and two doors, one on each end. Smoke traveled through an opening in the roof. People slept on platforms covered with mats.

Some villages were protected by wooden palisades made of split tree trunks or stout poles 10 to 12 feet high. The palisades were sometimes covered by bark for added protection. These stockades might surround a whole village but more commonly protected the chief's house and a wide enough area to harbor all the people if attacked by an enemy.

Implements and weapons were made of stone, wood, tooth, and shell. Knives were made of sharpened shells. A chisel was produced by setting a beaver tooth into a wood handle. Hatchets were made of a long stone sharpened at both ends and put through a piece of wood. Arrows were tipped with flint points. They carried shields of bark. Dugout canoes of up to 50 feet were made of a single log by charring and then scrapping with shells and sharp stones.

Each family had an extensive garden of 100 to 200 square feet, in which was grown corn, beans, peas, squash, pumpkin, and sunflower. Tobacco, primarily used for ceremonial purposes, was grown apart from the rest of the crops. To clear the land, the trees were girdled by bruising the bark and when sufficiently dry were felled with stone axes. A wooden spade was used for planting in a sitting position. Holes were made in the ground at about three-foot intervals into which four seeds of corn and two beans were set and covered. Pumpkins, squash, and sunflower were planted in the space between. When the corn was about half high it was mounded with soil. Women and children kept the gardens well weeded, and small platforms were erected with shelters for children to occupy and chase away birds.

Although the gardens were an important food source, the Powhatan relied on many other sources of food, including shellfish from the waterways; nuts, fruits, and berries from the woods; and hunting. Men took great pride in their hunting ability. All kinds of game were hunted for food and their skins, including squirrels, rabbits, deer, turkeys, grouse, waterfowl, and fish. Fish were caught by hook and line, nooses, dip-nets, weirs, spears, and bow and arrow. Individuals would stalk prey wearing the skin of a deer with head and legs attached. Occasionally large groups of both men and women would go on grand hunting expeditions to the mountains traveling for three or four days. The men would encircle deer by fire and noise to a central location where they were dispatched. They could take six to 15 deer in this manner (Willoughby 1907).

There was a strong seasonal pattern in the acquisition of food.

> In March and April, they fed primarily on turkeys, squirrels and fish. In May and June, they planted their fields and subsisted on fish, acorns, and walnuts; or they would disperse in small companies and collect fish, game, crabs, oysters, land tortoises, and wild fruits. In June, July and August their food consisted mostly of fish, berries, green corn, and roots of the tuckahoe [underground fungus in sandy pine barrens]. ... In the fall the natives fared quite well sumptuously on the products of their fields. After the harvest came their customary hunting expedition westward toward the mountains in search of deer and other game that had become scarce in the vicinity of their villages. During the winter months, their food consisted of corn, beans, nuts and acorns, dried fruit and berries, and what game they could secure. Fish and meat were preserved by drying upon hurdles over the fire and then prepared by boiling [Willoughby 1907, 85].

Maize was at the center of their diet year-round.

## Twelve

# Jamestown Teeters but Survives
## 1608–1622

### Setting the Stage: Captain Smith Takes Charge

In 1608, Smith was finally elected governing council president, leading them through that very difficult winter. Smith may have been headstrong and difficult to like, but he had proven instrumental in the colonists' early survival in his expeditions to Powhatan villages to secure food.

Among the first colonists, John Smith was by far the most prepared for the rigors and demands of wilderness settlement (Barbour 1964). His father was a yeoman farmer, and as a young man Smith had lived by himself in a wooded pasture, living off the land in a shelter built of tree branches. He then became an experienced soldier, fighting the Spanish in France and the Netherlands and then the Ottoman Turks in Slovenia, Hungary, and Transylvania (Romania). He was captured and enslaved during this war, finally escaping and traveling across Russia, Ukraine, Germany, France, Spain, and Morocco before finally making it home in 1604. Smith's military exploits greatly impressed the organizers of the Virginia Company, especially Gosnold, who was able to convince him to join the colonists.

Once in charge, Smith demanded a staunch work ethic from the settlers and utilized harsh measures to keep them in line. He demanded that they live by the New Testament aphorism "Those who do not work, will not eat" and did his best to stay in favor with Wahunsenacawh, whose patience was wearing very thin, as the colonists kept stealing food and taking land without compensation.

To describe the period of Smith's governorship and his explorations of the Chesapeake region, I use his *Generall Historie of Virginia, New England, and the Summer Isles*, originally published in 1609.

## Newport Brings Relief

When Smith returned from his last Chesapeake exploration on September 7, 1608, he found Jamestown still in dire straits. He reports:

> We safely arrived on the 7th of September, 1608. There we found Mr. Scrivener, and diverse others well recovered: many dead; some sick: the late President prisoner for mutiny: by the honest diligence of Master Scrivener, the harvest gathered, but the provision in the store much spoiled with rain. Thus was that summer (when little wanted) consumed and spent, and nothing done (such was the government of Captain Ratliffe) but only this discovery; wherein to express all the dangers, accidents, and encounters this small number passed in that small barge, by the scale of proportion, about three thousand miles, with such watery diet in those great waters and barbarous countries (till then to any Christian utterly unknown) [Smith 1907, 136–37].

On October 1, 1608, Captain Christopher Newport arrived back in Jamestown with a shipment of urgently needed supplies and an additional 70 colonists. Included in this group were Thomas Graves, one of the original stockholders of the Virginia Company, and the first two women—Margaret Forrest (married to Thomas Forest, Esquire) and Anne Burras, with her maid. Also included were the first non-English settlers (Dutch, Polish, and Slavic), who had been recruited as skilled craftsmen and industry specialists in lumbering and milling. They were sent to manufacture profitable export products such as pitch, tar, glass, and soap ashes, and erect sawmills (Hatch 1941).

Newport had been sent back to Virginia with several additional instructions in addition to bringing relief. He was to search for survivors of the Lost Colony of Roanoke, look for gold mines, and coronate Wahunsenacawh as a sub-king under James I, to cement a friendship.

The coronation proved to be a farce. Wahunsenacawh refused to go to Jamestown for the ceremony, insisting that he was already a king. The English were in fact under his rule, and they survived only because of his beneficence. Newport and Smith were forced to go to Wahunsenacawh's capital of Werowocomoco, where one side thought it was crowning a king while the other believed it was receiving tribute from its subjects. Wahunsenacawh was given a canopy bed and a scarlet cloak, and in exchange he gave Newport an old, worn pair of shoes and the mantle off his back.

Before heading back to England, Newport searched briefly and unsuccessfully for the lost colonists and gold, but to no avail. When he set sail for England, his ships bore no lost colonists or gold, but they did carry in their holds the first practical products of the settlers' labors: clapboard, wainscot, "pitch, tarre, glasse, frankincense, and sope ashes" ("Glassmaking at Jamestown" 2015). He arrived back in London in mid-January 1609.

## Smith Expands the English Settlement

In 1609, to feed the hungry settlers, Smith devised a plan to spread the Jamestown population out from the falls of the James River to its mouth on the Chesapeake Bay so they could source food from a wider range of native communities. The local communities at Paspahegh and Kecoughtan were now refusing to trade any more corn to the colonists. Smith's hope was that the Nansemond further down the river and the Powhatan (Wahunsenacawh's home villiage) at the falls would help them, even though they had not previously treated the Nansemond and the Powhatan any better than the Paspahegh and Kecoughtan. Smith also hoped to gain control of the whole James River Valley.

Overall, these moves did little to help feed the colonists. When Captain John Martin and his men tried to take over an island with a Nansemond village, they were faced with stiff resistance and were forced to retreat. When he returned later to search for survivors, he found only corpses with their mouths stuffed with bread (Ragan 2005).

At the falls of the James River, Francis West and John Smith demanded that Wahunsenacawh there pay tribute to them for protection against the Monacans. West required that all households pay a yearly tribute of a bushel of corn (Ragan 2005). Not surprisingly, Wahunsenacawh scorned this offer and continued raiding. West was forced to give up and return to Jamestown.

At the end of 1609, the colonists had been in Virginia for two and a half years and were still starving. However, they had made no effort to produce their own food.

## Samuel Argall Finds a Shorter Route to Jamestown

In early 1609, Captain Samuel Argall was commissioned to find a shorter, more direct route from England across the Atlantic Ocean to the colony at Jamestown. Rather than sailing the normal route south to the tropics and then west with the trade winds, Argall followed the 30th parallel, north of the traditional Caribbean route directly to the mouth of the Chesapeake Bay. His voyage took only nine weeks and six days, even with two weeks becalmed, rather than the three to five months of the previous fleets. This direct route allowed the English to save on provisions and avoid the hostile Spanish ships plying the Caribbean.

When he arrived, Argall found the colonists again in dire straits, as most of their stored maize had been destroyed by rot and an infestation of rats. He resupplied the colony with as much food and wine as he could spare and assured them that a rescue mission was being organized in England. Argall also found that John Smith had been incapacitated and was not expected to live.

As Kevin Miller (2018) describes in his blog "Pocahontas Lives!":

> Smith's account was that while he was asleep on a small boat while returning from an expedition upriver, a spark of unspecified origin caught his gunpowder bag on fire. The resulting burst of flame burned his body in an area 9 or 10 inches square where his torso meets his thigh (i.e., the groin area), causing him to jump into the river to put the fire out. His companions pulled him out of the river, nearly drowned, and in excruciating pain. He made the long trip back to Jamestown and was relieved of his duties. He was then put on a boat for England, a boat whose departure was purposely delayed for weeks, with Smith receiving inadequate treatment for his wound. He was not expected to live, and the Powhatan Indians were told that he had perished.

Argall returned to England in October 1609 with Smith aboard. He did ultimately recover.

George Percy replaced Smith as governor, but under his rule, discipline once again lagged, Indian relations deteriorated, and the colony entered its most harrowing time. The winter of 1609–10 became known as the "starving time," and 80 percent of the colonists died.

## Another Starving Time

At this point, Wahunsenacawh had lost all his patience with the encroaching colonists, and he decided that it was time to starve the English into submission. He ordered them to move back into their settlement and stopped trading with them. He also directed his people to kill any colonists found outside its boundaries.

As Tomečková (2021, 17) tells it:

> Due to a lack of food, the settlers started to eat their horses, dogs, cats, milk cows, and later even snakes, rats, and roots. The Indians saw the weakness of the English, and raided their settlements several times, killing them and their cattle in the process. The Indians hoped to intimidate the English and drive them off their land. The settlers who entered the forests in search of food were ambushed and killed by the Indians. With nothing left to eat, the colonists consumed trash, leather goods, and even animal excrement. Fearing attack if they left the colony's confines, they also started dismantling abandoned buildings for firewood. Ultimately, they dug up their dead and ate the bodies. One crazed man even murdered his pregnant wife in her sleep; he cut her open and took out the fetus and threw it in the river, then he salted the chopped body of his wife and ate it; he was later burned at the stake for the crime. Those who did not succumb to cannibalism either starved to death or joined the Natives.

During the starving time, John Ratcliffe led an expedition to the Powhatan capital at Orapakes to try and obtain food from the Indians. Most of the party were killed and he was captured and tortured to death. He was tied to a stake in front of a fire, skinned alive with mussel shells and ultimately burned at the stake.

## A Failed Relief Mission

In June 1609, seven ships carrying supplies set off from England to provision the colonists at Jamestown and replenish their numbers (Doherty 2008). Only a few days away from Jamestown, on July 24, the fleet was hit by a hurricane that separated the ships. A pinnace, *Catch*, sank with everyone aboard being lost. The largest ship, the *Sea Venture*, with more than 100 would-be colonists, was shipwrecked on the coast of Bermuda. Once on land, the settlers wanted to stay put, having now heard about the true conditions in Jamestown, but they were forced to build two new ships from *Sea Venture*'s wreckage. These were the second and third ships built by the English in America, the first being the 1607–8 construction of the *Virginia* by the Popham colony of New England. Finally on May 10, 1610, 143 survivors set sail for Jamestown, and upon arrival found it in such a horrible state that everyone decided to flee and return to England.

Wahunsenacawh had won the first round, but it would be a short-lived victory.

## Deliverance

As the retreating English ships descended the James River, they met another relief mission commanded by Newport and returned to Jamestown. The relief ships carried more settlers, soldiers, and a year's worth of provisions. Onboard were also the three men who would turn the colony's fortunes around: John Rolfe, Thomas West (Lord De La Warr), and Thomas Gates. Gates would take over as governor, Thomas West took charge of day-to-day affairs and relationships with the Powhatan, and Rolfe would learn to grow tobacco, which ultimately became the lifeblood of the colony.

Under West's leadership, the fort was rebuilt and martial law was instituted to prevent the cruel time from repeating itself. He instituted a set of rules that came to be known as the *Lawes Divine, Morall and Martiall* (Tarter 2020). Any colonists who traded individually with the Powhatan, killed livestock, stole from the storehouse, or refused to work were punished with whipping, hanging, or burning at the stake.

As the colony's population began growing, a new plan was created to establish new settlements along the James River to disperse the population. West totally rejected Smith's attempts at an amicable relationship with the Powhatan and decided to institute harsher policies; no longer would there be compromise. This set off the First Anglo-Powhatan War (1610-4), which became an ugly series of guerrilla strikes and counteroffensives.

The English began raiding the Amerindian settlements, often taking captives in the process (Ragan 2005). West had Sir Thomas Gates attack the Kecoughtan, and sent two other commanders, James Davis and George Percy, to accost the Paspahegh in August of 1610. Davis and Percy captured and burned down the Paspahegh capital and destroyed their fields of almost ripe maize, killing more than 60 inhabitants. They also kidnapped one of the chief's wives and two of her children. The children were subsequently murdered by throwing them into the James River and blowing their brains out. The English considered burning the wife at the stake but she was ultimately taken into the woods and stabbed. West then sent Dale against the Arrohateck nation, driving them from their lands and establishing a new colony at Henricus north of Jamestown.

Today, this ill-treatment of the Amerindians seems quite counterproductive. "It seems irrational that the settlers at Jamestown, who could not and would not feed themselves, went so far out of their way to kill Indians who willingly grew corn for the English," Ragan (2005) suggests.

Thomas West continued his atrocities up and down the James River until his poor health (dysentery, gout, and scurvy) forced him back to Jamestown and then to England (Ragan 2005).

When West returned to England, Samuel Argall became deputy governor.

## Argall Captures Pocahontas

In March 1613, Argall sailed to the Potomac River to trade with the still-friendly Patawomeck. Argall had to go so far to trade because of the ongoing war with the Powhatan. The Patawomeck were semi-independent of the Powhatan Confederacy.

While there, Argall learned that Pocahontas was visiting the Patawomeck to trade, and he decided that he would capture her and hold her as a bargaining chip with Wahunsenacawh. There are many versions of this story, but in the most popular one, Argall pressured a local chief Japazaws (Iopassus) to help him entice Pocahontas onto his ship (Miller 2020). Japazaws pleaded that if he helped him, it would bring the wrath of Wahunsenacawh upon his people. Argall assured him that the English would protect his people, and he offered him a copper kettle as a reward. Japazaws relented and had his wife ask Pocahontas to board the ship with her "on the pretext that Japazaws's wife wanted to see it and needed Pocahontas to accompany her" (Miller 2020). Argall subsequently captured Pocahontas, hoping to exchange her for English captives and some stolen weapons and tools. Wahunsenacawh returned the captives, but kept most of the weapons and tools, and a long standoff ensued.

While in captivity, Pocahontas, now 18, learned the English language and met John Rolfe, who asked the governor for permission to marry her. By now the war had grown sufficiently tiresome for both sides, prompting Wahunsenacawh and Governor Dale to use the marriage to establish a truce.

In April 1614, Pocahontas was baptized Rebecca and married Rolfe. With peace thus established, Jamestown began to prosper, and the colony spread. By the end of 1614, around 90 self-sufficient smallholdings were established in Jamestown (Horn 2018).

The abduction of Pocahontas (1624) by Johann Theodor de Bry after Georg Keller (The Virginia Historical Society / Wikimedia Commons).

## Argall Finds and Destroys the Last French Colony in New England

In the early seventeenth century, while Jamestown grew in strength, the French quietly held onto small footholds in New England at Port Royal and Mount Desert Island. The English would not discover the French presence there until 1613, when Thomas Argall stumbled onto the colony at Mount Desert during a fishing trip. He would subsequently destroy it.

When the Sieur de Monts was forced to leave Port Royal in 1607, he gave the rights to the place to Jean de Biencourt de Poutrincourt. Henry IV ratified the transaction, with the stipulation that Jesuit missionaries accompany any new expedition to New England. Poutrincourt sailed to Port Royal with a small group of settlers at the end of February 1610, and on June 22, 1611, was joined by the Jesuits Father Pierre Biard and Father Énemond Massé. Poutrincourt then returned to France to raise support for the colony, leaving his son Charles de Biencourt in charge.

When the elder Poutrincourt left, Biencourt set off to explore the New England coast with Father Biard, and reaching the Kennebec River towards the end of October, they learned about the failed Popham colony. They then headed back to Port Royal on November 4 or 5, visiting the site of the Saint Croix settlement, and arrived back on November 26 as the snow began to fall.

The Jesuits and the other settlers did not get along very well that winter. As Burrage states (1919, 103–4):

> The relation of the Jesuits to the other members of the colony at Port Royal during the winter that followed was by no means a harmonious one. Evidently, complaints of hindrances of various kinds, if not ill-treatment and open opposition, were made by the Jesuits to their friends in France. Meanwhile, the missionaries devoted themselves to the study of the language of the natives, and to other such matters as opportunity offered, displaying considerable adaptability to their surroundings.

The missionaries were relieved from this unhappy situation the following summer when Madame de Guercheville and her friends in France outfitted a vessel to carry the Jesuits to a more desirable place. Madame de Guercheville was the première dame d'honneur, or chief lady-of-honor, to the queen of France, Marie de' Medici, and was a particularly active supporter of French colonization.

The new expedition was led by the Sieur de la Saussaye and included 18 crew members, 27 colonists, and two Jesuits—Father Quantin and lay brother Gilbert du Thet. Charles Flory was the master of the vessel, which was loaded with sufficient supplies for a year, including horses and goats and four large royal tents or pavilions.

When the ship arrived at Port Royal, Biard, Massé, and their servant were waiting along with only two other colonists. Father Biard wrote in his *Relations de la Nouvelle France*, originally published in 1616: "Biencourt and the rest of the people were all quite far away, some here, some there." La Saussaye had been told to grab everything he could from Port Royal and had left behind only "a barrel of bread and some bottles of wine" (Prins and McBride 2007, 97).

The expedition then headed down the Penobscot River, into the Bay of Fundy, passing Grand Manan Island and Schoodic Point, finally arriving at Mount Desert Island. Father Biard wrote:

> The pilot turned to the eastern shore of the island, and there located us in a large and beautiful port, where we made our thanksgiving to God, raising a cross and singing to God his praise with the sacrifice of the holy mass [Prins and McBride 2007, 98].

The port was today's Bar Harbor. The local Etchemin chief, Asticou, welcomed them warmly and encouraged them to settle there. He hoped a French armed presence could offer protection against the Tarrentine raiders from Down East.

> Of course, the French Jesuits had made their own political calculations. With good reason, these "Black Robes" (as they came to be known) could expect that control over their own operational base in the center of the Gulf of Maine would give them direct access to Eastern and Western Etchemin communities who could be converted to Christianity, and at the same time provide their financial backers with a never-ending flow of furs to support their missionary project [Prins and McBride 2007, 100].

After considerable debate, the work of establishing a settlement commenced. However, rather than work on fortifications, la Saussaye focused on cultivating the rich soil, while the settlers lived in the royal tents.

> The French commander seems not to have had even a dream of insecurity for himself and his colony and was in no wise moved by the appeals of Father Biard and his associates. How long la Saussaye was left to his enjoyment in the cultivation of the rich, fertile soil of this delightful location is unknown. It may have been several weeks, and perhaps months. But the day for which la Saussaye had not looked, and for which he was wholly unprepared, at length came [Burrage 1914, 109].

## *The Colony Is Destroyed*

The lack of work on fortifications would prove disastrous to the French colonists.

> The fact that the Popham Colony at Kennebec had failed just five years earlier did not stop Gorges and his wealthy business associates in England from

sending fishing and fur-trading ships to the Wabanaki coast northeast as far as Penobscot Bay. As already noted, some of these English fishing boats did not come from across the Atlantic but sailed from the newly established colony at Jamestown, Virginia [Prins and McBride 2007, 101].

In July 1613, Samuel Argall, on a fishing trip from Jamestown, arrived at Mount Desert Island and learned from the Etchemin that there were white colonists in the neighborhood, who he surmised were French, that needed to be exterminated. Sir Thomas Dale, governor of Virginia, had given him orders to expel any French he came upon who had settled within the limits of King James's patent of 1606. Father Biard wrote:

"with the banners of England flying, and three trumpets and two drums making a horrible din," the Argall's *Treasurer* entered Somes Sound "swifter than an arrow." Heavily armed with "fourteen pieces of artillery [cannon] and sixty musketeers, trained to serve on ships, etc., [it] came to attack us...." The first Volley from the English vessel was terrible, the whole ship being enveloped in fire and smoke [Biard quoted in Prins and McBride 2007, 102].

In the battle, du Thet was killed and several other Frenchmen were wounded.

Of the 48 Frenchmen who had settled at Mount Desert, 15 were away fishing during the attack. The other 30 who had been captured were divided into two groups: one half, including Father Biard, were taken aboard the English ship, and the other half, with Father Massé, were allowed to sail to Cape Breton in a shallop (Prins and McBride, 2007). As the second group sailed off, they accidentally met another shallop carrying the French sailors who had been away and had escaped capture. They then sailed together around Cape Sable and headed to Port Mouton on Nova Scotia's Atlantic coast. Here they found two French ships anchored from Saint-Malo. Father Massé and the others returned to France in one of these. Father Biard's group was taken back to Jamestown and then England before being given their freedom in Calais.

After he got back to Jamestown, Governor Dale ordered Argall to return to Mount Desert Island and completely destroy the settlement. Upon arrival, the English took whatever they could find of value and destroyed what little remained after the brief French presence. Argall then sailed to Saint Croix Island, where he burned down the remains of the earlier French settlement.

Not knowing how to reach Port Royal, Captain Argall then captured a sagamore named Ouagimou, who showed him the way. Argall caught Port Royal off guard and destroyed it, although the two French noblemen, Biencourt and La Tour, and several others escaped and took refuge among the Mi'kmaq. They subsequently engaged in a guerrilla war against the English (Prins and McBride, 2007).

## Jamestown Finally Turns a Profit

Tobacco would become the crop that made Jamestown rich, as its popularity burgeoned in England. The man responsible for Jamestown's growing tobacco was John Rolfe, who got seeds of it from Trinidad. While everyone else was focused on finding gold and pillaging the Amerindians for corn, Rolfe honed his skills in the art of growing and curing tobacco. He sent his first small shipment to England in 1613 and caused quite a stir. His tobacco had a much sweeter and more aromatic flavor than that coming from the Spanish colonies. Tobacco would become "the first marketable commodity produced in Virginia" (Ragan 2005).

Rolfe and his Indian bride Pocahontas took his first commercial crop to England in 1616 to great acclaim. Baron De La Warr and his wife, Cecilia Shirley West, introduced Rolfe and Pocahontas into English society. The public was fascinated by Pocahontas and enamored with the taste and smell of Rolfe's signature tobacco. By then, he had branded it "Orinoco." Unfortunately, Pocahontas died that year in England, but Rolfe returned to Virginia in 1617 with the economic future of the colony set. He arrived just in time for the first Thanksgiving festival, a fitting celebration.

Now, everyone in the colony began planting tobacco on any spare piece of land they could find, and Amerindian land was now more coveted than ever. The pressure on the Algonquian communities further increased along the lower peninsula when an epidemic hit Virginia in the summer of 1617. Samuel Argall wrote of "a great mortality ... , far greater among the Indians and a morrain [plague] amongst the deer as well. All life suffered in the Chesapeake that year. The Indians [were] so poor [they couldn't] pay their debts and tribute" (Kingsbury 1907, 92). Argall had just arrived as the colony's new governor to discover that most settlers had abandoned their corn fields that flourished under Dale's martial law. Now, they planted tobacco instead of corn. Consequently, the English were set to starve again come winter. Making matters worse, there was a severe drought that burnt most of the corn and a hailstorm that battered what survived (Ragan 2005).

However, throughout Virginia, shipments of tobacco to England rose steadily from year to year. What was 20,000 pounds in 1618 became 60,000 in 1622, even though the colony would suffer an Indian massacre of a third of its population. Jamestown was finally a profitable entity after over a decade of struggle. Tobacco had become Atlantic America's first successful export crop.

In the 1620s, a tobacco boom would sweep all across Virginia (Dunkerly 1998). The population dramatically increased as new settlers grabbed more land to cultivate. By 1622, English settlements ringed both banks of the James River from Hampton Roads to the present site of Richmond. This rising tide of colonists would lead Wahunsenacawh's son Opechancanough to begin a concerted effort to drive the English out by attacking these settlements in a coordinated effort. Thus would begin another bloody Anglo-Powhatan War.

### Thirteen

# John Smith's Chesapeake Voyages
## 1608

## Setting the Stage: Exploratory Voyages of John Smith

In 1608, John Smith made two exploratory voyages into the Chesapeake Bay Region from Jamestown. Over a four-month period, he sailed all across the bay, noting the twists, turns, and tributaries of the Chesapeake and confronting the dense population of people who inhabited the region. He recorded these voyages and produced a detailed map showing the locations of many dozens of Amerindian villages. Included in his work were two of the earliest depictions of the Indigenous people of New England ("John Smith's Map of Virginia: A Closer Look" 2023).

Smith produced the first version of his map while he was still living in Jamestown and sent it back to England, where it fell into Spanish hands and became known as the Zúñiga chart, named after the Spanish ambassador to England (Farrell 2002). When Smith returned to England in 1609, he prepared what became the definitive version of this map as "A Map of Virginia. With a Description of the Countrey, the Commodities, People, Government and Religion." Smith included alongside the map a description of the nature of the Chesapeake region and its Indigenous people.

The detailed reports of his Chesapeake travels Smith published included (1) *A true relation of such occurrences and accidents of noate as hath happened in Virginia* in 1608, (2) *The general history of Virginia, New England & the Summer Isles* in 1624, and (3) *The True Adventures and Observations of Captain John Smith* in 1630. The quotes contained below come from a 1907 reprint of Smith's *General History of Virginia*.

The maps and chronicles of Smith's voyages throughout the Chesapeake Bay provide a remarkable description of Amerindian life in southern New England and the people's reactions to the European presence.

## Smith's Chesapeake Voyage 1

On June 2, 1608, Smith and 14 men headed north from Jamestown along the eastern shore and on the second day came upon their first two Amerindians.

> They crossed the Bay to the Eastern shore, and fell with the Isles called Smiths Isles, after our Captain's name. The first people we saw were two grim and stout savages upon Cape Charles, with long poles like javelins, headed with bone, they boldly demanded what we were, and what we would; but after many circumstances, they seemed very kind, and directed us to Accomack, the habitation of their Weroance, where we were kindly intreated [Smith 1907, 115].

Continuing north along the shore the next day, they found themselves in a violent thunderstorm and were unable to reach land before it hit them.

> Seeing many Isles in the midst of the Bay we bore up for them, but before we could obtain them, such an extreme gust of wind, rain, thunder, and lightening happened, that with great danger we escaped the unmerciful raging of that ocean-like water [Smith 1907, 116].

After about three days of travel, along the Watts and Tangier islands, the group ran short of fresh water, forcing them to search the mainland, where they encountered a village of the Algonquian Wighcocomoco.

> The next day searching the islands for fresh water, we could find none, the defect whereof forced us to follow a channel, which brought us to the river of the Wighcocomoco. The people at first with great fury seemed to assault us, yet at last with songs and dances and much mirth became very tractable, but searching their habitations for water, we could fill but three barrios [kegs]. ... We dug and searched in many places, but before two days expired, we would have refused two barrios of gold for one of Wighcocomoco puddle water. Being past these Isles which are many in number, but all naught for habitation, falling with a high land upon the main, we found a great Pond of fresh water, but so exceedingly hot we supposed it some bath [Smith 1907, 116].

For the next two days, Smith and crew continued exploring along the eastern shore, only to have another severe storm tear their sail and break their mast.

> Being thus refreshed in crossing over from the main to other Isles, we discovered the wind and waters so much increased with thunder, lightning, and rain, that our mast and sail blew overboard and such mighty waves.... For two days we were forced to inhabit these uninhabited Isles which for the extremity of gusts, thunder, rain, storms, and ill weather we called Limbo [Smith 1907, 117].

Finally able to continue down the river, they ran into another local nation, called the Kuskarawaok, who immediately began firing arrows upon them from the shore:

## Thirteen. John Smith's Chesapeake Voyages 167

> Repairing our sail with our shirts, we set sail for the main and fell with a pretty convenient river on the East called Kuskarawaok, the people ran as amazed in troupes from Kuskara—place to place, and getting into the tops of trees, they were not sparing of their arrows, nor the greatest passion they could express of their anger. Long they shot, we still rode at anchor outside their reach making all the signs of friendship that we could. The next day they came unarmed, with everyone a carrying basket, dancing in a ring, to draw us on shore: but seeing there was nothing in them but villainy, we discharged a volley of muskets charged with pistol shot, whereat they all lay tumbling on the ground, creeping some one way, some another into a great cluster of reeds nearby, where their companies lay in ambush.
>
> Towards the evening we waited and approaching the shore, discharged five or six shots among the reeds, we landed where there lay many baskets and much blood, but saw not a Savage. A smoke appearing on the other side of the river, we rowed thither, where we found two or three little houses, in each a fire, there we left some pieces of copper, beads, bells, and looking glasses, and then went into the bay, but when it was dark, we came back again [Smith 1907, 117–18].

The next day they encountered another small group of Amerindians who were unaware of the previous battles and were very friendly.

> Early in the morning four Savages came to us in their canoe, whom we used with such courtesy, not knowing what we were, nor had done, having been in the bay fishing, bade us stay and before long they would return, which they did and some twenty more with them; with whom after a little conference, two or three thousand men women & children came clustering about us, everyone presenting us with something, which a little bead would so well requite, that we became such friends they would contend who should fetch us water, stay with us for hostage, conduct our men any whither, and give us the best content [Smith 1907, 118].

At this point, Smith crossed the bay to travel along the western shore. Along the way, he explored the Patapsco River and was assaulted by a huge group of warriors that may have been sent by Wahunsenacawh, who was angered by his presence in the region.

> For two or three days we experienced wind & weather, whose adverse extremities added such discouragement, that three or four fell sick, whose pitiful complaints caused us to return, leaving the bay some nine miles broad, at nine and ten fantom water. The 16th of June we fell with the river Patowomek [Patapsco] … for thirty miles sailed, we could see no inhabitants, then we were conducted by two savages up a little bayed creek, towards Onawmanient, where all the woods were laid with ambush to the number of three or four thousand savages, so strangely painted, grimed and disguised, shouting, yelling and crying as so many spirits from hell could not have been more terrible. Many bravados they made, but to appease their fury, our Captain prepared with as seeming a willingness (as they) to encounter them. But the grazing of our bullets upon the water (many being shot on purpose they might see them) with the Echo of the woods so amazed them, as down went their bows and arrows.

James Watkins was sent six miles up the woods to their Kings habitation. We were kindly used of those Savages, of whom we understood, they were commanded to betray us, by the direction of Wahunsenacawh, and he so directed from the discontents at Jamestown, because our Captain did cause them [to] stay in their country against their wills [Smith 1907, 120].

From June 18 to July 16, Smith continued down the Potomac River, stopping at many villages along the way and meeting a Wighcocomoco man named Mosco, who he decided must be of European descent. Mosco then guided them across a portion of the Potomac.

Here we encountered our old friend Mosco, a lusty Savage of Wighcocomoco upon the river of Patawomek [Potomac], we supposed him some Frenchman's son, because he had a thick black bush beard, and the Savages seldom have any at all, of which he was not a little proud, to see so many of his Countrymen. Wood and water he would fetch us, guide us anywhere, cause diverse of his Countrymen help us tow against wind or tide from place to place till we came to Patawomek: there he rested till we returned from the head of the river [Smith 1907, 127–28].

On July 17, Smith was wounded by a stingray while fishing near the mouth of the Rappahannock River. He suffered mightily but recovered.

We spied many fishes lurking in the reeds: our Captain sporting himself by nailing them to the ground with his sword set us all fishing in that manner: we took more in one hour than we could eat. But it chanced that our Captain taking a fish from his sword (not knowing her condition) being much of the fashion of a Thornback, but a long table like a riding rod, whereon the middle is a most poisoned sting, of two or three inches long, bearded like a saw on each side, which she struck into the wrist of his arm near an inch and a half: no blood nor wound was seen, but a little blue spot, but the torment was instantly so extreme, that in four hours had so swollen his hand, arm, and shoulder, we all with much sorrow concluded his funeral and prepared his grave in an Island by, as himself directed: yet it pleased God by a precious Docter Russell at the first applied to it when he sounded it with probe (ere night) his tormenting pain was so well asswaged that he ate of the fish to his supper, which gave no less joy and content to us than himself, for which we called the Island Stingray Isle after the name of the fish [Smith 1907, 122–23].

Smith and crew then headed back to Jamestown and arrived home on July 21.

## Smith's Chesapeake Voyage 2

Smith set back out almost immediately on another expedition from Jamestown on July 24. His first stop was at present-day Hampton Roads, where he stayed with the Kecoughtan nation for two days.

The wind being contrary caused our stay two or three days at Kecoughtan: the King feasted us with much mirth.... In the evening we fired a few rackets, which flying in the air so terrified the poor savages, they supposed nothing impossible we attempted and desired to assist us [Smith 1907, 124].

From July 27 to 30 they then sailed north to the head of the bay, and on July 31 came upon a group of Massawomeck at the mouth of the Sassafras River. At this point, most of the crew were sick, and fearing an attack, they perched hats on their guns to make their party appear larger.

In crossing the Bay, we encountered 7 or 8 canoes full of Massawomecks, we seeing them preparing to assault us, left our oars and made way with our sails to encounter them, yet were we but five with our Captain that could stand, for within 2 days after we left Kecoughtan, the rest (being all of the last supply) were sick almost to death, until they were seasoned to the country. Having shut them under our Tarpaulin, we put their hats upon sticks by the barge's side, and betwixt two hats a man with two pieces, to make us seem many, and so we think the Indians supposed those hats to be men, for they fled with all possible speed to the shore, and there stayed, staring at the sailing of our barge till we anchored right against them. Long it was before we could draw them to come unto us. At last, they sent two of their company unarmed in a canoe, the rest all followed to second them if need required. These two being presented with a bell, brought aboard all their fellows, presenting our Captain with venison, bears flesh, fish, bows, arrows, clubs, targets, and bearskins. We understood them nothing at all, but by signs, whereby they signified unto us they had been at war with the Tockwoghes, which they confirmed by showing us their green wounds, but the night parting us, we imagined they appointed the next morning to meet, but after that, we never saw them [Smith 1907, 125].

Traveling down the Sassafras River on August 1, they met a group of Tockwogh, who were angered that they possessed weapons from the Massawomeck, their enemies. Smith convinced them that they took the weapons in battle rather than via trade. The Tockwogh took them to their palisaded town, and there Smith asked them where they got their metal tools, and the Tockwogh answered that they came from the Susquehannock, who lived to the north along the Susquehanna River. Smith asked them to send a messenger to request a meeting with them.

Entering the river of Tockwogh, the Savages all armed, in a fleet of boats, after their barbarous manner, round environed us; so it chanced one of them could speak the language of Powhatan who persuaded the rest to a friendly parley. But when they saw us furnished with the Massawomeks weapons, and we pretending to have taken them by force; they conducted us to their palisaded town, mantled with the bark of trees, with scaffolds like mounts, breasted about with breasts very formally. Their men, women, and children with dances, songs, fruits, furs, and what they had, kindly welcomed us, spreading mats for us to sit on, stretching their best abilities to express their love.

> Many hatchets, knives, pieces of iron and brass, we saw amongst them, which they reported to have from the Sasquesahanocks, a mighty people and mortal enemies with the Massawomeks. The Sasquesahanocks inhabit upon the chief spring of these four branches of the bays head, two days journey higher than our barge could pass for rocks, yet we prevailed with the Interpreter to take with him another interpreter, to persuade the Sasquesahanocks to come visit us, for their language are different [Smith 1907, 126].

While Smith waited to hear from the Susquehannock, he explored the Susquehanna and Elk Rivers from August 2 to 7. On August 7, they were greeted by 60 Susquehannock who had rowed down to the Tockwogh town.

> Three or four days we expected their return, then sixty of those giant-like people came down, with presents of venison, tobacco pipes three feet in length, baskets, targets, bows and arrows. Five of their chief Weroances came boldly among us to cross the Bay for Tockwhogh, leaving their men and canoes; the wind being so high they could not pass.
>
> Our order was daily to have prayer, with a Psalm, at which solemnity the poor Savages much wondered, our prayers being done, a while they were busied with a consultation until they had contrived their business. Then they began in a most passionate manner to hold up their hands to the sun, with a most fearful song, then embracing our Captain, they began to adore him in like manner: though he rebuked them, yet they proceeded till their song was finished: which done with a most strange furious action, and a hellish voice, began an oration of their loves; that ended, with a great painted bear skin they covered him: then one ready with a great chain of white beads, weighing at least six or seven pounds, hung it about his neck, the others had 18 mantels, made of diverse sorts of skins sewed together; all these with many other toys they laid at his feet, stroking their ceremonious hands about his neck for his creation to be their Governor and Protector, promising their aid, victuals, or what they had to be his if he would stay with them, to defend and revenge them of the Massawomeks [Smith 1907, 126–27].

From August 8 to 13, Smith headed south, where he explored the Patuxent River and had friendly encounters with the local people. They then arrived at the mouth of the Rappahannock River and traveled upstream to the town of Moraughtacund. There, Smith reunited with Mosco, who warned him not to travel further upriver into the Rappahannock territory, as they were at war with the Moraughtacund. Not heeding Mosco's warning, Smith continued up the Rappahannock and indeed was attacked.

Mosco described that they should not travel further upriver into Rappahannock territory,

> for they would kill us for being friends with the Moraughtacunds that but lately had stolen three of the King's women. This we did think was but that his

friends might only have our trade: so we crossed the river to the Rapahanocks. There some 12 or 16 standing on the shore, directed us to a little creek where there was a good landing, and commodities for us in three or four canoes we saw lying there: but according to our custom, we demanded to exchange a man in a sign of love, which after they had a little consulted, four or five came up to the middles, to fetch our man, and leave us one of theirs, showing we need not fear them, for they had neither clubs, bows, nor arrows. Notwithstanding, Todkill, being sent on shore ... perceived two or three hundred men behind the trees ... that he called to us we were betrayed, and by that he had spoken the word, our hostage went over-board, but Watkins his keeper slew him in the water. Immediately we let fly amongst them, so that they fled, & Todkill escaped, yet they so fast that he fell flat on the ground where he could recover the boat.

Here Massawomek shields stood us in good stead, for upon Mosco's words, we had set them about the forepart of our boat like a forecastle, from hence we securely beat the savages from off the plain without any hurt: yet they shot more than a thousand arrows, and then fled into the woods. Arming ourselves with these light shields (which are made of little small sticks woven between strings of their hemp and silk grass), as is our cloth, but so firmly that no arrow can possibly pierce them: we rescued Todkill, who was all bloody by some of them who were shot by us that held him, but as God pleased he had no hurt; and following them up to the woods, we found some slain, and in diverse places much blood. It seems all their arrows were spent, for we heard no more of them. Their Canoes we took; the arrows we found we broke, save them we kept for Mosco, to whom we gave the canoes for his kindness, that entertained us in the best triumphing manner, and warlike order in armies of conquest he could procure of the Moraughtacunds [Smith 1907, 128–29].

On August 21, crew member Richard Fetherstone died, probably of malaria.

There it pleased God to take one of our Company called Mr. Fetherstone, that all the time he had been in this Country, had behaved himself, honestly, valiantly, and industriously, where in a little Bay, we called Fetherstones Bay we buried him with a volley of shot: the rest notwithstanding their ill diet, and bad lodging, crowded in so small a barge, in so many dangers never resting, but always tossed to and again, had all well recovered their health [Smith 1907, 130].

On August 22, they reached the fall line of the Rappahannock River, where they were attacked again by Manahoac. Smith took in an injured Amerindian and had him treated by the expedition's doctor. The next day his kinfolk returned with reinforcements and attack, forcing Smith downstream. Eventually the captive, named Amoroleck, convinced his brothers to stop the ambush, and the two sides commenced trading.

There were about a hundred nimble Indians skipping from tree to tree, letting fly their arrows so fast as they could: the trees here served us for Barricades.

But Mosco did us more service than we expected, for having shot away his quiver of Arrows, he ran to the Boat for more. The Arrows of Mosco at first made them pause upon the matter, thinking by his bruit and skipping, there were many Savages. For about half an hour this continued, then they all vanished as suddenly as they approached. Mosco followed them so far as he could see us, till they were out of sight. As we returned there lay a savage as dead, shot in the knee ... so we had him to our Boat, where our surgeon who went with us to cure our Captains hurt from the Stingray, so dressed this Savage that within an hour after he looked somewhat carefully, and did eat and speak.

...it was not long before we heard their arrows dropping on every side of the boat; we caused our Savages to call unto them, but such a yelling & hallowing they made that they heard nothing.... More than 12 miles they followed us in this manner; then the day appearing, we found ourselves in a broad Bay, out of danger of their shot, where we came to anchor, and fell to breakfast. Not so much as speaking to them till the Sunne rose; being well refreshed, we untied our shields that covered us as a deck, and all showed ourselves with those shields on our arms, and swords in our hands, and also our prisoner Amoroleck; a long discourse there was between his Countrymen and him, how good we were, how well we used him, how we had a Patawomek with us, loved us as his life, that would have slain him had we not preserved him, and that he should have his liberty would they be but friends; and to do us any hurt it was impossible. Upon this, they all hung their bows and quivers upon the trees, and one came swimming aboard us with a Bow tied on his head, and another with a quiver of arrows, which they delivered to our Captain as a present, the Captain having used them so kindly as he could, told them the other three Kings should do the like, and then the great King of our world should be their friend, whose men we were. It was no sooner demanded but performed, so upon a low Moorish point of Land we went to the shore, where those four Kings came and received Amoroleck: nothing they had but bows, arrows, tobacco-bags, and pipes: what we desired, none refused to give us, wondering at everything we had, and heard we had done: our pistols they took for pipes, which they much desired, but we did content them with other Commodities, and so we left four or five hundred of our merry Mannahocks, singing, dancing, and making merry, and set sail for Moraughtacund [Smith 1907, 130–31].

From August 24 to August 30, Smith traveled back down the river and was convinced by werowances of friendly nations to make peace with the Rappahannocks. Smith succeeded in this endeavor, and their werowance offered Smith the three wives taken by them. Not wanting them himself, Smith gave them away.

...where Rapahanock presented his bow and arrows and confirmed all we desired ... [and] would give him the three women Moraughtacund had stolen.... The 3 women were brought to our Captain, and to each he gave a chain of beads: and then causing Moraughtacund, Mosco, and Rapahanock to stand before him, bid Rapahanock take her he loved best, and Moraughtacund choose next, & to Mosco he gave the third. Upon this away went their canoes over the water, to fetch their venison and all the provision they could, and they that wanted boats swam over the river: the dark commanded us then to rest.

The next day there were of men, women, and children, as we conjectured, six or seven hundred, dancing, & singing, and not a bow nor arrow seen amongst them.... All promising ever to be our friends, and to plant Corn purposely for us; and we to provide hatchets, beads, and copper for them, we departed, giving them a Volley of shot, and they us as loud shouts and cries as their strength could utter [Smith 1907, 134].

From August 31 to September 7, Smith and his crew continued their travels, exploring the Piankatank, Elizabeth, and Nansemond Rivers. On the Nansemond River, they were attacked by the local people, responded with gunfire, and were able to seize the chief's weapons, a chain of pearls, and 400 baskets of corn.

On September 7, Smith returned to Jamestown. He recorded,

There we found Mr. Scrivener, and the others well recovered: many dead; some sicke: the late President prisoner for mutiny: by the honest diligence of Master Scrivener, the harvest gathered, but the provision in the store much spoiled with rain. Thus was that summer (when little wanted) consumed and spent, and nothing done (such was the government of Captaine Ratliffe) but only this discovery; wherein to express all the dangers, accidents, and encounters this small number passed in that small Barge, by the scale of proportion, about three thousand miles, with such watery diet in those great waters and barbarous Countries (till then to any Christian utterly unknown) [Smith 1907, 137].

## Lifeways of the Chesapeake Societies Encountered by Smith

The Chesapeake Bay region was densely packed with many different distinct groups, each with its own leaders. Most of the peoples John Smith came in contact with were Algonquian-speaking and most were in the Powhatan Confederacy. The exceptions were the Massawomeck and Susquehannock, which were Iroquois-speaking and were at war with the Powhatan. Another group, the Manahoac, may have been Siouan and were at war with both the Powhatan and Iroquois.

The Chesapeake peoples lived in riverine communities, drawing their sustenance from farming and the waterways. Smith's choice to explore by boat put him in easy contact with them. Most of the groups numbered in the hundreds, but those in the Powhatan Confederacy could count on one another for mutual defense. There may have been as many as 30 Algonquin nations scattered around Chesapeake Bay.

Details about the lifeways of the Powhatan and Iroquois were discussed earlier (Chapters 6 and 11). Most of the Chesapeake groups were expert farmers, drying corn and beans for later consumption. The women and children interplanted in their fields beans, corn, pumpkins, squash, sunflowers, and tobacco. From the wild, they gathered nuts, berries, and edible plants of all kinds. In the summer months, they ate lots of seafood, including clams, crabs, eels, mussels, oysters, and fish, that they caught with baskets, nets, snares, and spears made by the men. The men also hunted for squirrels, turkeys, deer, opossums, rabbits, bears, partridges, ducks, and geese. Larger game was hunted using bows and arrows, and for smaller animals snares were employed. Food was roasted over open fires or boiled in clay pots as a stew.

## Fourteen

# The Enduring Dream of Ferdinando Gorges
## 1611–1619

### Setting the Stage: Gorges's New England Expeditions

Ferdinando Gorges was certainly discouraged by the failure of the Popham colony, but he was by no means deterred in his desire to colonize New England. He continued his search for economic opportunities and possible settlement sites in New England even as the fledgling Jamestown colony began to win its struggle for survival in Virginia.

Over about a decade, Gorges, with the help of other investors, sponsored several major expeditions to the coast of Maine and New England led by a diverse cast of characters, including Edward Harlow, John Smith, Thomas Hunt, Martin Pring, Nicholas Hobson, and Thomas Dermer. These missions had a hodgepodge of specific goals, ranging from fishing to finding gold to further mapping the coastline to abducting local people as scouts and slaves.

### The Nefarious Deed of Edward Harlow

In the summer of 1611, Captain Edward Harlow was commissioned by Sir Ferdinando Gorges and the Earl of Southampton, Henry Wriothesley, to explore the New England coast and capture some locals for interrogation about the region (Swett 1899; "Epenow, the Wampanoag who tricked his way home from England in 1614" 2022). Harlow was chosen for his previous experience in New England as the master of ordnance for the Popham colony.

Few details exist of Harlow's voyage except his success at abduction. Harlow first sailed to Monhegan Island, and upon arrival he enticed three Wabanaki to board his ship and he seized them unceremoniously. Remarkably, this was the same place where Waymouth had taken his five captives in 1605. Two of Harlow's abductees, Monopet and Peckenine, were quickly subdued, but the third, Peckmo, was able to break away and leap overboard. Upon hitting the shore, he alerted his brethren, and they rushed in their canoes to try to rescue the other two captives. Under heavy fire, they could not get on board, but they were able to cut loose the longboat of the ship. This they dragged to shore and filled with sand, waiting with their arrows poised for a recovery attempt.

When several crewmen arrived to retrieve the ship, the Wabanaki attacked fiercely and several of them along with three of Harlow's men were seriously wounded. A spooked Harlow and crew decided to leave the boat behind and set sail immediately to Capawack (named Martha's Vineyard by Gosnold) with the two captives held securely in their hold.

Here Harlow continued his nefarious deeds, by luring another three unsuspecting local Nauset—Sackaweston, Coneconum, and Epenow (also spelled Epanow)—on board for trade and then forcing them below deck with the other two captives. These wretched five were then spirited back to London by Harlow, leaving behind a legacy of hate and distrust. These kidnappings make an indelible impression on the Algonquians of Monhegan and Capawack, who vowed to never let Europeans again set foot on their land.

Upon their arrival in England, this group of five were treated with much less dignity than the abductees of Waymouth. They were exhibited as New World exotics all across the city of London, to the thrill of the populace. Epenow, in particular, was exhibited as a physical marvel. His cries of "Welcome! Welcome!" were well-known among Londoners who frequented coffeehouses and taverns. Shakespeare was probably referring to him when he mentioned a "strange Indian" in his play *Henry VIII* ("Epenow, the Wampanoag who tricked his way home from England in 1614" 2022):

> What should you do, but knock 'em down by the dozens? Is this Moorfield's to muster in or have we some strange Indian with the great tool come to court, the women so besiege us?

The ultimate fate of the five captured by Harlow is largely unknown, except for Epenow, whose story is related below. He wound up as a resident on Ferdinando Gorges's estate with two of Waymouth's captives and later blazed a historical trail back home to Capawack. As for the others, Monopet may also have moved in with Gorges, after spending some time with the Earl of Southampton, and likely made the trip to Capawack with Epenow. John Smith (1907) reported that Sackaweston lived for many years in

England and fought in the wars of Bohemia, and that Coneconum died of exposure near Plymouth after escaping into the woods. The fate of Peckenine is totally lost.

## Gorges Sends John Smith to New England

In 1614, Gorges and the Plymouth Company engaged Captain John Smith, now fully recovered from his burns at Jamestown, to sail to New England ostensibly to hunt whales for oil and search for gold and copper. If these endeavors failed, fish and furs were to be the backup. With Smith on this mission were Thomas Hunt, who would soon go rogue and become a slaver, and Thomas Dermer, who would later explore New England with one of Hunt's captives.

Smith recorded the highlights of this mission in his book *A Description of New England* (1616), which contains the first map that accurately displays the coast of Maine and Massachusetts Bay. In it he raved endlessly about the promise of New England and how the Amerindians could be easily subjugated to serve the settlers. Herein, I quote from an 1865 edition of this book published by James MacLehose and Sons.

On Smith's voyage, it was the backup that proved most profitable. As Smith related:

> We found this whalefishing a costly conclusion—we saw many, and spent much time in chasing them; but could not kill any.... For our gold, it was rather the master's device to get a voyage that projected it, than any knowledge he had at all of such a matter. Fish and furs was now our guard [Smith 1865, 3].

Smith soon grew bored with fishing and left his companions to the task while he explored what he dubbed "New England." In Smith's words (1865, 25):

> That part we call New England is between the degrees of 41 and 45: but that part that this discourse speaks of, stretched but from Penobscot to Cape Cod, some 75 leagues by a right line distant each from other: within which bounds I have seen at least 40 habitations upon the Sea Coast and sounded about 25 excellent good harbors; In many whereof, there is anchorage for 500 ships of any burthen; in some of them for 5000: And more than 200 Iles overgrown with good timber, of diverse sorts of wood, which do make so many harbors as required a longer time than I had, to be well discovered.

Of Monhegan Island and the coast of Maine, Smith (1865, 34–35) wrote:

> First, the ground is so fertile, that questionless it is capable of producing any grain, fruits, or seeds you will sow or plant, growing in the regions afore named: But it may be, not every kind to that perfection of delicacy; or some

tender plants may miscarry, because the summer is not so hot, and the winter is more cold in those parts we have yet tried near the seaside, then we find in the same height in Europe or Asia; Yet I made a garden upon the top of a rocky ile in 43½, 4 leagues from the maine [land] in May, that grew so well, as it served us for salads in June and July. All sorts of cattle may here be bred and fed in the islands, or peninsulas, securely for nothing. In the interim until they increase if need be (observing the seasons) I do undertake to have corn enough from the savages for 300 men, for a few trifles; and if they should be untoward (as it is most certain they are) thirty or forty good men will be sufficient to bring them all in subjection, and make this provision; if they understand what they do: 200 whereof may nine months in the year be employed in making merchantable fish, till the rest provide other necessaries, fit to furnish us with other commodities.

In March, April, May, and half of Iune, here is cod in abundance; in May, June, July, and August mullet and sturgeon; whose roes do make caviar and puttargo [relish]. Herring, if any desire them, I have taken many out of the bellies of cod, some in nets; but the savages compare their store in the sea, to the hairs of their heads: and surely there is an incredible abundance upon this coast. At the end of August, September, October, and November, you have cod again to make cor-fish or Poore Iohn: and each hundred is as good as two or three hundred in Newfoundland. So that half the labor in hooking, splitting, and turning, is saved: and you may have your fish at what market you will before they can have any in Newfoundland: where their fishing is chiefly but in Iune and July: whereas it is here in March, April, May, September, October, and November, as is said. So that by reason of this plantation, the merchants may have fraught both out and home: which yields an advantage worth consideration.

Of Cape Cod, Smith (1865, 47–48) wrote:

The waters are most pure, proceeding from the inside of rocky mountains; the herbs and fruits are of many sorts and kinds: as alkermes, currants, or fruit like currants, mulberries, vines, raspberries, gooseberries, plums, walnuts, chestnuts, small nuts, &c. pumpkins, gourds, strawberries, beans, peas, and maize: a kind or two of flax ... the chief wood; of which there is a great difference in regard of the soil where it grows, fir, pines, walnut, chestnut, birch, ash, cypress, cedar, mulberry, plumtree, hazel, saxifrage, and many other sorts.

Oak, is the chief wood; of which there is a great difference in regard of the soil where it grows, fir, pine, walnut, chestnut, birch, ash, elm, cypress, cedar, mulberry, plum-tree, hazel, saxifrage, and many other sorts.

Eagles, snipes, diverse sorts of hawks, cranes, geese, brants, cormorants, ducks, sheldrakes, teal, gulls, turkeys, dive-doppers, and many other sorts, whose names I know not.

Whales, grampus, porpoises, turbot, sturgeon, cod, hake, haddock, cole, cusk, or small ling, shark, mackerel, herring, mullet, base, pinbacks, cunners, perch, eels, crabs, lobsters, mussels, oysters, and diverse others etc.

Moose, a beast bigger than a stag; deer, red, and fallow; beavers, wolves,

### Fourteen. The Enduring Dream of Ferdinando Gorges

foxes, both black and other; wild-cats, bears, otters, martins, fitches, and diverse sorts of vermin, whose names I know not. All these and diverse other good things do here, for want of use, still increase, and decrease with little diminution, whereby they grow to that abundance. You shall scarcely find any bay, shallow shore or cove of sand, where you may not take many clams, or lobsters, or both at your pleasure, and in many places load your boat if you please; Nor Iles where you find not fruits, birds, crabs, and mussels, or all of them, for taking, at low water. And in the harbors we frequented, a little boy might take of cunners, and pinacks, and such delicate fish, at the ship's stern, more than six or ten can eat in a day; but with a casting net, thousands when we pleased ... if he has sense, strength, and health: for there is no such penury of these blessings in any place, but that a hundred men may, in one hour or two, make their provisions for a day: and he that hath experience to manage well these affairs, with forty or thirty honest industrious men, might well undertake (if they dwell in these parts) to subject the savages, and feed daily two or three hundred men, with as good corn, fish and flesh, as the earth hath of those kinds, and yet make that labor but their pleasure.

As he moved along the coast, he actively traded with the people he met. He came home with 11,000 beaver skins and 100 each of marten and otter skins which he had traded for rifles.

## The Foul Deed of Thomas Hunt

When he had finished exploring New England, Smith returned home, leaving behind his lieutenant, Captain Thomas Hunt, with one of the expedition's ships. Hunt's instructions were to continue fishing and trading until his ship's hull was full before returning. Hunt's mission took a dark and ominous turn, however, when he decided to engage in the slave trading business as a means of enhancing his personal profit from the voyage. He seized at least 20 people from Patuxet and seven from Nauset to sell in Spain.

As Sir Ferdinando Gorges described the incident in his *A Brief Relation of the Discovery and Plantation of New England*:

> It happened that there had been one Hunt (a worthless fellow of our nation) set out by certain merchants for love of gain; who (not content with the commodity he had by the fish, and peaceable trade he found among the savages) after he had made his dispatch, and was ready to sail, (more savage like than they) seized upon the poor innocent creatures, that in the confidence of his honesty had put themselves in his hands. And stowing them under the hatches, to the number of twenty-four, carried them to the Straits [Burrage 1923, 144].

The captives were carried off to Malaga, Spain, where Hunt tried to sell them at £20 each. Some of the local monks discovered what was happening and took the remaining Indians from Hunt in order to instruct them in the Christian faith, "thus disappointing this unworthy fellow of the hopes of gain he conceived to make by this new and devilish plot" (Burrage 1923, 144). One of the Amerindians, named Tisquantum (more commonly known as Squanto), lived with the monks for a year or two until he made his way to London under the care of John Slaney, a merchant, treasurer of the Newfoundland Company, and a shipbuilder. As will be described below more fully, Tisquantum would become a key player in the English exploration and settlement of America.

## Later Voyages of John Smith

Smith made two more attempts to return to New England in 1614 and 1615, both with Gorges's support. In the first, a storm dismasted his ship, and he was forced to return home. In the second attempt, French pirates captured him off the coast of the Azores and held him captive for several weeks before he managed to escape and make his way back to England.

After this last adventure, Smith wrote and published his *Description of New England*. It promoted Smith as a potential travel guide who could serve as an important resource for people wanting to migrate to New England. The Pilgrims nearly selected him in 1620 to be their advisor but instead selected Miles Standish. They did, however, use his map of New England to find their way to Plymouth. Smith himself would never again return to New England and died in London on June 21, 1631.

## Epenow Finds His Way Home

After his abduction by Harlow, Epenow appeared to settle in well with Gorges. Sir Ferdinando wrote:

> There came one Harlow unto me bringing with him a native of the island of Capawick, a place seated to the southward of Cape Cod, whose name was Epenow. He was a person of goodly stature, strong and well proportioned....
> How Captain Harlow came to be in possession of this savage I know not; but I understood by others how he had been shown in London for a wonder. It is true, as I have said, that he was a goodly man, of a brave aspect, stout, and sober in his demeanor [Baxter 1890, 20–21].

Once placed under Gorges's umbrella, however, Epenow developed a shrewd plan to get back home, by telling the English exactly what they wanted to hear. He told them that he knew of a gold mine in Cape Cod, hoping that they would send him back as a guide. He brought into his plan Waymouth's captive Assacomet, who was by then back with Gorges.

## Fourteen. The Enduring Dream of Ferdinando Gorges

Gorges bought their story and decided to send both to Capawack to lead an expedition to the mine. He approached his old friend the Earl of Southampton, who for the third time was willing to finance a voyage to the area. To lead the mission they selected one of the earl's men from the Isle of Wight, a Captain Nicholas Hobson, who was also willing to contribute a hundred pounds to the venture.

Thus, a third English expedition to Capawack was organized. The ship sailed in June 1614 with Hobson, who had been with Harlow in 1611 when Epenow was kidnapped, as captain. Also on board were Gorges's son Robert, who would serve as scribe, and three Algonquian: Epenow, Assacomet, and probably Monopet.

When the English and their captive company arrived on the coast of Cape Cod, "they were piloted from place to place by the natives as well as their heart could desire" (Baxter 1890, 23). However, Monopet died under unknown circumstances, and the other two's willingness to help the Englishmen soon began to wane when they began to communicate with their local brethren. Epenow and Assacomet were likely shocked to learn that there had been new abductions made at Patuxet and the Cape by Captain Hunt.

When Captain Hobson arrived at the harbor at Capawack, many of the most important men of the place, including Epenow's brothers and cousins, came aboard the ship. They were warmly received by the captain and allowed to confer with Epenow. While the Nauset must have been filled with rage at the recent abductions, they probably peaceably came on board to scope the situation out. The captain himself would not have known about the fresh enslavements. After a short visit, the Amerindians promised to return the next day to trade.

On the following day, at least 100 Nauset arrived in 20 canoes with bows ready. They refused to board the ship, even when beckoned by the captain. Gorges continues the story:

> The captain speaks to Epenow to come to him where he was, in the forecastle of the ship. He then being in the waist of the ship, between two of the gentlemen that had him in guard, starts suddenly from them and coming to the captain, calls to his friends in English to come aboard; in the interim slips himself overboard, and although he was taken hold of by one of the company, yet being a strong, heavy man, could not be stayed, and was no sooner in the water but the natives sent such a shower of arrows, and withal came so desperately near the ship, that they carried him away in spite of all the musketeers aboard, who were for the number as good as our nation did afford [Baxter 1890, 24–25].

In the ensuing melee, the master of the ship and many others were wounded, including Nauset and Englishmen alike. The English were sure that Epenow had been killed as he swam, and while trying to recover the dead body, the master of the ship and many of the crew were wounded (Dunn 1993). Spooked, Captain Hobson decided to return to England with no gold and little else accomplished. Ferdinando Gorges and his collaborators must have been greatly chagrined upon their return.

## Thomas Dermer and Squanto Explore New England

In 1616, while on a fishing and exploration visit to Newfoundland, Captain Thomas Dermer met Hunt's former captive Squanto, who had been sent there from England by the London merchant John Slaney as a guide (Hunt 2003b). Dermer met Squanto at the village of Cupids at Conception Bay.

Dermer immediately realized that Squanto would be an invaluable asset as a guide and interpreter on other missions to New England. In a letter to Ferdinando Gorges, he wrote that he had found Squanto in Newfoundland and asked what he should do with him (Burrage 1923). His reply is lost, but it must have been a request for Squanto's return, because Dermer took him back to England. How willingly he returned is not known.

In 1619, Gorges organized another expedition to New England. Captain Dermer and Squanto were sent to fish, further explore New England's natural resources, and reinitiate trade with the Indigenous people along that coast. At the end of this expedition, Squanto was to be returned to his home at Patuxet.

A letter by Thomas Dermer describing this expedition was published in *Purchas his Pilgrimes*, London (1625). I quote from a reprint of this letter found in G.P. Winship's (1905) *Sailors Narratives of Voyages Along the New England Coast, 1524-1624*.

When the expedition arrived at Monhegan, Dermer and Squanto left the fishermen and set sail southward in a small pinnace of five tons towards Patuxet. As they proceeded down the coast, they were traveling amongst Indigenous people still very charged with indignity about Hunt's foul play in 1614. In fact, when a French fishing ship was shipwrecked on the shores of Cape Cod in 1617 all but a few were enslaved, and the rest killed by the Nauset. Dermer in his short chronicle of the trip (1619) suggested that he himself might also have been killed at Cape Cod, had not Squanto entreated hard for him.

To their horror, when they arrived at Patuxet, Dermer and Squanto found that every man, woman, and child had been wiped out by the plague. Epidemics had swept across New England and the Canadian Maritimes between 1614 and 1620 and had devastated the Nauset, Wampanoag, and Massachusetts, with mortality reaching 100 percent in many mainland villages.

As Dermer described:

> [We] passed along the Coast where I found some ancient Plantations, not long since populous now utterly void; in other places, a remnant remains, but not free of sickness. Their disease is the Plague, for we might perceive the sores of some that had escaped, who described the spots of such as usually die [Dermer 1905, 251].

After surveying the tragedy at Patuxet, Dermer and Squanto headed inland to search for survivors and information about what had happened. After a day of travel, they found the still inhabited village of Namasket (Middleborough, Massachusetts) and learned of the tragedy that had destroyed the local population.

While at Namasket, Dermer was visited by two sachems, Massasoit and his brother Quadequina from nearby Pokanoket (Bristol) near the ocean. As Dermer (1905, 252) tells it:

> Whence came to see me two kings, attended with a guard of fifty men, who being well satisfied with what my savage (Tisquantum) and I discoursed unto them, (being desirous of novelty,) gave me content in whatsoever I demanded, where I found that, former relations were true.

Dermer was able to redeem "a Frenchman, and afterward another at Mastachusit, who three years since escaped shipwreck at the north-east of Cape Cod."

Dermer and Squanto then returned to Patuxet, and explored the islands of Boston Harbor looking for gold. In mid–June Dermer and his crew headed back to Monhegan leaving Squanto behind. Squanto would later play a central role as an interpreter and guide when the *Mayflower* landed in Cape Cod Bay in 1620 (Mark 2020).

At Monhegan, Dermer supervised the dispatching of the fishing vessels to England, and then headed south in his pinnace to further explore the eastern coastline of America from Monhegan to Virginia. During the voyage, Dermer and crew endured many storms, leaks, and attacks. At one critical point they had to throw most of their provisions overboard to keep control of the ship, before it dashed upon the rocks. His relations with the local people were now very tenuous without Squanto's help.

Dermer and his crew were attacked by the Nauset on the southern tip of Cape Cod. He was only able to escape by taking a Nauset leader and two others as hostages. Remarkably, he was able to ransom them back for a few hatchets and a canoe full of corn and then hastily depart for Capawack.

There he found Epenow alive and well, and even friendly. Dermer (1905, 255) wrote: He "was reported to have been slain with diverse of his countrymen by sailors, which was false. With him, I had many conferences, who gave me very good satisfaction in everything almost I could demand." Dermer left Epenow on good terms and continued his voyage, "searching every harbor, and compassing every cape-land till he arrived in Virginia."

Dermer and crew spent the winter of 1619 in Plymouth Harbor. He became very ill that winter but recovered. In the spring he headed south to New York, where he found a number of Dutch ships in Manhattan that he warned were trespassing on English ground (Dermer 1905). He then traveled back to Plymouth Harbor, where five months later the *Mayflower* would arrive carrying 102 Pilgrims.

Dermer would be at the end of a long line of explorers to visit Plymouth Harbor before the Pilgrims arrived in 1620. As Arthur Lord (1920, 55–56) pointed out:

> Where on that wide-flung seacoast line along the Atlantic could a little band of Englishmen in December, 1620, have found another harbor where during the twenty years before their landing the ships of three nations had anchored ... or where the coastline had been so ... thoroughly mapped and charted, sounded and named, as in that sheltered bay of Plymouth.

Englishmen Martin Pring, John Smith, and Thomas Dermer had been in the bay, and Bartholomew Gosnold had passed by it but had not landed. The Frenchman Pierre Dugua de Monts had also made short stays there. "Maps circulating in England, France, Holland, and Spain during the first decades of the seventeenth century all indicated the presence of the harbor, and some depicted its configurations quite accurately" (Rutman 1960, 164).

## *Final Fate of Dermer and His Legacy*

The final fate of Dermer is a bit cloudy. Most reports suggest he was mortally wounded in an ambush while trying to trade with Nauset. This ambush may have been led by Epenow, who might have turned against him. John Smith in his *History of Virginia* suggests that he survived multiple wounds (as many as 14) but was able to return to Virginia where he later died.

As Dunn tells the story, Dermer stopped at Nantucket and Martha's Vineyard, where Epenow bragged about his escape. In questioning Dermer about Gorges's intent, Epenow got angry, and he and his companions attacked Dermer and his crew.

> Dermer received fourteen or fifteen wounds. All of Dermer's men were slain except for one who had stayed in the boat. While Dermer tried to get into the

boat, Epanow and company would have cut off Dermer's head upon a small cabin in the boat, if Dermer's man had not rescued Dermer with a sword and escaped with him to Virginia, where Dermer died from his wounds or from a disease [Dunn 1993, 41].

Whatever his fate, Dermer's overall mission can be considered a success, as he had made great inroads towards repairing relationships with the Amerindians of New England after the repeated kidnapping done by the Europeans. The Nauset continued to be hostile, but the Wampanoag would be more lenient towards the colonists, particularly after the epidemics of 1616 and 1618.

Hunt (2003b) tells us that Dermer emerges from the records as a man of exemplary character:

> This worthy gentleman ... giving us good content in all he undertook. In particular, his dealings with the Indians appear to have won their confidence and esteem. Standing high in their good graces, he was warmly welcomed all along the coast. In no small measure, therefore, he paved the way for the Pilgrim Fathers who landed in New England 11 Dec. 1620.

## Fifteen

# Henry Hudson and the Early Dutch Expeditions
## 1609–1621

### Setting the Stage: Henry Hudson's Fateful U-Turn

It was not until the seventeenth century that a Dutch group supported a voyage to North America, and it was not their original intention. It took the Englishman Henry Hudson's U-turn, pursuing the Northwest Passage to China, to point them in that direction.

Before his fateful turnabout, Hudson had made two previous trips to find a Northwest Passage. In 1607, he had been sent by the English Muscovy Company to find an ice-free sea that would lead west from Europe to China. The plan was to sail northeast past the northern tip of the Scandinavian peninsula, then cruise along the northern coast of Russia, and enter the North Pacific Ocean through the Bering Strait. Unfortunately, Hudson was stopped by ice near the Svalbard archipelago and had to return home. A year later, he made another trip east for the Muscovy Company but only got as far as the islands of Novaya Zemlya before being set upon by ice fields and being forced back.

Seeing little hope of being sent on a third mission by the English, Hudson began to look to the Continent for another opportunity. In 1609, he was able to convince the Dutch East India Company to support another mission east. He was given a vessel of about 30 tons and was to depart about April 1, proceeding along pretty much the same route as before. He was then to return and report to the Dutch East India Company's director and provide him with all journals, logs, and charts of the trip. The contract also stated that his wife and children were required to live in Holland to encourage his return. Their expenses would be covered while in residence.

On March 25, 1609, Hudson and a crew of 16 sailed a ship called the

*Half Moon* into the North Sea. The crew was a rowdy mix of English and Dutch sailors who did not speak each other's language. Hudson himself did not speak Dutch. The *Half Moon* weighed between 60 and 80 tons and was about 85 feet in length.

For almost two months, the ship sailed northeast, only to be stopped again by ice. At this point, Hudson made the inconceivable decision to turn around and travel west toward North America rather than return to Amsterdam as agreed. There is no written record of why he made this decision, but it is known that he had had correspondence with John Smith, who was then leading the Jamestown colony and was convinced that the Northwest Passage lay through the middle of North America. Hudson may also have been faced with a mutinous crew who would no longer travel east into a sea of ice and found the maritime Atlantic more inviting.

## Who Was Henry Hudson?

Very little is known about Henry Hudson except for his roaring ambition. His passion was to find a passage to the Orient through arctic waters, even though many others had failed. The Portuguese had grown rich following a southern route along Africa and around the Horn to South Asia, and Hudson wanted to be the one who found another route across the top of the world. This became his passion, and this passion would ultimately lead to his death. In Ian Chadwick's delightful online biography of Hudson, he suggests "that Hudson must have learned his craft and skills by traveling with contemporary seafarers, probably British mariners and explorers (possibly even sailing with John Davis on one of his voyages to the Arctic) or even in one of the fishing fleets that crossed the Atlantic for the rich banks off Newfoundland." He could also have sailed on one of the English ships that fought the Spanish Armada in 1588, but there are simply no records of his early exploits.

## Hudson's Third Voyage

A complete log of Hudson's first North American voyage has survived, written by Robert Juet (1625), an English sailor who had also accompanied Hudson on his previous Arctic trips. It was first published in *Purchas His Pilgrimage* (Volume 13) in 1614. I quote from a reprint of this work published by James MacLehose and Sons in 1906. Hudson also wrote of this journey, but most of this report is lost except for pieces of it recorded in Dutch by Johannes De Laet in his *Extracts from the New*

*World, or, a History of the West Indies* (1625). I quote from an English translation of this work made by George Folsom in 1841.

The *Half Moon* sailed slowly westward, losing its foremast in a storm on June 15. In early July, Hudson arrived at the Grand Banks of Newfoundland, which he found to be well-populated with French cod fishing boats. Hudson lingered in the region for a few days, and over a five-hour period, his crew caught 118 cod themselves.

Hudson continued sailing southwesterly and on July 12 anchored in Penobscot Bay off the coast of Maine in a heavy fog. When the fog cleared a few days later, Hudson and his crew had their first encounter with the local people when two canoes approached their ship manned by six Etchemin. These men greeted them warmly and wanted to trade. They had obviously been in contact with traders before. Hudson gave them food and drink, along with some trinkets he had brought for trading.

The next day they moved to the mouth of the Penobscot River and a landing party was sent ashore to cut down a huge pine to replace their broken mast. After delivering the new mast, the sailors went back to shore to fill their water barrels and caught 31 lobsters in the shallow water. More Etchemin came to visit their ship, and they were able to do more trading, but the sailors started getting nervous about the ultimate intent of the local people, despite their friendly overtures. The Etchemin bartered beaver skins and other furs for a few red gowns.

On the evening of July 24, the sailors decided that instead of waiting for the Etchemin to start something, they would initiate hostilities. What triggered this reaction is unknown. The next morning, they went on shore and stole a canoe and then, without provocation, attacked a village, chased the inhabitants out of their homes, and pillaged the village for food. A sad action, particularly on top of George Waymouth's abductions in the Gulf of Maine only four years earlier.

Fearing reprisals, the *Half Moon* immediately sailed south and a week later arrived at Cape Cod. After anchoring, the sailors heard a mysterious sound from the shore that they took to be "Christians" calling to them. As described by Juet (1906, 351):

> We stood to the North-west two watches, and one South in for the Land, and came to an Anchor at the Northern end of the Headland and heard the voice of men call. Then we sent our Boat on shore, thinking they had been some Christians left on the land: but we found them to be savages, which seemed very glad of our coming. So we brought one aboard with us, and gave him meat, and he did eat and drink with us. Our Master gave him three or four glasses and sent him on land with our shallop again. And at our boats coming from the shore, he leaped and danced, and held up his hands, and pointed us to a river on the other side: for we had made signs that we came to fish there.

The *Half Moon* continued on, and by August 18 it was off the coast of Virginia, where Hudson's friend John Smith and the Plymouth Colony were struggling for survival. Interestingly, Hudson did not try to visit the colonists—perhaps because he was sailing under the Dutch flag, or maybe he didn't feel he had the resources to share with the colonists if they were in need. The settlers were indeed in pretty dire straits, even though they had recently received some relief supplies from England.

## New York Bay and the Hudson River

The *Half Moon* then turned north, and on August 28 reached Delaware Bay. This sea they initially thought might be the Northwest Passage, but it proved too shallow. They continued north and, on September 2, reached New York Harbor and the mouth of what came to be called the Hudson River. While Hudson is often considered its European discoverer, he was actually the third explorer to set his eyes on the harbor. The first two had been Giovanni da Verrazzano and Estêvão Gomes, nearly a century earlier.

Hudson spent the next five weeks exploring the river and interacting with the local Lenape. These interactions swung back and forth wildly, from friendly to hostile, depending on the mood of Hudson and his crew, and that of the local nations.

On September 5, the crew landed and had a couple of congenial meetings with the Lenape. Juet (1906, 364–65) writes:

> Our men went on Land there, and saw great store of men, women, and children, who gave them tobacco at their coming on Land. So they went up into the woods and saw a great store of very goodly oaks, and some currants. One of them came aboard and brought some dried, and gave me some, which were sweet and good. This day many of the people came aboard, some in mantles of feathers, and some in skins of diverse sorts of good furs. Some women also came to us with hemp. They had red copper tobacco pipes and other things of copper they did wear about their necks. At night they went on land again, so we rode very quietly, but did not trust them.

Hudson observed in another encounter:

> When I came on shore, the swarthy natives all stood around, and sung in their fashion; their clothing consisted of the skins of foxes and other animals, which they dress and make the skins into garments of various sorts. Their food is Turkish wheat [maize or Indian corn], which they cook by baking, and it is excellent eating. They all came on board one after another in their canoes, which are made of a single hollowed tree; their weapons are bows and arrows, pointed with sharp stones, which they fasten with hard resin. They had

no houses, but slept under the blue heavens, sometimes on mats of bulrushes interwoven, and sometimes on the leaves of trees. They always carry with them all their goods, such as their food and green tobacco, which is strong and good for use. They appear to be friendly people, but have a great propensity to steal, and are exceedingly adroit in carrying away whatever they take a fancy to (Laet and Folsom 1841, 299).

## The Lenape Attack

On September 6, Hudson sent John Colman and four others to sound a nearby river. Here they were attacked by Lenape in two canoes, and Colman was killed by an arrow through his neck. They then retreated, and the sailors and their dead mate were left adrift on a dark, rainy night. They spent the night rowing about, fearing another attack, and it wasn't until 10 o'clock the next day that they reached the *Half Moon*. After they were pulled on board, the crew barricaded the sides of their ship with waste boards and nervously awaited attack. Colman's death confirmed the crew's misgivings about the Lenape and thereafter, even the most peaceful meetings were considered suspicious.

Later that day and again the next, a couple of small, peaceful groups of Lenape came alongside them in canoes to trade, showing no apparent remorse or fear from the attack the day before. The sailors, ignoring their friendly gestures, took revenge by preventing two of the visitors from leaving, employing the now time-honored tradition of Europeans abducting Indigenous people. These two captives managed to escape 10 days later by jumping overboard and swimming to shore.

In this ever-shifting sea of hostility and congeniality, Hudson went on land on September 18 and made a peaceful visit to a local village. He relates:

> I sailed to the shore in one of their canoes, with an old man, who was the chief of a tribe, consisting of forty men and seventeen women; these I saw there in a house well-constructed of oak bark, and circular in shape so that it had the appearance of being well built, with an arched roof. It contained a great quantity of maize or Indian corn, and beans of last year's growth, and there lay near the house for the purpose of drying, enough to load three ships, besides what was growing in the fields. On our coming into the house, two mats were spread out to sit upon, and immediately some food was served in well-made red wooden bowls; two men were also dispatched at once with bows and arrows in quest of game, who soon after brought in a pair of pigeons which they had shot. They likewise killed a fat dog and skinned it in great haste with shells that they had got out of the water. They supposed that I would remain with them for the night, but I returned after a short time on board the ship. The land is the finest for cultivation that I ever in my life set foot upon, and it

also abounds in trees of every description. The natives are a very good people, for when they saw I would not remain, they supposed that I was afraid of their bows, and taking their arrows, they broke them in pieces, and threw them into the fire [Laet and Folsom 1841, 300].

On September 21, near Albany, Hudson entertained a group of chiefs on board the *Half Moon* in his cabin. He plied them with much alcohol "to try whether they had any treachery in them" (Powys 1928, 110). They became very inebriated, and one old man became so drunk that he passed out. This so alarmed his compatriots that they left and came back later with strings of wampum, to make an offering to free him from the evil that befell him. By the next day, he was okay, having slept off his stupor, and his grateful brethren thanked Hudson profusely and gave him tobacco, more wampum, and freshly dressed venison.

On September 26, Hudson had another friendly encounter with an old man they had apparently previously met. Juet (1906, 370–71) writes:

> This morning, two canoes came up the river from the place where we first found loving people, and in one of them was the old man that had lay aboard of us at the other place. He brought another old man with him, which brought more straps of beads, and gave them to our Master, and showed him all the country there about, as though it were at his command. So he made the two old men dine with him, and the old man's wife: for they brought two old women, and two young maidens of the age of sixteen or seventeen years with them, who behaved themselves very modestly. Our Master gave one of the old men a knife, and they gave him and us tobacco. And at one of the clock they departed down the river, making signs that we should come down to them; for we were within two leagues of the place where they dwelt.

The *Half Moon* continued down the river, and on October 1, while the crew was otherwise occupied in trading for furs, a Lenape near the stern of the ship climbed up the rudder and through the window of Juet's cabin, where he stole a pillow, two shirts, and two cutlasses. When his deed was discovered, an alarm went out and the man was shot in the chest as he tried to escape and was killed. Total chaos erupted as the Lenape dove overboard. The crew scrambled into their canoe to make chase, and one poor swimmer had his hand cut off when he tried to overturn their boat. As Juet (1906, 372) describes, "Then one of them that swam got hold of our Boat, thinking to overthrow it. But our Cooke took a Sword and cut off one of his hands, and he was drowned."

Upon retrieving the stolen items, Hudson set sail and traveled as far downriver as possible before night fell to avoid further confrontation. However, the next day, a flotilla of canoes appeared alongside the *Half Moon* and sent a volley of arrows into the ship after they were denied boarding. The crew retaliated by firing six muskets toward the boats and killing two people. A group of 100 Lenape then assembled on the shore and began raining arrows upon the *Half Moon*. Juet shot a cannon at them and killed two more. Most of them then fled into the shelter of the woods, but nine or 10 got into a canoe and paddled rapidly toward the ship. Juet discharged a second round from his cannon, which killed another Lenape and sunk their canoe. Other crew members picked off another three or four others with their muskets.

As Juet (1906, 372) described the attack:

> But we perceived their intent, and suffered none of them to enter our ship, Whereupon two canoes full of men, with their bows and arrows shot at us after our sterne: in recompense whereof, we discharged muskets and killed two or three of them. Then about a hundred of them came to a point of land to shoot at us. There I shot a falcon at them, and killed two of them: whereupon the rest fled into the woods. Yet they manned off another canoe with nine or ten men, which came to meet us. So I shot at it also a falcon and shot it through, and killed one of them. Then our men with their muskets, killed three or four more of them. So they went their way, and within a while after, we got down two leagues beyond that place, and anchored in a bay, clear from all danger of them on the other side of the river.

Thus ended the skirmish. The *Half Moon* sailed down the river through the night without further incident and then headed home across the ocean, arriving in Dartmouth, a little over a month later.

Upon landing, Hudson sent word of his return to his Dutch employers, along with a request to return to Newfoundland for further exploration before heading back to Amsterdam. The Dutch directors denied this request and demanded that he and his crew return at once. However, he was prevented from leaving by the English government, which accused him of having gone on a mission to the detriment of his own country and forbade him and his crew to leave. It wasn't until July of the following year that Hudson and his men were finally allowed to sail to Amsterdam.

## *The English Send Hudson on His Last Mission*

In 1610, three influential Englishmen banded together, with the support of Prince Henry, to send Hudson again to North America—Sir Thomas Smith, who held the royal charter for the London Virginia Company, which had established the Jamestown colony in 1607; Sir Dudley Digges, the author of *Of the circumference of the earth, or a treatise of the Northwest passage*; and Master John Wolstenholme, a wealthy financier who was knighted in 1617. The voyage was organized to find the Northwest Passage, focusing on the Davis Strait.

## Fifteen. Henry Hudson and the Early Dutch Expeditions

Sir Thomas Smith had a particularly active career as an international merchant (Wolfe 2021). His father was a founding member of the Muscovy Company, which was chartered in 1555 to trade with Russia. He was also a charter member of the Company of Merchant Adventurers, a governor himself of the Muscovy and Levant Companies, and was the first governor of the East India Company, chartered in 1600. He also had invested in Sir Walter Raleigh's unsuccessful attempt to establish the colony at Roanoke, Virginia, in 1584.

Henry Hudson's fourth voyage began on April 17, 1610, on the ship *Discovery*, previously sailed by Waymouth in his search for the Northwest Passage. The most important chronicler of this voyage would be its navigator, Abacuk Pricket, who, after the voyage, published *A Journal of Mr. Hudson's Last Voyage for the Discovery of a North-West Passage*. His account is generally considered quite self-serving. Herein, I rely heavily on Llewelyn Powys's account of the fourth voyage in his *Henry Hudson* (1928).

The *Discovery* was manned with what proved to be a particularly fractious crew. Included were Hudson's former chronicler John Juet as mate, experienced navigator Robert Bylot, the surgeon Edward Wilson, Abacuk Pricket, the mathematician and nautical expert Thomas Wydowse, and Henry Greene, "a dissolute young man, disowned by his well-to-do Kentish family, whom Hudson had apparently befriended" (Neatby 2003).

Greene would be at the center of all the contentious controversies that arose during the voyage. As Powys (1928, 125–26) describes him:

> [He] was a self-willed scapegrace. His parents, respectable people living in Kent, had been outraged by the conversation and manner of life of their offspring, who preferred above everything the company of bawds, panders, pimps, and trollops. He belonged to the underworld, was clever, physically strong, and turn his hand to anything.... Hudson had apparently taken a fancy to this ne'er-do-well, and had offered him a berth in his ship, promising upon his return to England to use his influence with Prince Henry, to have Greene made one of his guards.

The *Discovery* sailed from London and put into a bay in Iceland on May 18 to wait for the ice fields to the west to dissipate. Here came the first discordance among the crew (Neatby 2003). Greene quarreled with Wilson and beat him severely. While the crew was greatly upset by Greene's actions, Hudson shielded him and suggested that it was Wilson who was responsible for the fight. Once at sea, a drunken Juet, who had already come to detest Wilson, declared to all that Greene was on board as a stool pigeon to spy on the officers and men. Hudson flew into a rage and was barely persuaded not to turn back to Iceland and dump off Juet.

After sailing towards Greenland and then across Davis Strait, Hudson turned into the bay that now carries his name. Hudson was by no means the first to chart it. The bay had been entered by Waymouth and Frobisher, and a number of Portuguese navigators between 1558 and 1569. All had found the bay to be tough going due to the ice floes.

Hudson also ran into ice and spent a considerable amount of time weaving among the floes. The masses of ice floated back and forth, driven by the tides, making movement difficult and filling the crew's minds with terror. Hudson spent several weeks sailing to and fro but never finding a clear opening. Near Akpatok Island, along the northern coast of Québec, Juet organized a mutiny and the crew begged Hudson to turn their ice-battered ship around, but Hudson narrowly won out. Juet was arraigned before the crew, convicted of inciting disobedience, and his office of mate was transferred to Robert Bylot.

By November, it became clear to Hudson that they would need to ground the ship to relieve the pressure of ice on the hull and build a shelter to house the crew. Hudson chose the southeast corner of James Bay at the mouth of the Rupert River. This decision brought more consternation to the crew since only a week earlier, Hudson had impatiently rejected a suggestion from the ship's carpenter, Philip Staffe, to erect such a house. Staffe declared that it had now grown too cold to do the construction and that "he neither could nor would go in hand with such work.... Hudson ferreted him out of his cabin to strike him, calling him by many foul names, and threatening to hang him" (Powys 1928, 147). After a day or two, tempers cooled, and the house was built. Bad blood, however, still seethed.

In the middle of November, the gunner John Williams died of exposure and was buried in a shallow grave scraped out of the hard, frozen soil. Greene asked Hudson for the dead man's heavy gray cloak, and Hudson gave it to him, greatly angering the crew. Hudson's action went against naval tradition. Usually, when a sailor died, his clothes and other belongings were auctioned to the crew and the proceeds were taken back to the sailor's next of kin.

The next day, Greene and Staffe went out hunting together, causing Hudson to change his mind about the dispersal of Williams's coat, and he gave it to Robert Bylot. "Greene challenged Hudson to keep his promise, but Hudson railed at Greene with so many words of disgrace, saying his friends would not trust him (Greene) with 20 shillings" (Chadwick 2007).

## *The Harsh Winter*

It was a long, harsh winter. While the crew was able to supplement their short rations with wildfowl and fish in the early months, these became scarce as winter progressed, and many suffered from scurvy. A local Amerindian came to their aid briefly in the depth of winter, but an ungrateful Hudson destroyed the possibility of further help. As Powys (1928, 153) tells it:

> About the time that the ice broke up the explorers were visited by an Indian who after a kind reception took his leave promising by signs to return "after so many sleeps." When he returned, he came drawing behind him a sled, on which were two deerskins, two beaver skins, and some meat. "When, therefore, the Indian offered to barter one of the deer skins for a hatchet, Hudson insisted that the implement was worth both the skins." The native consented to the explorer's exaction at the time, but evidently formed a secret resolution never to come near him again.

And indeed, the travelers never saw him again. "In desperation, Hudson took the shallop and went in search of an Amerindian encampment to obtain food. He discovered their settlement, but they refused all intercourse with him and even set the woods on fire to keep the unwelcome visitors at a distance" (Neatby 2003).

On June 12, 1611, after a long and arduous winter, they were once again ready to set sail, but the demand for food was now a great issue.

> By now provisions are running very low and Hudson orders a search of the ship to find hidden stores. He then divides up the remaining food, including that which is spoiled, but some feel cheated.... The mutual distrust that now pervaded the ship was not improved by the fact that Hudson had in the boat certain favorites, amongst them the young surgeon, whom he used to ask into his cabin, to enjoy, so the hungry men imagined, ampler fare. Indeed, it seems almost certain that Hudson did not act with complete honesty over the distribution of the remaining stores [Powys 1928, 158].

## A Mutiny

Events reached a head on the evening of June 23. Wilson and Greene entered Pricket's cabin and told him how they and their associates were determined to put Hudson and all the sick men into the shallop and let them shift for themselves. A stunned Pricket concurred after some argument. Juet then came next into Pricket's cabin and declared that he would join the mutiny, followed by four other crewmen conspirators.

The next day, the quartermaster King was the first to be grabbed by the mutineers and was shoved into the hold. Next, Hudson appeared, and his arms were pinned and tied behind his back. Several of the sick crew members were then taken captive. Juet went into the hold to fetch King, but to his surprise, King had found a sword and attacked. Juet's cries brought help, and King was overpowered. Two other sick crewmen were then captured, as was Hudson's son John. Then, the most unthinkable thing was done—Henry Hudson, his son, and six other sick men were put in the shallop and were sent adrift, along with loyal Staffe, who voluntarily followed his captain. None of them was ever seen or heard from again.

As Powys tells it (1928, 166–67):

> And now, the shallop still being in tow, they stood out of the ice; and when they were nearly out of it, they cut her head fast from the stern of the ship, and with top-sails up, steered away into an open sea, leaving their captain and his son, with seven poor sailors, abandoned and exposed, without food, drink, fire, clothing, or other necessaries, in the great unexplored bay. There he sat in the tiny boat, dressed in a motley gown, the possessed sea captain who had sailed to the North, sailed to the East, and sailed to the West to find a passage through the ice-bound ramparts of the planet itself. There he sat, this dreamer, in his coat of many colors, until to the eyes of the mutineers, who watched the shallop grow smaller and smaller in the wake of their stolen vessel, he became a mote, a speck, a nothing, lost to sight on the unresting waves of the wharfless wilderness that had been by him, so resolutely, so desperately discovered.

By the force of his character, Greene took over leadership of the diminished band and restored Bylot to the post of mate. He piloted the ship to the Digges Islands, where they encountered some Indigenous people, whom they were sure would give them food. Greene landed with an unarmed party and confronted a group of frightened and wary locals, who immediately set upon them and mortally wounded two men. The survivors moved to another part of the island, where they were able to catch some wildfowl for the trip home.

Bylot managed to get the starving group to Ireland, where help was obtained. Of the 12 conspirators, four died on the way home, including Robert Juet. When they arrived in England, they were questioned and it was recommended that they hang, but the sentences were never carried out.

## *The Legacy of Henry Hudson*

It took the English several years to understand the full worth of Hudson's discovery of the Hudson River. However, Dutch merchants were quick to see the Hudson as a new opening into the lucrative fur trade and soon began sending ships to Manhattan (Jacobs 2013).

Dutch traders began flocking to the Hudson Valley, as the French had a few years earlier in the St. Lawrence Valley. A few even pushed westward to the Delaware River. They came strictly to trade and not to settle. The Amerindians usually welcomed them and gladly exchanged furs for trinkets, kettles, knives, hatchets, and guns.

Along with the French efforts in the St. Lawrence, the activity in the Hudson Valley commenced a great assault on the beaver. As Powys (1928, 120) puts it:

> But now, all at once, the demand for the pelts of the sagacious creatures was increased to proportions of unprecedented severity. A wholesale massacre began, a massacre of these rodents who had learned through long ages of trial and error to fell trees, build dams, and to sink logs for their winter food, with an ingenuity unrivaled in the animal world. We read of ships leaving the Hudson with cargoes of seven thousand skins. Indeed, there was not an animal whose coat could provide a covering for a hairless man that was not trapped, hunted, and killed.

## Early Dutch Activities in the Hudson Valley

The first ship to reach the Hudson in 1610 was commanded by Hendrick Christiaensz, but little else is known about this visit (Jacobs 2013). Captain Cornelis Rijser in the *St. Pieter* followed this voyage in 1611 and, in 1612, two ships, the *Fortuyn* under captain Adriaen Block and the *Jonge Tobias* captained by Thijs Volckertsz Mossel, made the journey.

With two ships in the bay, there was immediately competition for fur trade. The two captains had different sponsors: Block was sponsored by the Van Tweenhuysen Company, Mossel by the Hans Claesz Company. Mossel initially offered the traders twice as much for their beaver as Block, which led to heated negotiations. The two captains finally agreed to a predetermined price per beaver pelt, and Block, who got there first, would receive two-thirds of the profits and Mossel one-third.

In 1613, the Van Tweenhuysen Company sent out two ships, the *Fortuyn*, under Hendrick Christiaensz, and the *Tijger*, under Block, while the Hans Claesz Company sent out the *Nachtegael*, captained by Mossel. Once again, the rivals reached an agreement on price, but this time Mossel was to get two-fifths of the total profit, while Block and Christiaensz received three-fifths. Block also agreed to move further south to trade.

Ice floes delayed Block's departure, and in January he was still trapped in Upper New York when a fire destroyed his ship. Mossel tried to jump on Block's misfortune by offering to help him if he would flip the previously agreed sharing ratio. An indignant Block refused and ordered his ship's carpenter to build another small boat, which he named the *Onrust* ("Unrest" or "Restless"). Before this ship was completed, however, part of his crew mutinied and took over Mossel's ship. The mutineers then sailed away and became Caribbean pirates.

The competition in Hudson Bay continued to grow hotter and hotter as more ships arrived from other companies. The first of these, also called the *Fortuyn*, was commanded by Cornelius Jacobsz May, and was sent by a company of merchants from the city of Hoorn in the northern part of Holland. The other new arrival was the *Vosje*, captained by Pieter Franz, which had left Amsterdam almost a year earlier to search for the Northwest Passage. "The arrival of these two ships made it necessary to revise the earlier allocation ratio. Each of the four companies now was to receive one-quarter of the beaver pelts, which meant the previously dominant position of the Van Tweenhuysen Company was further eroded" (Jacobs 2013, 64).

## Block's Voyage of Discovery

Block and his remaining crew were forced to overwinter on Manhattan Island while they finished the *Onrust* with the help of the local Lenape. Finally, in the spring of 1614, Block completed his ship and sailed down the East River through some whirlpools he named Hellegat (Hell Gate) and into Long Island Sound. Block then became the first European to explore the Connecticut River, whose shorelines were inhabited by thousands of Amerindians with extensive fields of maize.

Block wrote about his travel down the Connecticut:

> Next, on the same south coast, succeeds a river named by our countrymen Fresh River, which is shallow at its mouth.... In some places it is very shallow.... There are few inhabitants near the mouth of the river, but at the distance of fifteen leagues above they become more numerous.... The natives there [South Windsor] plant maize, and in the year 1614 they had a village resembling a fort for protection against the attacks of their enemies [Howe 1969, 221].

Block was a careful notetaker and cartographer. Stapler (n.d.) wrote:

> The potential of the region for commercial exploitation of its resources, and particularly the rich fur trade with the natives, was carefully noted and fortified trading posts were established at present Albany and Manhattan Island. One of the most historically important results of this exploration was the so-called "Figurative Map of Capt. Adriaen Block." This map details the area of the 1611–1614 explorations plus the collective knowledge of the time. It was published after the return of Block to Amsterdam in July of 1614.

Back in the Dutch Republic, the fierce competition on the Hudson River finally pushed the four rival companies to approach the government for a joint monopoly. They joined together to form the Compagnie van Nieuwnederlant (New Netherland Company), and on October 1614, the States General granted a patent to them. They were given exclusive rights to make four voyages over three years to the area between the 40th and 45th parallels but excluding the Delaware River.

## First Dutch Settlements

The New Netherland Company established the first Dutch trading post in the Americas in 1615 at Fort Nassau, on Castle Island along the Hudson, near present-day Albany. Because of flooding, it was relocated in 1617 to the mouth of the Normans Kill on the Hudson River near today's Bethlehem. In 1618, this new fort was also flooded, and the site was abandoned for good.

The New Netherland Company applied for a new monopoly in October 1618, but the States General decided to reject the application, and New Netherland Company came to an end, opening the fur trade again to all (Jacobs 2013).

In 1621, the United Provinces charted a new company, the Dutch West India Company (Westindische Compagnie or WIC). It was given a trading monopoly in the Americas and was charged with forming a new province called New Netherland. They sent their first colonists into the New World in 1624; they settled at Fort Orange near the old Fort Nassau. In 1626, the WIC purchased the island of Manhattan from the Lenape and built Fort Amsterdam at its tip, which became the main port and capital of New Netherland.

# Epilogue
## Northern Atlantic America in the Early Seventeenth Century

### Setting the Stage: Activities in the Sixteenth Century

The exploration of Atlantic America started in Newfoundland. The first explorer to visit was Venetian John Cabot in 1497, who followed the annual migration of European fishermen to the Grand Banks in hopes of finding a passage to China.

In the first half of the sixteenth century, England was largely content with focusing on its North Sea fisheries and privateering in the Caribbean for international profit. It wasn't until the middle of the century that influential writers such as Richard Hakluyt and John Dee began to pressure Elizabeth to build her own overseas empire. Martin Frobisher was the first explorer to garner the queen's support, and in the 1570s he made three expeditions to the North Atlantic. In these voyages, he discovered Frobisher Bay, extensively charted Greenland, and alternately traded and skirmished with the Inuit. He also took back two boatloads of minerals that proved to be worthless.

Englishman John Davis would make three quests to find the Northwest Passage between 1585 and 1587. All these failed, but he did chart long stretches of Greenland, Baffin, and the Labrador coasts and made numerous careful observations on the terrain, rock formations, weather, and fauna. He provided one of the earliest descriptions of the Inuit, which was both accurate and sympathetic.

As fishing activity in the Grand Banks reached a fever pitch in the 1580s, the kings of England and France deemed it prudent to encourage exploration and colonization of the region. In 1583, Englishman Humphrey Gilbert led an expedition to Newfoundland in which he took possession of the port of St. John's and explored a large portion of the coastline. He was followed by Étienne Bellenger, who traveled to Cape Breton in 1583 and traded extensively with the local Innu; Marquis de la Roche-Mesgouez, who established a short-lived colony on Sable Island in 1598; and John Guy, who built the first enduring colony in Newfoundland at Cuper's Cove in 1610.

As the sixteenth century closed, the English became convinced that the climate of the mid–Atlantic would prove to be more favorable for colonization than that of the cold North. In 1584, Queen Elizabeth directed Sir Walter Raleigh to send the first English expedition to the mid–Atlantic. This group landed on the Outer Banks of North Carolina and had very friendly interactions with the local Roanoke people. Encouraged by this welcoming, Sir Walter dispatched another group of colonists the following year. Things appeared to start out well for this group, but when a supply ship returned to the colony after five years away, the settlement was found to be abandoned. No one knows for sure what happened to these colonists, but the most likely explanation is that relations with the Roanoke became contentious, and all the settlers were massacred.

## The French in Canada

Lower Canada would be thoroughly investigated in the sixteenth and early seventeenth centuries by the likes of the Frenchmen Jacques Cartier, François Gravé Du Pont, and Samuel de Champlain. About the time that Spaniard Cabeza de Vaca was emerging from the wilderness of Texas, the French explorer Jacques Cartier was beginning his first exploration of Canada. He would make three voyages between 1534 and 1542. He began along the west coast of Newfoundland, then discovered Prince Edward Island, sailed up the St. Lawrence River as far as Montréal, and claimed all of L'Acadie for France. As he traveled, Cartier had intimate, friendly contact with the Innu and St. Lawrence Iroquoian peoples.

In the second half of the sixteenth century, the estuary of the St. Lawrence River became a hotbed of French trade and exploration. In 1600, Pierre de Chauvin de Tonnetuit, was awarded the first monopoly by King Henry, and he tried to establish a colony at Tadoussac. All perished except for five who took refuge with an Innu community. In 1603, Aymar de Chaste dispatched three ships to New France, two small ones for trade and a larger one, the *Bonne Renommée*, mostly for exploration. This ship was commanded by Gravé Du Pont, aided by Samuel de Champlain. These two explored the St. Lawrence River as far as the Lachine Rapids, visited the Gaspé and the Acadian Peninsulas, and made friends with a number of Algonquin nations in the region.

In 1604, King Henry granted Pierre Dugua de Monts another fur trade monopoly in New France. He dispatched three ships to L'Acadie, with the largest again being commanded by François Gravé Du Pont with Samuel de Champlain's help. The first summer, they built a fort on Saint Croix Island and suffered a terrible winter. Of the 79 men who wintered there, 35 died of scurvy and 20 more were severely debilitated when spring finally came. The co-adventurers relocated their small settlement across the Bay of Fundy to Port Royal, next to a friendly Innu community. Here, they were blessed with much milder conditions, and although scurvy again proved to be a problem, the colony lost only five of its residents. Champlain spent each of the summers charting the coastline of New England and interacting with the local people.

In 1608, de Monts sent another three vessels to New France. One, captained by Pierre Champdoré, was to continue trading for furs at Port Royal. The other two, captained by François Gravé Du Pont and Champlain, were to travel to the St. Lawrence. Du Pont was commissioned to trade at Tadoussac, while Champlain was to establish a new colony at Québec. Champlain and his men endured another terrible, cold winter, where only eight of their original party survived, but the colony would persist. The following summer, Champlain joined a war party of several hundred Innu, Algonquin, and Wendat and explored the interior of Québec. Somewhere in the area near Ticonderoga and Crown Point, Champlain and his party encountered a huge group of Haudenosaunee ready for battle and defeated them.

## *The English and Dutch in New England*

While Du Pont and Champlain were successfully anchoring a lucrative fur trading network in the St. Lawrence Valley, several English explorers began to search New England in earnest for potential profits and possible places to settle. Three major English missions would set out for the Gulf of Maine and New England between 1602 and 1605: Bartholomew Gosnold, who briefly settled on Cuttyhunk Island near Cape Cod in 1602; Martin Pring, who harvested sassafras at the mouth of the Pamet River near Cape Cod in 1603, and George Waymouth, who explored Monhegan Island off the coast of Maine in 1605. All had initially warm interactions with the local people, but their stays ended with major confrontations. Waymouth's was the most grievous, as he abducted five Wabanaki before heading home.

In 1606, King Henry chartered the Virginia Companies of London and Plymouth to colonize the eastern coast of North America. The London

Company was the first to organize an expedition, and on December 20, 1606, three ships carrying 105 English men and boys left London for Virginia, arriving at Jamestown on April 26, 1607. From the very beginning, the colony struggled mightily. They became almost totally dependent on trade with the local Powhatan, who themselves had little food to spare and became increasingly aggressive. The colony would barely be kept solvent by three resupply missions in 1608 and 1609, and John Smith's ascension to the presidency.

Only a few months after the London Company established Jamestown, Sir Ferdinando Gorges and the Plymouth Company sent about 120 colonists to build a settlement at the mouth of the Kennebec River in Maine. The colonists succeeded in building a fort, and all of them survived the winter except for Popham. He was replaced by headstrong Raleigh Gilbert, who turned out to be an ineffective manager who destroyed the colonists' fragile relationship with the Etchemin. Fearful for their survival, the exhausted colonists returned to England that spring only 14 months after they had landed.

While disappointed with the failure of the Popham colony, Gorges kept the faith and sponsored many more expeditions to New England. In the summer of 1611, Captain Edward Harlow was commissioned to explore the New England coast and along the way abducted two Wabanaki and three Nauset. In 1614, John Smith was sent to New England to whale, fish, and trade for furs, and he produced the first detailed maps of the New England coast. One member of Smith's expedition, Thomas Hunt, went rogue and seized 50 Indigenous people to sell as slaves. Also in 1614, Captain Nicholas Hobson went on a fruitless trip for gold to Capawack, directed by three Amerindian guides who had been staying at the estate of Gorges. They all escaped while on the island. In 1616, Thomas Dermer led a mission to explore the eastern coastline of America, taking along one of Hunt's old captives, Tisquantum, as a guide. To their horror, when they arrived at Tisquantum's old home at Patuxet, they found that every man, woman, and child had been wiped out by the plague.

From 1607 to 1611, Henry Hudson undertook four major expeditions in search of a route to the Orient. In the first two, he traveled east into the Arctic Ocean until he was stopped by ice and had to return home. On his third trip, sailing for the Dutch East India Company, he again headed east, but this time he turned around when blocked by ice and headed back across the ocean to North America. There he explored the Grand Banks of Newfoundland, anchored in Penobscot Bay, and then spent five weeks traveling down the Hudson River. Along the way, he had many friendly-to-hostile interactions with the Indigenous communities, depending on his mood. In Hudson's fourth voyage, he sailed directly west towards Greenland and then across the Davis Strait into the bay that now carries his name. After a long, harsh winter, his starving crew mutinied and put Hudson, his son, and six other sick men into a shallop and sent it adrift, never to be heard from again.

Soon after Hudson's third voyage, Dutch fur traders began arriving in large numbers in the Hudson Valley. The New Netherland Company established the first Dutch trading post in the Americas in 1615: Fort Nassau, on Castle Island, near present-day Albany. Because of flooding, it was relocated in 1617 to the mouth of the Normans Kill on the Hudson River near today's Bethlehem. In 1618, this new fort was also flooded, and the site was abandoned for good. The Dutch West India company (Westindische Compagnie or WIC) sent its first colonists into the New World in 1624; they settled at Fort Orange near the old Fort Nassau. The WIC purchased the island of Manhattan from the Lenape in 1626 and built Fort Amsterdam at its tip, which became the main port and capital of New Netherland.

## *The Conquest of Atlantic America Begins*

It took about 13 years of struggle for Jamestown to become a profitable entity. In 1620, tobacco had become Atlantic America's first successful export crop. The European conquest of Atlantic America would now begin in earnest, as the farmers of Virginia began pushing for far more of the Indigenous people's land.

By this time, most of the nooks and crannies of the Atlantic coast had been carefully charted and mapped from the Florida Keys to Newfoundland. It was now abundantly clear that a huge continent stood between Europe and Asia, and it was highly unlikely that there was a major seaway that passed through it to Oriental riches. It was also clear to the European invaders that they were unlikely to find mother lodes of mineral wealth on the North American coast and would have to find another path to riches in their New World.

The early Spanish attempts at occupying southeastern Atlantic America had largely sputtered and died, but the English were now well-rooted in Jamestown, Virginia, and were ready to begin a push into New England. France was also well positioned in Ontario to build a great fur trading network across America. The Dutch were making their first settlements in New Netherlands based on the explorations of Hudson. Within a few years, the Plymouth Company (1620), the Massachusetts Bay Company (1629), the Company of New France (1627), and the Dutch West India Company (1621) would begin to send thousands of colonists, including families, to North America.

European colonization and settlement of North America would be an invasion of territory that had been controlled and settled for centuries by the Indigenous people. These groups perceived the Europeans' arrival rightly as an encroachment, and they pursued any number of avenues to deal with that invasion. As the English diaspora continued, and their lust for land continued to grow, the colonies would increasingly come in conflict with the Indigenous people, leading to the so-called Pequot War (1636–8) and later King Philip's War (1675–8). The colonists would prove victorious in both these wars and would continue to take over most of the Indigenous-occupied land, forcing the original occupants into reservations, slavery, or a migration west.

# Bibliography

Abler, T.B. 2019. "Kanyen'kehà:ka (Mohawk)." The Canadian Encyclopedia. https://thecanadianencyclopedia.ca/en/article/mohawk.
Adams, J.R. 2015. "Alien abductions: How the Abenaki discovered England." *American Indian* 16(3): 1–8. https://www.americanindianmagazine.org/story/alien-abductions-how-abenaki-discovered-england.
Allaire, B. 2013. "Jacques Cartier." The Canadian Encyclopedia. https://www.thecanadianencyclopedia.ca/en/article/jacques-cartier.
Bailey, A.G. 1969. *The Conflict of European and Eastern Algonkian Cultures 1504–1700: A Study in Canadian Civilization*. 2nd ed. University of Toronto Press.
Barbour, P.L. 1964. *The Three Worlds of Captain John Smith*. Houghton Mifflin.
Baxter, J.P. 1890. *Sir Ferdinando Gorges and His Province of Maine*. Prince Society.
Béreau, S. 2020. "Membertou (baptized Henri)." Dictionary of Canadian Biography, Vol. 1. University of Toronto/Université Laval. https://www.biographi.ca/en/bio/membertou_1E.html.
Bicheno, H. 2012. *Elizabeth's Sea Dogs: How England's Mariners Became the Scourge of the Seas*. Conway Maritime.
Biggar, H.P. 1901. *The Early Trading Companies of New France: A Contribution to the History of Commerce and Discovery in North America*. Vol. I. University of Toronto Library.
Biggar, H.P. 1903. *The Voyages of the Cabots and of the Corte-Reals to North America and Greenland, 1497–1503*. Macon, Protat, Fréres Imprimeurs.
Biggar, H.P. 1911. *The Precursors of Jacques Cartier 1497–1534: A Collection of Documents Relating to the Early History of the Dominion of Canada*. Ottawa Government Printing Bureau.
Biggar, H.P. 1922. *The Works of Samuel de Champlain. Vol. 1: 1599–1607*. The Champlain Society.
Biggar, H.P., W.L. Grant, and W.F. Ganong. 1907. *Lescarbot: History of New France*. Vol. I. The Publications of the Champlain Society.
Black, M.J, and Z. Parrott. 2018. "Algonquin." The Canadian Encyclopedia. https://www.thecanadianencyclopedia.ca/en/article/algonquin.
Bourque, B.J., and R.H. Whitehead. 1985. "Tarrentines and the introduction of European trade goods in the Gulf of Maine." *Ethnohistory* 32(4): 327–41.
Burrage, H.S., ed. 1906. *Early English and French Voyages Chiefly from Hakluyt 1534–1608*. Charles Scribner's Sons.
Burrage, H.S. 1914. *The Beginnings of Colonial Maine 1602–1658*. Marks Printing House.
Burrage, H.S. 1923. *Gorges and the Grant of the Province of Maine 1622: A Tercentenary Memorial*. State of Maine, Portland.
Butman, J. n.d. *Sir Ferdinando Gorges and His Impossible Dream of Maine*. Maine, Boats, Homes and Harbors. https://www.maineboats.com/print/issue-153/sir-ferdinando-gorges-and-his-impossible-dream-maine.
Cell, G.T. 1969. *English Enterprise in Newfoundland 1577–1660*. University of Toronto Press.
Chadwick, I. 2007. *Henry Hudson's Fourth Voyage 1610: The Northwest Passage*. www.ianchadwick.com/hudson/hudson_04.htm.

Clément, D. 1996. *The Algonquins*. University of Ottawa Press.
Collinson, R. 1867. *The Three Voyages of Martin Frobisher, in Search of a Passage to Cathaia and India by the North-west, A.D. 1576–8*. Reprinted from the first edition of *Hakluyt's Voyages*, with selections from manuscript documents in the British Museum and State Paper Office. Hakluyt Society.
Cooke, A. 2003. "Frobisher, Sir Martin." Dictionary of Canadian Biography, Vol. 1. University of Toronto/Université Laval. http://www.biographi.ca/en/bio/frobisher_martin_1E.html.
Cormack, W.E. 1928. *A Journey across the Island of Newfoundland in 1822*. Longmans, Green.
Cronon, W. 1983. *Changes in the Land: Indians, Colonists, and the Ecology of New England*. Hill and Wang.
"The Cupids Colony and John Guy." 2008. Heritage Newfoundland and Labrador. https://www.heritage.nf.ca/articles/exploration/cupids.php.
Day, G.M. 1953. "The Indian as an ecological factor in the Northeastern Forest." *Ecology* 14(2): 329–46.
De Costa, B.F. 1884. "Chapter VI. Norumbega and its English explorers." In *Narrative and Critical History of America*, Vol. 3, edited by J. Winsor. Houghton, Mifflin and Co.
De Costa, B.F. 1891. "The Voyage of Pierre Angibaut, known as Champdoré, Captain in the Marine of New France, Made to the Coast of Maine, 1608." Maine History Documents, 634. https://digitalcommons.library.umaine.edu/cgi/viewcontent.cgi?article=1634&context=mainehistory.
Denevan, W.M. 1992. "The pristine myth: the landscape of the Americas in 1492." *Annals of the Association of American Geographers* 82(3): 369–85.
Dermer, T. 1905. "Thomas Dermer, 1619." In *Sailors Narratives of Voyages Along the New England Coast, 1524–1624*, edited by G.P. Winship. Houghton Mifflin & Company.
Dickason, O. 1996. "Huron/Wyandot." In *Encyclopedia of North American Indians*, edited by F.E. Hoxie. Houghton Mifflin Harcourt.
Dickenson, V. 2008. "Cartier, Champlain, and the fruits of the New World: Botanical exchange in the 16th and 17th centuries." *Scientia Canadensis* 31(1): 27–47.
Dobyns, H.F. 1983. *Their Number Became Thinned*. University of Tennessee Press.
Doherty, K. 2008. *Sea Venture: Shipwreck, Survival, and the Salvation of Jamestown*. St. Martin's Griffin.
Dunbabin, T. 2003. "Waymouth, George." Dictionary of Canadian Biography, Vol. 1. University of Toronto/Université Laval. www.biographi.ca/en/bio/waymouth_george_1E.html.
Dunkerly, R. 1998. "Growth and settlement beyond Jamestown." Historic Jamestowne. U.S. National Park Service. https://www.nps.gov/jame/learn/historyculture/growth-and-settlement-beyond-jamestown.htm.
Dunn, J.P. 1993. "Squanto before he met the Pilgrims." *Bulletin of the Massachusetts Historical Society* 54 (1): 38–42.
"Epenow, the Wampanoag who tricked his way home from England in 1614." 2022. New England Historical Society. https://www.newenglandhistoricalsociety.com/epenow-wampanoag-conned-way-home-england/.
Farrell, C. 2002. "Zúñiga Chart." Encyclopedia Virginia. https://encyclopediavirginia.org/entries/zuniga-chart.
Fisher, D.H. 2008. *Champlain's Dream*. Simon & Schuster.
Fossett, R. 2001. *In Order to Live Untroubled: Inuit of the Central Arctic, 1550–1940*. University of Manitoba Press.
Gagné, M. 2015. "St. Lawrence Iroquoians." The Canadian Encyclopedia. https://www.thecanadianencyclopedia.ca/en/article/st-lawrence-iroquoians#.
Galasso, S. 2014. "When the last of the Great Auks died, it was by the crush of a fisherman's Boot." *Smithsonian Magazine*. https://www.smithsonianmag.com/smithsonian-institution/with-crush-fisherman-boot-the-last-great-auks-died-180951982/.
Gallant, D.J., and M. Filice. 2022. "Beothuk." The Canadian Encyclopedia. https://development.thecanadianencyclopedia.ca/en/article/beothuk.

Ganong, W.F., ed. 1922. *The Works of Samuel de Champlain, Vol. I, Part III, The Voyages 1613: Acadia and New England, 1604–1607.* Champlain Society.
Gilbert, W. 1990. "'Divers Places': The Beothuk Indians and John Guy's voyage into Trinity Bay in 1612." *Newfoundland Studies* 6(2): 147–67.
Gilbert, W. 2002. "Russell's Point (CiAj-1): A Little Passage/Beothuk site at the bottom of Trinity Bay." MA thesis, Memorial University of Newfoundland.
"Glassmaking at Jamestown." 2015. Historic Jamestowne. National Park Service. https://www.nps.gov/jame/learn/historyculture/glassmaking-at-jamestown.htm.
Grant, W.L., ed. 1907. *Voyages of Samuel de Champlain 1604–1618.* Charles Scribner's Sons.
Handcock, G. 2000. "English settlement." Heritage Newfoundland and Labrador. https://www.heritage.nf.ca/articles/society/settlement.php.
Hatch, C.E. 1941. "Glassmaking in Virginia, 1607–1625." *The William and Mary Quarterly* 21(2): 119–38.
Heidenreich, C.E., and M. Filice. 2018. "Wendat (Huron)." The Canadian Encyclopedia. https://www.thecanadianencyclopedia.ca/en/article/huron.
Hiller, J.K. 2004. "The Portuguese Explorers." Heritage Newfoundland and Labrador. https://www.heritage.nf.ca/articles/exploration/portuguese.php.
Holly, D.H. 2000. "The Beothuk on the eve of their extinction." *Arctic Anthropology* 37 (1): 79–95.
Holly, D.H., C. Wolf, and J. Erwin. 2010. "The ties that bind and divide." *Journal of the North Atlantic* 3: 3–44.
Horn, J.P. 2018. *1619: Jamestown and the Forging of American Democracy.* Basic.
Howe, H.F. 1969. *Prologue to New England: The Forgotten Century of the Explorers.* Kennikat Press, Inc.
Huck, B. 2002. *Exploring the Fur Trade Routes of North America: Discover the Highways that Opened a Continent.* Heartland.
Hunt, E. 2003a. "Easton, Peter." Dictionary of Canadian Biography, Vol. 1. University of Toronto/Université Laval. http://www.biographi.ca/en/bio/easton_peter_1E.html.
Hunt, E. 2003b. "Dermer, Thomas." Dictionary of Canadian Biography, Vol. 1. University of Toronto/Université Laval. http://www.biographi.ca/en/bio/dermer_thomas_1E.html.
Huntley, D. 2023. "Bartholomew Gosnold—How England Settled in the New World." British Heritage Travel. https://britishheritage.com/history/bartholomew-gosnold-englands-settled-new-world.
Jacobs, J. 2013. "Early Dutch explorations in North America." *Journal of Early American History* 3: 59–81.
"John Smith's Map of Virginia: A Closer Look." 2023. Captain John Smith Chesapeake National Historical Trail. National Park Service. https://www.nps.gov/articles/000/smith-map-of-virginia.htm.
Jones, E.T. 2008. "Alwyn Ruddock: John Cabot and the discovery of America." *Historical Research* 81(212): 224–54.
Juet, R. 1906. "The Third Voyage of Master Henrie Hudson." In *Hakluytus Posthumus, or Purchas his pilgrimes: Containing a history of the world in sea voyages and lande travells by Englishmen and others*, Vol. 13, edited by S. Purchas. James MacLehose and Sons.
Kingsbury, S.M. 1906. *Records of the Virginia Company.* 4 Vols. Library of Congress.
Koch, A., C. Brierley, M.M. Maslin, and S.L. Lewis. 2019. "Earth system impacts of the European arrival and Great Dying in the Americas after 1492." *Quaternary Science Reviews* 207: 13–36.
La Roque de Roquebrune, R. 2003. "La Roque, Marguerite de." Dictionary of Canadian Biography, Vol. 1. University of Toronto/Université Laval. http://www.biographi.ca/en/bio/la_roque_marguerite_de_1E.html.
Laet, J.D., and G. Folsom, tr. 1841. *Extracts from the New World, or, a Description of the West Indies.* https://www.loc.gov/item/11022409/.
Lanctot, G. 2003a. "Aubert, Thomas." Dictionary of Canadian Biography, Vol. 1. University of Toronto/Université Laval. http://www.biographi.ca/en/bio/aubert_thomas_1E.html.
Lanctot, G. 2003b. "La Roche de Mesgouez, Troilus de." Dictionary of Canadian Biography,

Vol. 1. University of Toronto/Université Laval. http://www.biographi.ca/en/bio/la_roche_de_mesgouez_troilus_de_1E.html.

Larnder, M.M. (2003). Davis (Davys), John (d. 1605). *Dictionary of Canadian Biography*, vol. 1, University of Toronto/Université. Laval. https://www.biographi.ca/en/bio/davis_john_1605_1E.html.

Levermore, C.H. 1912. *Forerunners and Competitors of the Pilgrims and Puritans.* 2 Vols. New England Society.

Lord, A. 1920. *Plymouth and the Pilgrims.* Houghton Mifflin Company.

MacBeath, G. 2003. "Dugua de Monts (Du Gua, de Monts)." Dictionary of Canadian Biography, Vol. 1. University of Toronto/ Université Laval. http://www.biographi.ca/en/bio/du_gua_de_monts_pierre_1E.html.

Mark, J.J. 2020. "Plymouth Colony." World History Encyclopedia. https://www.worldhistory.org/Plymouth_Colony/.

Mark, J.J. 2021a. "Wampanoag Confederacy." World History Encyclopedia. https://www.worldhistory.org/Wampanoag_Confederacy/.

Mark, J.J. 2021b. "Jamestown Colony of Virginia." World History Encyclopedia. https://www.worldhistory.org/Jamestown_Colony_of_Virginia/.

Mark, J.J. 2021c. "Popham Colony." World History Encyclopedia. https://www.worldhistory.org/Popham_Colony/.

Markham, A.H., ed. 1880. *The Voyages and Works of John Davis, the Navigator.* The Hakluyt Society.

Markham, C.R. 1889. *The Life of John Davis, the Navigator (1550–1605), Discoverer of the Davis Straits.* Dodd, Mead and Company.

Marsh, T.N. 1962. "An unpublished Hakluyt Manuscript?" *The New England Quarterly* 35(2): 247–52.

Marshall, I. 1996. *A History and Ethnography of the Beothuk.* McGill-Queens University Press.

Marshall, I. 1998. "Beliefs and practices." Beothuk Institute, St. John's, Newfoundland. https://beothuinstitute.ca/the-beothuk/beliefs-and-practices/.

McCoy, R.M. 2014a. "Explorer Martin Frobisher infects the Queen with gold fever. Part 1." *Explorers' Tales* (blog). https://www.newworldexploration.com/explorers-tales-blog/explorer-martin-frobisher-infects-the-queen-with-gold-fever-part-1.

McCoy, R.M. 2014b. "Explorer Martin Frobisher infects the Queen with gold fever. Part 2." *Explorers' Tales* (blog). https://www.newworldexploration.com/explorers-tales-blog/explorer-martin-frobisher-infects-the-queen-with-gold-fever-part-2.

McFee, W. 1928. *Sir Martin Frobisher.* John Lane the Bodley Head LTD.

McGhee, R. 2001. *Ancient People of the Arctic.* UBC Press.

McLeod, S. 2019. "First British Settlement at Cuper's Cove, Newfoundland." Fascinating Canadian History. https://glimpsesofcanadianhistory.ca/first-british-settlement-in-cupers-cove-newfoundland/.

McManamon F.P. 2022. "The French along the Northeast Coast—1604–1607." Saint Croix Island International Historic Site. National Park Service. https://www.nps.gov/articles/the-french-along-the-northeast-coast-1604-1607.htm.

Merás, L.M. 1993. *Cartografía Marítima Hispana: La Imagen de América.* IGME.

Miller, K. 2018. "Was Smith's gunpowder accident actually a murder plot?" *Pocahontas Lives!* (blog). https://www.pocahontaslives.com/was-smiths-gunpowder-accident-actually-a-murder-plot.html.

Miller, K. 2020. "How was Pocahontas captured?" *Pocahontas Lives!* (blog). https://www.pocahontaslives.com/how-was-pocahontas-captured.html.

Morison, S.L. 1971. *The European Discovery of America: The Northern Voyages, A.D. 500–1600.* Oxford University Press.

Morley, W.F.E. 2003. "Chauvin de Tonnetuit, Pierre de." Dictionary of Canadian Biography, Vol. 1. University of Toronto/Université Laval. http://www.biographi.ca/en/bio/chauvin_de_tonnetuit_pierre_de_1E.html.

Munn, W.A. 1934. "History of Harbor Grace: Chapter 5." *Newfoundland Quarterly* 34 (3): 5–8.

Nabokov, P. 1996. "Architecture." In *Encyclopedia of North American Indians*, edited by F.E. Hoxie. Houghton Mifflin Harcourt.
Neatby, L.H. 2003. "Hudson, Henry." Dictionary of Canadian Biography, Vol. 1. University of Toronto/Université Laval. http://www.biographi.ca/en/bio/hudson_henry_1E.html.
Otis, C.P. 1880. *Voyages of Samuel de Champlain: Translated from the French*. Prince Society.
Pastore, R.T. 1998. "Beothuk culture." The Newfoundland and Labrador Heritage Website. https://www.heritage.nf.ca/articles/indigenous/beothuk-culture.php.
Pedersen, M., Z. Parrott, and D. Gallant. 2010. "Inuit." The Canadian Encyclopedia. https://www.thecanadianencyclopedia.ca/en/article/inuit.
Pendergast, J.F. 1997. "The confusing identities attributed to Stadacona and Hochelaga." *Journal of Canadian Studies* 32(4): 149–67.
Pope, P. 2009. "Early migratory fishermen and Newfoundland's seabird colonies." *Journal of the North Atlantic*, Special Volume 1: 57–74.
Pope, P. 2015. "Bretons, Basques, and Inuit in Labrador and northern Newfoundland: The control of maritime resources in the 16th and 17th centuries." *Études/Inuit/Studies* 39(1): 15–36.
Powys, L. 1928. *Henry Hudson*. Harper and Brothers Publishers.
Pringle, H. 1997. "Cabot, cod and the colonists." *Canadian Geographic* 31(30): 33–39.
Prins, H.E.L., and B. McBride. 2007. *Asticou's Island Domain: Wabanaki Peoples at Mount Desert Island 1500–2000*. Acadia National Park. Ethnography Program. National Park Service.
Quinn, D.B. 1962. "The voyage of Étienne Bellenger to the Maritimes in 1583: A new document." *Canadian Historical Review* 43(4): 328–43.
Quinn, D.B. 2019. "Gilbert (Gylberte, Jilbert), Sir Humphrey." Dictionary of Canadian Biography, Vol. 1. University of Toronto/Université Laval. http://www.biographi.ca/en/bio.php?BioId=34374.
Quinn, D.B. 2003a. "Parkhurst, Anthony." Dictionary of Canadian Biography, Vol. 1. University of Toronto/Université Laval. http://www.biographi.ca/en/bio/parkhurst_anthony_1E.html.
Quinn, D.B. 2003b. "Bellenger, Étienne." Dictionary of Canadian Biography, Vol. 1. University of Toronto/Université Laval. http://www.biographi.ca/en/bio/bellenger_etienne_1E.html.
Quinn, D.B., and A.M. Quinn. 1983. *The English New England Voyages 1602–1608*. Vol. 161 of the Hakluyt Society.
Ragan, E. 2005. "Chapter 6: A brief survey of Anglo-Indian interactions in Virginia during the seventeenth century." In D. Moretti-Langholtz, *Colonial: A Study of Virginia Indians and Jamestown. The first century*. National Park Service. https://www.nps.gov/parkhistory/online_books/jame1/moretti-langholtz/chap6.htm.
Rountree, H.C. 1990. *Pocahontas's People: The Powhatan Indians of Virginia through Four Centuries*. University of Oklahoma Press.
Ruddock, A.A. 1974. "The reputation of Sebastian Cabot." *Historical Research* 47: 95–99.
Rutman, D.B. 1960. "The Pilgrims and their harbor." *The William and Mary Quarterly* 17 (2): 164–84.
St-Pierre, C.G. 2016. "Iroquoians in the St. Lawrence River Valley before European Contact." *Ontario Archaeology* 96: 47–64.
Sauer, C.O. 1941. "The settlement of the humid East." In *Climate and Man: Yearbook of Agriculture*. United States Department of Agriculture.
Sheler, J.L. 2005. "Rethinking Jamestown." *Smithsonian Magazine*. https://www.smithsonianmag.com/history/rethinking-jamestown-105757282/.
Skelton, R.A. 2003. "Cabot, Sebastian." Dictionary of Canadian Biography, Vol. 1. University of Toronto/Université Laval. http://www.biographi.ca/en/bio/cabot_sebastian_1E.html.
Smith, J. 1865 [1615]. *A Description of New England or Observations and Discoveries in the North of America in the Year of our Lord, 1615*. William Veazie.
Smith, J. 1907 [1622]. *The Generall Historie of Virginia, New England, and the Summer isles:*

*Together with the true travels, adventures and observations, and A sea grammar.* James MacLehose and Sons, Publishers to the University New York, The Macmillan Company.

Snow, D.R. 1994. *The Iroquois.* Blackwell Publishers.

Stapler, M. n.d. "1614—Adriaen Block." The Society of Colonial Wars in the State of Connecticut. https://www.colonialwarsct.org/1614.htm.

Strachey, W. 1849. *The Historie of Travaile into Virginia Britannia.* Edited by R.H. Major. Hakluyt Society.

Swett, S. 1899. *Stories of Maine.* American Book Company.

Tanner, A. 1999. "Innu culture." Heritage Newfoundland and Labrador. https://www.heritage.nf.ca/articles/indigenous/innu-culture.php.

Tarter, B. 2020. "Lawes Divine, Morall and Martiall." Encyclopedia Virginia. https://encyclopediavirginia.org/entries/lawes-divine-morall-and-martiall.

Tattrie, J. 2014. "Sable Island: Criminal colonists settle on a desert island." Nova Scotia In Depth. CBC News. https://www.cbc.ca/news/canada/nova-scotia/sable-island-criminal-colonists-settle-on-deserted-island-1.2755143.

Tomečková, M. 2021. "Jamestown, 1607–1624." Bachelor's thesis, Univerzita Tomáše Bati ve Zlíně.

Tremblay, R. 2006. *The St. Lawrence Iroquoians: Corn People.* Pointe-à-Callière and Éditions de l'Homme.

Trigger, B.G. 1962. "Trade and tribal warfare on the St. Lawrence in the sixteenth century." *Ethnohistory* 9(3): 240–56.

Trigger, B.G. 1971. "Champlain judged by his Indian policy: A different view of early Canadian history." *Anthropologica* 13: 85–114.

Trigger, B.G. 1987. *The Children of Aataentsic: A History of the Huron People to 1660.* McGill-Queen's University Press.

Trudel, M. 2003. "Donnacona." Dictionary of Canadian Biography, Vol. 1. University of Toronto/Université Laval. http://www.biographi.ca/en/bio/donnacona_1E.html.

Tuck, J.A., D.J. Gallant, and M. Filice. 2022. "Beothuk." The Canadian Encyclopedia. https://www.thecanadianencyclopedia.ca/en/article/beothuk.

Turgeon, L. 1998. "French fishers, fur traders, and Amerindians during the sixteenth century: History and Archaeology." *The William and Mary Quarterly* 55(4): 585–610.

Tyler, L.G. 1907. *Narratives of Early Virginia, 1606–1625.* Barnes and Noble, Inc.

Vigneras, L.A. 2003. "Corte-real, Gaspar." Dictionary of Canadian Biography, Vol. 1. University of Toronto/Université Laval. http://www.biographi.ca/en/bio/corte_real_gaspar_1E.html.

Wallace, B. 2003. "The Norse in Newfoundland: L'Anse aux Meadows and Vinland." *Newfoundland Studies* 19(1): 5–43.

Warrick, G. 2000. "The precontact Iroquoian occupation of southern Ontario." *Journal of World Prehistory* 14 (4): 454–57.

Weinstein-Farson, L. 1989. *The Wampanoag (Indians of North America).* Chelsea House Publishers.

Williams, M. 1989. *Americans and Their Forests: A Historical Geography.* Cambridge University Press.

Williams, S. 1904. "The Iroquois Confederacy." *Proceedings of the New York State Historical Association* 4: 9–18.

Willoughby, C.C. 1907. "The Virginia Indians in the seventeenth century." *American Anthropologist* 9: 57–86.

Wolfe, B. 2021. "Sir Thomas Smythe (ca. 1558–1625)." Encyclopedia Virginia. https://encyclopediavirginia.org/entries/smythe-sir-thomas-ca-1558-1625.

Zacek, N. 1921. "Edward Maria Wingfield (1550–1631)." Encyclopedia Virginia. https://encyclopediavirginia.org/entries/wingfield-edward-maria-1550-1631.

# Index

Abenaki  32, 91, 102, 103, 108, 116, 136
L'Acadie  71
Accomack  166
Algonquian  33, 73, 80, 115, 122, 143, 150, 163, 166, 173, 176
Algonquin  78, 80, 83, 123, 125, 127, 128, 173, 181, 202, 203
Amooret  116, 132, 137
Amoret  116
Anglo, Jean  15
Anglo-Powhatan War  158, 164
L'Anse aux Meadows  11
Assacomet  116, 117, 132, 180, 181
Asticou  101
Aubert, Thomas  15
Auks  20, 21, 24

Baffin Island  11, 36, 37, 49, 56, 201
Bashabes  102, 103, 116, 117, 136
Basque  19, 48, 57, 61, 68, 71, 73, 108, 119, 134
Bellenger, Étienne  63
Beothuk  14, 15, 16, 20, 22, 69
Best, George  34, 35, 36, 37, 38, 39, 40, 41, 42, 43, 44
Block, Adriaen  197, 198
Boullé, Hélene  124
Bristol  11, 14, 40, 65, 68, 111, 133
Brittany  19, 65, 76
Brulé, Étienne  125
Bylot, Robert  193, 194, 196

Cabot, John  11
Cabot, Sebastian  14
Cabot Strait  16
Capawack (also Martha's Vineyard)  176, 181, 183
Cape Breton  13, 15, 16, 57, 60, 63, 64, 71, 72, 97, 132, 162, 202
Cape Cod  1, 2, 3, 5, 71, 74, 99, 103, 105, 108, 109, 111, 112, 130, 139, 140, 177, 178, 180, 181, 182, 183, 188, 203

Cartier, Jacques  4, 19, 72, 74, 78, 118, 120, 123, 125
Champdoré  91, 97, 98, 100, 118, 119
Champlain, Samuel de  73, 75, 76, 78, 79, 80, 83, 86, 87, 88, 89, 90, 91, 94, 95, 96, 97, 98, 100, 102, 103, 116, 118
Charlesbourg-Royal  28
Chaste, François Aymar de Clermont de  76, 77, 85
Chefdostel, Thomas  66
Christiaensz, Hendrick  197
Cod  52, 57, 65, 67, 71, 74, 99, 103, 105, 106, 108, 110, 178, 188
Columbus  11, 12
Compagnie van Nieuwnederlant  198
Coneconum  176, 177
Corte-Real, Gaspar  15
Corte-Real, Miguel
Cudouagny  25
Cuper's Cove  68, 70

Davis, John  46
Davis Strait  11, 55, 192, 193, 205
Day, John  11
Dee, John  34, 47, 59, 201
Dermer, Thomas  177, 182, 183, 184, 185
Donnacona  22, 23, 24, 25, 26, 27, 28
Drake, Bernard  65
Drake, Francis  34
Du Pont, François Gravé  75, 76, 77, 78, 79, 80, 86, 88, 91, 97, 118, 119, 120, 121, 123, 125
Duval, Jean  119

Easton, Peter  68, 69
Elizabeth  34, 37, 38, 41, 47, 54, 55, 107, 131
Epenow  139, 175, 176, 180, 183, 184
Etchemin  32, 73, 74, 78, 86, 88, 89, 91, 94, 96, 97, 102, 103, 114, 115, 116, 124, 132, 134, 135, 161, 162, 188, 204

213

## Index

Fagundes, João Álvares 15
Fernandez, Francis 14
Fort Amsterdam 199
Fort Nassau 199
Fort Orange 199
Frobisher, Martin 34
Frobisher Strait 36, 42

Gates, Thomas 130
Gilbert, Adrian 47
Gilbert, Bartholomew 134
Gilbert, Humphrey 47, 58, 132
Gilbert, Raleigh 47, 131, 132, 134, 135, 136, 137, 138, 204
Gilbert Sound 49, 50, 52, 53, 54
*Golden Hind* 60, 61, 63
Gomes, Estêvão 16
Gonzales, Joao 14
Gorges, Ferdinando 117, 131, 132, 133, 134, 138, 139, 161, 175, 177, 179, 180, 181, 182
Gosnold, Bartholomew 73, 74, 105, 106, 107, 111, 130, 140, 146, 153, 176, 184
Great Auk 20
Great Dying 9, 103
Greene, Henry 193, 194, 195, 196
Greenland 11, 13, 15, 35, 38, 42, 45, 46, 48, 49, 50, 51, 53, 54 55, 56, 193
Guy, John 68, 69, 70

Hakluyt, Richard 34, 35, 46, 58, 59, 60, 63, 64, 106, 107, 111, 130, 134, 201
*Half Moon* 187, 188, 189, 190, 191, 192
Hans Claesz Company 197, 198
Harlow, Edward 175, 176, 180, 181
Haudenosaunee Confederacy 30, 82, 121
Hawkins, John 34, 47, 58
Hayes, Edward 106
Hobson, Nicholas 181, 182
Hochelaga 24, 25, 26, 29, 125
Hudson, Henry 186
Hudson Bay 14, 43, 127, 197
Huguenot 74, 85
Hunt, Thomas 177, 179
Huron 72, 82, 128

Innu 22, 29, 64, 73, 75, 76, 78, 79, 86, 87, 89, 122, 123, 124, 202, 203
Inuit 37, 38, 39, 45, 49, 51, 52, 54, 55, 56, 201
Iouaniscou 102
Iroquois 72, 78, 79, 82, 121, 122, 123, 124, 125, 128, 129, 150
Island of Birds 24

James I 130, 154
Jamestown 140, 153

Janes, John 46, 47, 48, 49, 50, 53, 54, 55
Juet, John 187, 192, 193, 194, 195, 196

Kecoughtan 144, 155, 158, 168, 169
Kichesipirini 127
Kuskarawaok 166, 167

Lachine Rapids 80
Lenape 5, 189, 190, 191, 192, 198, 199
Lescarbot, Marc 98, 99, 100, 102, 103
Loc, Michael 35, 37, 38, 42, 44
London Company 130, 138, 140

Manahoac 171, 173
Maneddo 116
Manido 116, 132
Marquerite 28
Martha's Vineyard (also Capawack) 103, 109, 110, 117, 132, 150, 176, 184
Martin, John 155
Mason, John 70
Massasoit 183
Massawomeck 169, 171, 173
Matoaka *see* Pocahontas
Mawooshen Confederacy 102, 103, 117, 134, 135, 136, 137
Membertou 102, 103
Micmac 20, 64, 108, 119; *see also* Mi'kmaq
Mi'kmaq 20, 31, 45, 73, 102, 103, 108
Mohawk 72, 83, 84, 121, 123
Monacans 155
Monhegan Island 105, 113, 116, 134, 175, 177, 182, 183
Monopet 176, 181
Montagnais 29, 78, 121, 123, 124, 125
Monts, Pierre Dugua de 75, 85, 86, 87, 88, 89, 90, 91, 92, 93, 94, 95, 96, 97, 98, 99, 102, 118, 120, 126, 160, 184
Moraughtacund 170, 171, 172
Mosco 168, 170, 171, 172
Mossel, Volckertsz 197
Mount Desert Island 88, 91, 102, 160, 161, 162

Naskapi 29
Nauset 103, 108, 109, 111, 112, 113, 176, 179, 181, 182, 183, 184, 185
New France 75, 76, 77, 79, 102, 118, 123, 124, 126, 129
Newport, Christopher 140, 145, 146, 150, 154, 157
Normandy 66, 71, 131
Northwest Passage 12, 14, 16, 25, 29, 34, 38, 43, 46, 47, 49, 50, 58, 59, 113, 186, 187, 189, 192, 193, 198, 201

Ouagimou 102

Panounias 91, 102, 103, 162
Paspahegh 155, 158
Paspihae 145
Patuxet 179, 181, 182, 183
Peckenine 176, 177
Peckmo 176
Penobscot Bay 59, 89, 102, 111, 134, 162, 188, 212
Percy, George 140, 142, 143, 144, 145, 146, 148, 156, 158
Plymouth Company 130, 131, 132, 138, 177
Pocahontas 148, 156, 158, 159, 163
Popham, Francis 138
Popham, George 131, 133, 135, 136, 138
Popham, John 117, 131, 132, 133
Popham colony 134, 157, 160, 161, 175
Port Royal 7 171, 85, 87, 96, 97, 98, 99, 100, 103, 118, 119, 160, 161, 162
Powhatan 142, 143, 144, 145, 146, 148, 150, 153, 155, 156, 157, 158, 159, 169, 173
Powys, Llewelyn 193
Prévert, Jean Sarcel de 78, 79, 80
Pricket, Abacuk 193
Pring, Martin 106, 111, 132, 133
Pristine forest 7
Province of Maine 139

Quadequina 183
Québec 22, 28, 29, 31, 75, 118, 124, 194

Raleigh, Walter 34, 47, 59, 60, 61, 65, 106, 107, 110, 111, 131, 140, 202
Rapahanock 171, 172
Ratcliffe, John 146, 147, 150, 157
Rijser, Cornelis 197
Roberval, Jean-François de La Rocque de 27, 29
Roche-Mesgouez, Marquis de la 65
Rut, John 16

Sable Island 62, 64, 66, 67, 202
Sackaweston 176
Saffacomoit 116
Saguenay River 28, 31, 71, 72, 73, 75, 78, 124
Saint Croix 37, 65, 86, 87, 88, 89, 90, 95, 96, 98, 160, 162
St. John River 73, 124
St. Lawrence Iroquoians 22, 30, 72, 115
St. Lawrence River 15, 19, 22, 23, 24, 27, 29, 30, 57, 72, 74, 75, 80, 83, 86, 105, 115, 118, 119, 121, 123, 124, 128, 196, 202
Sasquesahanocks 170
Sassafras 2, 109, 110, 111, 112, 137, 169
Secoudon 97, 98, 99, 102, 103
Siouan 173
Skicowaros 116
Skidwarres 116, 133, 134, 135, 137, 138
Smith, John 5, 134, 139, 145, 146, 147, 153, 154, 155, 165, 176, 179, 180, 184, 187, 189
Smith, Thomas 192, 193
Somers, George 130
Squanto 180, 182, 183
Stadacona 24, 25, 28, 29
Staffe, Philip 194, 196
Susquehannock 169, 170, 173

Tadoussac 11675, 78, 80, 86, 118, 119, 121, 123, 124, 126, 127
Tahánedo 116, 132, 135, 137, 138
Taignoagny 23, 24, 25, 115
Tarrentine 74, 97, 102, 161
Tessouat 127
Tisquantum (also Squanto) 180, 183
Tockwogh 169, 170
Tonnetuit, Pierre de Chauvin de 74, 75, 76, 78
Trinity Bay 69
Trois-Rivieres 75, 121, 124, 126
Tsenacommacah 150

Van Tweenhuysen Company 197, 198
Verrazzano, Giovanni da 3, 20, 59, 73, 107, 189
Vignau, Nicolas de 127
Vikings 11
Virginia Company 134, 138, 140, 141, 146, 153, 154, 193

Wabanaki 5, 7, 31, 73, 78, 86, 88, 91, 92, 95, 96, 114, 117, 136, 138, 162, 176, 203, 204
Wahunsenacawh 142, 143, 144, 148, 149, 150, 153, 154, 155, 156, 157, 158, 159, 167, 168
Walsingham, Francis 47, 50
Wampanoag 10, 103, 109, 110, 175, 176, 182, 185
Waroskoyack 147
Waymouth 113, 193, 194
whales 31, 42, 45, 47, 48, 54, 72, 177, 178
Wighcocomoco 166, 168
Wingfield, Edward Maria 130, 146
Wyandot 30, 81, 123

www.ingramcontent.com/pod-product-compliance
Lightning Source LLC
Chambersburg PA
CBHW032043300426
44117CB00009B/1168